MW01069553

A list of books in the series appears at the back of this book.

International Nietzsche Studies

Nietzsche has emerged as a thinker of extraordinary importance, not only in the history of philosophy but in many fields of contemporary inquiry. Nietzsche studies are maturing and flourishing in many parts of the world. This internationalization of inquiry with respect to Nietzsche's thought and significance may be expected to continue.

International Nietzsche Studies is conceived as a series of monographs and essay collections that will reflect and contribute to these developments. The series will present studies in which responsible scholarship is joined to the analysis, interpretation, and assessment of the many aspects of Nietzsche's thought that bear significantly upon matters of moment today. In many respects Nietzsche is our contemporary, with whom we do well to reckon, even when we find ourselves at odds with him. The series is intended to promote this reckoning, embracing diverse interpretive perspectives, philosophical orientations, and critical assessments.

The series is also intended to contribute to the ongoing reconsideration of the character, agenda, and prospects of philosophy itself. Nietzsche was much concerned with philosophy's past, present, and future. He sought to affect not only its understanding but also its practice. The future of philosophy is an open question today, thanks at least in part to Nietzsche's challenge to the philosophical traditions of which he was so critical. It remains to be seen—and determined—whether philosophy's future will turn out to resemble the "philosophy of the future" to which he proffered a prelude and of which he provided a preview, by both precept and practice. But this is a possibility we do well to take seriously. International Nietzsche Studies will attempt to do so, while contributing to the understanding of Nietzsche's philosophical thinking and its bearing upon contemporary inquiry.

—RICHARD SCHACHT

Reading Nietzsche

Reading Nietzsche

Mazzino Montinari

*Translated from the German
and with an Introduction by Greg Whitlock*

UNIVERSITY OF ILLINOIS PRESS

URBANA AND CHICAGO

Nietzsche Lesen © 1982 by Walter de Gruyter GmbH & Co. KG,
Berlin and New York
English translation © 2003 by the Board of Trustees
of the University of Illinois
All rights reserved
Manufactured in the United States of America
C 5 4 3 2 1

Library of Congress Cataloging-in-Publication Data
Montinari, Mazzino.
[Nietzsche lesen. English]
Reading Nietzsche / Mazzino Montinari; translated from the German
and with an introduction by Greg Whitlock.
p.   cm. — (International Nietzsche studies)
Includes bibliographical references and index.
ISBN 0-252-02798-1 (cloth: alk. paper)
1. Nietzsche, Friedrich Wilhelm, 1844–1900.
I. Title.
II. Series.
B3317.M59513   2003
193—dc21   2002009060

CONTENTS

TRANSLATOR'S INTRODUCTION

What distinguishes Mazzino Montinari's *Reading Nietzsche* is the author's perspective. The essays and lectures collected here resulted from a nearly unique manner of reading Nietzsche available to only a handful of people from each generation, those who, like Montinari, edited Nietzsche's works in the original manuscript form. But Montinari stands apart even within this exceptionally restricted group of Nietzsche readers, for he alone can claim to have edited a complete critical collection of the works of Friedrich Nietzsche—although, as Montinari insisted, his departed friend and fellow editor Giorgi Colli must share the honor in spirit.

Montinari faced a Herculean task in editing the complete collected juvenilia, philologica, published works, correspondence, and remaining notebooks from 1869 to Nietzsche's insanity in 1889; in its final printed form, the Colli-Montinari *Kritische Gesamtausgabe Werke* (*Critical Collected Works Edition*, or KGW) comprises thirty-three large volumes. This task had been attempted by more than one team of scholars, only to meet inadequacy, incompleteness, and scholarly or even ethical shipwreck. For example, the massive *Großoktavausgabe* (Large octave edition, or GOA; a list of abbreviations used follows this introduction), edited by Peter Gast, Elisabeth Förster, and several teams of other editors, ran aground without producing a genuinely *critical* edition— quite the opposite—and without publishing the literally *complete* works.

The next attempt, the Musarion edition of Nietzsche's works, comprised twenty-three volumes (including three volumes of indexes) and presented the published works, notebooks, and philologica according to a single chronological sequence. Although this edition contains more juvenilia than does the GOA, it limits itself to the GOA's 1,067 notes and twelve outlines.

Another attempt, the *Werke und Briefe: Historische-Kritische Gesamtausgabe*

(Historical-critical edition of the complete works and correspondence, or HKG), supervised by H. J. Mette, was never completed.

After the early death of his friend and colleague Colli, Montinari served as the sole editor-in-chief of the enormous KGW. Montinari's perspective on reading Nietzsche could not be fully shared even by Karl Schlechta, the premier midcentury Nietzsche scholar and the editor of Nietzsche's works and selected notes in three volumes (1954 to 1956), among other projects still important to Nietzsche scholarship. Indeed, it was Schlechta's standard that Colli and Montinari had to exceed. This may explain some of Montinari's antipathy to Schlechta (as when he portrays Schlechta as rejecting any importance for the *Nachlaß,* even though Schlechta proved its importance in project after project). Schlechta's achievements in Nietzsche scholarship went well beyond his three-volume collection to include a three-volume collection of Gersdorff's letters to Nietzsche with numerous comments by Schlechta, a chronology, an index to the works, several essays on Nietzsche's early development, several articles on aspects of Nietzsche's philosophy, a collection of his own essays and lectures on Nietzsche, the important study *Nietzsches grosser Mittag,* and in 1962, a collaborative work with Anni Anders detailing "the hidden origins" of Nietzsche's philosophy. Even so, Montinari's new critical edition of the works eclipsed Schlechta's editorial achievements and set him in a league of his own among Nietzsche editors.

Montinari was quick to point out, however, that his perspective was but one among many valid viewpoints. As Montinari suggests in his highly condensed and cryptic preface to the German edition of *Reading Nietzsche,* he was ultimately confined to his own philological, historical, and editorial perspective—a perspective that (so he intimated) obscured some critical element and thwarted his efforts to see his own activities objectively (as, of course, no one can). He left to the reader's investigations what these active but not entirely conscious forces might be. Montinari called the essays and lectures collected in *Reading Nietzsche* "mere preliminaries, mere warnings, mere assessments."

Even more important, Montinari insisted that his secondary work not replace each reader's own confrontation with Nietzsche. To the contrary, readers must have an adequate knowledge of Nietzsche to follow the trains of thought contained in the work at hand. We must be readers of Nietzsche before we enter into dialogue with Montinari.

At the same time, although highly accomplished Nietzsche scholars can learn a substantial amount from Montinari and find their own understandings and perhaps methods challenged, even initiates to Nietzsche scholarship will find a treasure trove of concrete images and solid methodological advice from this slim volume. Montinari specifically said, "The title—*Reading*

Nietzsche—should signify a (slow) process of acclimation to the turbulent waters of his thought." That slow, careful acclimation may begin in, continue with, or even culminate in actively engaging with Nietzsche's greatest editor on the topic of reading Nietzsche.

There is surprisingly little of Montinari's own voice in this short work. The book contains long passages from Nietzsche's lesser-known notebooks, juvenilia, and correspondence, as well as long documentary exhibits from a variety of early Nietzsche editors, including H. J. Mette, Peter Gast, C. G. Naumann, Raoul Richter, and others. It also reproduces lengthy quotations from Thomas Mann, Friedrich Engels, Alfred Bäumler, Georg Lukács, and other philosophers, as well as extremely rare quotations from Nietzsche's mother, sister, uncle, and father. It even includes a poem by Ludwig Hölty and a German proverb. I found myself translating these various voices as often as Montinari's own voice.

Indeed, this volume may seem to offer too little Montinari, but such a criticism misses the mark, for the guiding intention behind this motley choir of voices is Montinari's alone. Moreover, a discernible set of connections runs throughout Montinari's seemingly divergent thoughts: Nietzsche as a person and a family member, as a writer with a specific literary itinerary, as a human being living within a specific historical span in specific historical circumstances, and as the object of various attempted collected works. This matrix of connections structures the book's treatment of Nietzsche as a figure with a facet of enlightenment and another, darker one. The inner coherence and integrity of these essays and lectures will become clear to the attentive reader.

The first two chapters lay out the basic issues of Montinari's perspective: how one should read Nietzsche and how the collected works should be edited. Montinari then applies his method to salient issues in Nietzsche scholarship (for example, his relation to the Enlightenment), but from a perspective that is informed by a palette for the most obscure yet powerful passages from the works. Chapters 3 through 7 prove how satisfying the historical, philological, empirical approach can be.

Chapter 3 demonstrates the importance of *Human, All Too Human* in the works as a whole. Here Montinari employs the juvenilia to illuminate overlooked allusions in the well-known published works. For many readers, even longtime Nietzsche readers, this will be their first sustained look at the juvenilia. Indeed, without a Germanistic, historical-philological orientation to the works, any consideration of the juvenilia may seem irrelevant, but Montinari manages to connect recollections of childhood to rather poignant passages. For many other readers, the biographical information to be gleaned from Montinari's subtle use of the earliest notes will prove unique and valuable. In

chapter 3 Montinari further urges readers to take *Ecce Homo* (and, by extension, other autobiographical reports) as highly reliable, a thesis to which he
returns throughout the book. The denouement of this chapter comes when
Montinari uses his assembled fragments to incisively interpret an aphorism
from *The Wanderer and His Shadow*.

Chapter 4 offers a penetrating study of the Nietzsche-Wagner relationship.
Montinari found great serendipity in delivering this lecture on the one-hun-
dredth anniversary of Nietzsche's letter to Overbeck first alluding to *Human,
All Too Human*. Montinari treats the entire relationship as an intellectual decision on Nietzsche's part that clarified personal facts as much as vice versa.

Methodologically Montinari was far from a historical-philological reduc-
tionist. The connection he discerns between Wagner, on the one hand, and
Democritus and science, on the other, is understated and refined, but this
nexus (and connections to the pre-Platonic philosophers in general) later
proved to be a rich field of investigation. Moreover, by emphasizing Nietzsche's specific literary intentions in his method, Montinari shows the significance of a letter in which Nietzsche states that he wishes to return to his philologica for additional publications. (These include not only the Democritea,
which Montinari recognized as one possibility, but also, and more likely, the
Basel lectures on the pre-Platonics.) In fact, careful scholarship in Montinari's
fashion can demonstrate in greater detail that Nietzsche's reemerging interest in science spelled one of the final moments of the Nietzsche-Wagner relationship.

Further, when Montinari opened the question of symbiosis among Wagner, Feuerbach, and Nietzsche, he again unearthed fertile ground for research.

What we receive from Montinari, though, are only preliminary sketches,
ones that may well be misshapen or mistaken. For example, in this chapter
Montinari begins what I suggest is a rather tortured treatment of Nietzsche's
politics. He describes the genuine Nietzsche as antinationalist, anti-German,
antiromantic, anti-anti-Semitic, anti-obscurantist, antimetaphysical, anti-
irrationalist, antimythic, and anti-"Jesuit," as well as anti-Wagnerian, but nowhere does Montinari mention or describe Nietzsche as specifically *antileft-
ist,* even though he should be considered a virtual antipode to the dogmas of
socialism, Marxism, communism, and certain currents in the Young Hegelian
movement, regardless of whether he actually knew of them in detail or at all.

Chapter 5 delivers a fascinating look into Nietzsche's important relation
to the later Goethe, at the same time offering a masterful treatment of a certain complex of ideas surrounding enlightenment, reaction, and revolution.
Again, *Human, All Too Human* serves Montinari as a crucial text (specifically
aphorisms 26 and 221). Nietzsche is portrayed here as antirevolutionary and

antireactionary but also opposed to the Enlightenment as conventionally understood (i.e., as the triumph of reason).

As Montinari reads him, Nietzsche promoted his own interpretation of the Enlightenment project and rose above the conventional split between revolutionary and reactionary modes of thought. Montinari stresses the Enlightenment complex of ideas in the writings to the near exclusion of an irrational aspect. This chapter already presents the bulwark that Montinari later employs against Lukács: Nietzsche was a genuine, albeit idiosyncratic, figure of the ongoing Western Enlightenment who rose above conventional antirevolutionary thought. Properly understood, Montinari's insight proves to be exceptionally powerful, as the next chapter shows.

Chapter 6 builds on this strong foundation of Nietzsche as an errant Enlightenment thinker. Montinari here explores the then-understudied area of Nietzsche's relation to science. Indeed, to the extent that he lauded, promoted, and used (if abused) science in his writings, Nietzsche *is* an Enlightenment thinker. Although he wrote disappointingly little about this, Montinari had clearly rediscovered Nietzsche's hidden and difficult relation to the sciences. Drawing on Nietzsche's notebooks, personal library, and borrowings from university libraries, which were available to him as the editor of the KGW, Montinari discerned that Nietzsche never underwent a "positivist period" but rather maintained a strong, if briefly interrupted, lifelong interest in science. Only the alien interruptions from Schopenhauer's metaphysics and Wagner's aesthetics kept Nietzsche from science. Montinari's own writings argue that the Nietzsche who theorized the scientific notions of will to power and eternal recurrence is the "genuine Nietzsche." And the will to power's highest drive is none other than the human passion for knowledge. When Montinari describes this passion for knowledge, his essays and lectures recall Frau Lou Andreas-Salomé's early account of Nietzsche's hidden self. Montinari stresses the scientific interests of Nietzsche, however, whereas Andreas-Salomé accepts the misleading if not mistaken notion of "periods" in Nietzsche's development. (But why does Andreas-Salomé's reading differ from that of Montinari? For one thing, note the later editor's greater accessibility to documents; Andreas-Salomé had no knowledge of the notebooks, the complete correspondence, or *Ecce Homo* and the other then-unpublished late works, where scientific interests are expressed.)

Of course, Montinari was familiar with the studies by Alwin Mittasch and by Karl Schlechta and Anni Anders. Whereas Montinari stresses Mach's indubitable influence on Nietzsche, many others equaled his influence, and a number far exceeded it, as the wide scholarship on the subject demonstrates. Montinari even detected the influence of the almost entirely forgotten African Spir on Nietzsche, although in the scholarly apparatus to the KGW, Montinari simply yields to Schlechta and Anders on the matter of Boscovich, Spir, and Zöllner (Schlechta and Anders considered Boscovich a more important influence than Spir or Zöllner). Nonetheless, Montinari could already see the beginnings of a new scholarship on Nietzsche's relation to science, so more recent discoveries would not have surprised him in the least. Finally, Montinari's contrast between the scientific spirit and "Jesuitism" in this chapter is also noteworthy.

Chapter 7 offers further fruit of the historical-philological method. Montinari discovers two Zarathustras: the one in the well-known work bearing that name and the previously unknown one sketched before the full-length work. The "Zarathustra before *Zarathustra*" in some ways was surprisingly contrary to the final character. Montinari argues that the so-called Lou affair marks the abrupt turning point between the two, but since Montinari states this elegant and well-taken major claim only once, as is his wont, readers expecting main points to be highlighted and emphasized may easily overlook the point.

In fact, despite the dangers for American readers used to repetition, the subtle tones of Montinari's style only deepens the meaning of Montinari's essays and lectures. The style is understated, factual, analytic, and professorial, yet it is also full of subtle and delicious irony, sarcasm, and humor. Certainly one of the most elaborate and richest jokes to come out of Nietzsche's legacy is delivered here over several chapters, with the punchline delivered by Elisabeth Förster's "tool," Peter Gast. The full impact of this joke at her expense can be fully appreciated, though, only if the reader has followed Montinari's arguments, presented throughout this book, concerning the need for a critical, complete edition of the works, collected with integrity.

Indeed, only such an edition can provide us with "instructive glimpses" into thought processes; everything else is an uncertain reading. In seeking to prepare a truly critical edition, Montinari examined the *Nachlaß* with reference to Nietzsche's specific literary plans. Montinari presents his devastating case against any literary production with the title "Will to Power" with an atypically meticulous attention to detail.

Montinari concludes that "*Twilight of the Idols* and *Antichrist* were created from the notes for the 'Will to Power'; the rest is—*Nachlaß,* unpublished writings." Even more weighty for our image of Nietzsche is Montinari's conclusion that "the Turin catastrophe came when Nietzsche was literally entirely finished with everything."

The reader should recall that these essays and lectures were delivered to expert audiences of Montinari's fellow Nietzsche scholars. The German professorial aesthetic of the time rejected detailing one's entire case and making every point explicit. Only the crucial or novel points required stating; the audience was expected to make the logical connections and appreciate the dazzling and sometimes shocking discoveries for themselves. Just as Nietzsche said his best readers must have long legs with which to stride from scattered passage to passage, so Montinari's readers must be prepared to ponder his points as mountain peaks along a ridge, with not necessarily visible ground giving them orientation and scale.

In the powerful chapters 8 and 9 and the documentary supplement to chapter 9, Montinari develops a methodical, damning indictment of Elisabeth Förster and Peter Gast's edition of Nietzsche's works; specifically, and as already suggested, he dismisses the notion of a magnum opus called "Will to Power." In the process Montinari provides perhaps the literature's most penetrating and decisive treatment of Nietzsche's relation to his mother and sister.

In these two chapters, having already developed an appreciation of the historical-philological approach to reading Nietzsche, and having then shown its power in a series of chapters that paint a clear and deep image of Nietzsche, Montinari dispassionately yet resolutely depicts the virtual polar opposite approach to his own editing and reading Nietzsche, that of the philosopher's sister and her collaborator, Peter Gast. For any reader, from initiate to long-term enthusiast, the manner in which Montinari uncovers the Nietzsche family relations, the quality of his evidence, and his uncanny ability to produce such obscure evidence will prove magisterial. In chapter 8 any philologically defensible notion of a work called "Will to Power" disappears. (Readers may well find Montinari's distinction between the "two approaches" to Nietzsche's *Nachlaß* as somewhat stilted or relevant only to editors, however.)

Despite its forbidding title, the documentary supplement to chapter 9 is perhaps the high point of the collection at hand and is surely a "must read" for initiate and aficionado alike. The correspondence between the philosopher's sister, C. G. Naumann (Nietzsche's last publisher), and Raoul Richter (the first editor of *Ecce Homo*) is both deliciously tragic and comic. What develops is one of the most dramatic detective stories involving Nietzsche and his legacy. The entire intrigue surrounding the new section for *Ecce Homo* is explained here more thoroughly and decisively, I believe, than in any other treatment in any language to date.

Ironically, Montinari seems far less successful in the final chapter when indicting two other abuses of Nietzsche's legacy: Alfred Bäumler's and Georg Lukács's interpretations of the German philosopher. Although Bäumler and Lukács are as certainly guilty of their own charges as are Förster and Gast, Montinari takes a strange and unconvincing approach to them both individually and relative to each other.

In the case of Bäumler, Montinari presents the reader with a vague image of the role that Nietzsche's thought played in the Third Reich without any awareness of the Nazi party's internal intrigue surrounding the figure of Nietzsche (for his anti-Rome sentiments and thought, not the more usually cited nexuses with anti-Semitism and German nationalism). Using an apologetic characteristic of Walter Kaufmann, Montinari dismisses the equally crucial but separate question of a common ground in Nietzschean and Nazi worldviews. In Montinari's defense, though, the massive documentation of the Nationalsozialistische Deutsche Arbeiterpartei's (NSDAP) internal politics was still largely unavailable to scholars in the 1970s and 1980s. Nonetheless, Montinari uncharacteristically relies entirely on Langreder's dissertation to suggest that any real connection between Nietzsche's thought and National Socialism is absurd. In any event, this chapter was originally written as an article for a scholarly journal, so that Montinari simply could not launch a detailed defense of Nietzsche against Nazism here.

In the case of Lukács, Montinari leads the reader down a rather tortured path to the ironic suggestion that Nietzsche had no significant knowledge concerning the various leftist movements around him and that the German philosopher was a rather bourgeois provincial type from Thüringen.

Although these mouthpieces of, respectively, Nazi and Marxist ideology are relatively easy targets, Bäumler and Lukács seem to escape effective refutation in the individual cases. Indeed, Montinari's treatment of the two cases relative to each other should seem puzzling to the reader. Perhaps here the reader should recall Montinari's cryptic remark in the preface, where he suggests that not entirely conscious elements influenced his own historical-philological method: some of the forces at play in his approach are not unaffected by cold war politics, however much Montinari struggled to divorce them from his edition.

And so Nietzsche meant to direct all his derogatory remarks about the masses and demagogues almost exclusively toward his own middle class, for he apparently knew little of the neo-Hegelian leftist movement, socialism, or the early international communist movement. And so, conversely, Nietzsche was not really connected to irrationalism and actually approximated Friedrich Engel's dialectical materialist notion of eternal recurrence. Again, the crucial nexuses of Feuerbach and Dühring are not given adequate treatment—though, to be fair, this cannot be the standard by which to judge Montinari's chapter.

Montinari's investigations are, as he urged, "mere preliminaries," suggestions for research projects. Nonetheless, although countless suggestions arise from reading Montinari, it is his *historical-philological* or (as I would call it) *Germanistic* methodology, not the research particulars, that I intend to promote by translating his work for English-speaking readers.

• • •

Montinari's general readership may profit from a brief explanation of his rather elaborate argument concerning the "Will to Power," but those readers thoroughly familiar with the *Nachlaß* may choose to skip this section without consequence.

The German term *Nachlaß* means in various contexts (1) "leftovers" or "remainders" in general; (2) "remains," that is, a corpse; and (3) an estate or corpus, that is, what is left behind. A literary figure's various unpublished works, correspondence, notes, and even loose sheets of paper with penned words constitute that author's literary estate, or *Nachlaß*.

Nietzsche's particular *Nachlaß* comprises the extant juvenilia, correspondence, published works (from *Birth of Tragedy* to *Twilight of the Idols*), finished manuscripts intended for publication (including "Antichrist," "Ecce Homo," and "Dionysian Dithyrambs"), and a set of 106 notebooks containing partial essays, aphoristic notes, jottings, and even diagrams and other sorts of material. Scholars refer more specifically to these 106 notebooks, from 1870 to 1888, as the *Nachlaß*. The entirety of this literary estate, and it alone, constitutes the complete works of Nietzsche.

Consider the 106 notebooks from the standpoint of an editor. The notebooks are the natural organizing units for the notes, meaning that the notes should be organized according to the notebooks, grouped in chronological order where possible. Now we can consider the editorial policies of Förster-Nietzsche and Gast, who followed an illicit method: of the entire range of notes, they chose to edit none of the notes from 1870 to 1883. Of all the notes from 1883 to 1888, they chose only one-third, a total of 1,067 fragments, along with twelve outlines. In their *Großoktav* edition they further divided these 1,067 notes as volumes 15 (nn. 1–455) and 16 (nn. 456–1,067). These two volumes together, Förster-Nietzsche and Gast advertised, constituted the systematic magnum opus that Nietzsche intended to publish as "Will to Power."

The pseudowork was arranged by one of the outlines, which was given a pragmatic priority over the rest. The fragments were thus assembled artificially under keywords and by a partial numbering scheme that Nietzsche himself abandoned. This fabrication alone would have had little impact, but the consequent Musarion edition reproduced only the same 1,067 fragments and twelve outlines, which it published, in volumes 8 and 9, as the "Will to Power," employing the GOA numbering system. As did the next attempted complete works, the ill-fated HKW did not attain completeness.

As a further link in the causal chain, even Karl Schlechta's edition of the works in three volumes was constrained to the official 1,067 fragments and outlines, though he did not employ the GOA's numbering system.

When the Kröner publishing house published the "Will to Power," edited by Alfred Bäumler, it became a ready-made mainstay of the Nazi half-educated. Again, these were the same 1,067 GOA fragments, advertised as a systematic work. And when Walter Kaufmann published his English-language edition of "Will to Power," he too used these official 1,067 fragments, which for readers limited to English thus constituted the entirety of Nietzsche's notes. Moreover, both Bäumler and Kaufmann observed the GOA's numbering system.

What makes Montinari's KGW so monumental is that it preserves the natural integrity of the notebooks as an organizing principle. All notes are arranged according to the notebooks in which they are found, which are designated by a series letter and numeral and published complete in seven volumes of the KGW (and seven volumes in the shorter KSA). All the notes are included, not just those from 1883 to 1888. The edition thus allows the reader to follow the exact contents of each notebook; further, it provides a superior dating of the notebooks, allowing a more exact chronological order. No notes are divided and strewn about. The KGW avoids any selective organization or preference for some organizing principle favored in one note. Succinctly put, the KGW contains no remnant of the GOA's fabricated "Will to Power."

In *Reading Nietzsche* Montinari questions whether the KGW would be completed in his own lifetime. When he died unexpectedly in 1986, the edition was not yet complete.

• • •

It is not enough to write about reading Nietzsche or write about writing about reading Nietzsche, and so on, if we do not read Nietzsche himself extensively and intensively. Reading Nietzsche seriously means moving beyond the best-known published works to include the notebooks, correspondence, juvenilia, and philologica. Reading Nietzsche seriously means becoming conversant with his predecessors and immediate intellectual environment. Reading Nietzsche seriously means connecting his biographical information to his readings and writings. Montinari makes the crucial point that the serious student must not only read Nietzsche; he or she must also read *what Nietzsche read*.

Although Montinari does not emphasize or even elaborate one of his most important findings, he clearly considered *Human, All Too Human* as Nietzsche's turning point, for in that work the writer whom Montinari calls "the genuine Nietzsche" recovers himself from alien influences and returns to his earlier, unadulterated interests, especially the pre-Platonics and science. Of course, scholars beginning with Andreas-Salomé have widely recognized *Human, All Too Human* to be important for the break with Wagner. But anyone unaware or dismissive of Nietzsche's interest in science (and the Greeks later in life) cannot fully appreciate the ramifications of the self-liberation in *Human, All Too Human.*

Montinari also makes clear, however, that at the time this book was written, the real predecessors of and influences on Nietzsche in the realm of science had yet to be discovered. Montinari emphasizes the almost certain role Ernst Mach played in Nietzsche's thought. (Karl Schlechta had already proposed much of this orientation, especially in his 1962 work, although he emphasized Roger Joseph Boscovich, J. C. F. Zöllner, and African Spir rather than Mach as influences.)

Montinari approached each of Nietzsche's works as the philosophical and artistic shaping of a distinct, if fluid, line of thought from a distinct time. Each work is intimately connected to a relatively definite set of notes and to Nietzsche's works as a whole. The works stand in a mutual explanatory relation to one another. The notebooks are Nietzsche's thoughts in the process of becoming, as Montinari puts it. A true mastery of this broad collection of notes and texts must include the sort of reading and scholarship that successfully connects the works to the writer's predecessors, his immediate intellectual milieu, and his posterity. Only a historical-philological reading, preferably in the original language and optimally using the manuscripts at Weimar, can adequately provide a groundwork for Nietzsche interpretation. Montinari's own essays and lectures here are superb examples of the fruit a Germanistic method can yield. Although scholarship during and after Montinari's time has greatly accelerated dramatic discoveries in the identities and roles of Nietzsche's hidden influences, his point that much of the notebooks remains understudied is well taken.

Of course, the Germanistic perspective must be supplemented by as many other perspectives as possible. Montinari lauded some readings of Nietzsche, although he remained tactfully silent about others. And Nietzsche himself was a multiperspectivist, so to speak, but he also urged the good reader to read him historically and philologically, that is, carefully, extensively, intensively, and critically.

First and foremost, the Germanist or other serious reader of Nietzsche must become fluent in the controversy surrounding the so-called "Will to Power," which I will set in quotation marks, unlike most other titles cited in this translation (except the equally misunderstood title "Revaluation of All Values" or

provisional titles). Finally, note that all material enclosed in square brackets—
[ ]—is Montinari's; all material enclosed in angle brackets—<>—is mine.

· · ·

The German edition of *Reading Nietzsche* was dedicated to Montinari's wife. I
would like to dedicate this translation to Mazzino Montinari and, as he would
insist, Giorgio Colli. Perhaps more generally, though, it honors the passing of
German philologists and scholars who worked with Montinari in various ways:
Ernst Behler, Jörg Salaquarda, Wolfgang Müller-Lauter, and others. Without
their no-nonsense, careful, historical-philological scholarship, our understanding of Nietzsche would be unacceptably impoverished.

For the few quotations of Nietzsche's published works early on in this book,
I have used the translations of Walter Kaufmann, Gary Handwerk, and the
recently deceased R. J. Hollingdale, whose translations were enjoyed across the
globe. If I were to translate but one sentence of German as beautifully as Professor Hollingdale did, I would rest content.

On a happier note, I would like to thank Walter de Gruyter Verlag in Berlin
for permission to translate Mazzino Montinari's *Nietzsche lesen.* My thanks also
go out to Richard Schacht for his support on this project and otherwise. Benjamin Keller provided helpful suggestions for translation of the Ludwig Hölty
poem. Finally, I wish to thank Bruce Bethell for another superb copyedit.

Gutes lesen!

ABBREVIATIONS

CWFN   *Complete Works of Friedrich Nietzsche,* 3 vols. to date, ed. Ernst Behler (Stanford, Calif.: Stanford University Press, 1995–). Based on Friedrich Nietzsche, *Kritische Studienausgabe,* 15 vols., ed. G. Colli and M. Montinari.

GOA   *Friedrich Nietzsche, Werke* (the *Großoktavausgabe*), 20 vols., ed. Elisabeth Förster (Leipzig: Naumann/Kröner Verlag, 1894–1926).

HKG   *Friedrich Nietzsche, Werke und Briefe: Historische-Kritische Gesamtausgabe,* 9 vols., ed. H-J. Mette (Munich: Beck Verlag, 1933–42).

KGB   *Kritische Gesamtausgabe Briefwechsel, Nietzsche, Werke: Kritische Gesamtausgabe,* 22 vols. in 4 parts, ed. G. Colli and M. Montinari (Berlin: de Gruyter Verlag, 1975–84).

KGW   *Kritische Gesamtausgabe Werke, Nietzsche, Werke: Kritische Gesamtausgabe,* 33 vols. in 8 parts, ed. G. Colli and M. Montinari (Berlin: de Gruyter Verlag, 1967–).

KSA   *Friedrich Nietzsche, Sämtliche Werke: Kritische Studienausgabe,* 15 vols., ed. G. Colli and M. Montinari (Munich: Deutscher Taschenbuch Verlag; Berlin and New York: de Gruyter, 1980).

Reading Nietzsche

The essays and lectures assembled here are the products of a special sort of opportunity to read Nietzsche, that of the editor of his works. As such, I am aware of the fact that my practice of reading, the results of which I share here, is conditioned as *one single* perspective. In his practice the editor remains confined, at least provisionally, within the net of his historical, philological fore- and hindsight—so much so that the Nietzsche interpretation behind this volume is hidden from him, that it has, so to speak, eluded him, that it has not yet been discovered by him. We achieve here mere preliminaries, mere warnings, mere assessments from the retrospection of one possible reading of Nietzsche. The real matter of concern, though, direct confrontation with Nietzsche himself, appears to have been postponed, to have been moved to the indefinite future. Quite the opposite! My desire, as the author of this undertaking, is to open a dialogue with Nietzsche's *readers.* The title—*Reading Nietzsche*—should signify a (slow) process of acclimation to the turbulent waters of his thought. If everyone who enters them is destined to shipwreck, then every attempt at swimming in any possible fashion—including that of going against the current—is justified.

Mazzino Montinari
Academic Faculty
University of Berlin
Early March 1982

1   Reading Nietzsche

1

One rightfully expects that the editor of the new critical edition of Nietzsche's collected works and correspondence would have something to say on the topic of "reading Nietzsche," particularly since he has occupied himself almost exclusively with Nietzsche for twenty years, and the little that he has published other than the edition—such as the essays collected here—have no other purpose than as instruction on reading Nietzsche. The edition itself: what is it, when all is said and done, if not the suggestion to read Nietzsche anew and differently?

Today we experience a strange, noteworthy, but also dubious return of Nietzsche. We may even say that today a new myth is forming around Nietzsche within a gigantic cultural syncretism in which elements of conservative ideology coexist with those of Marxist or leftist and anarchist theories. Our edition has contributed to this return. I believe and hope that it, as a recommendation for the critical reading of Nietzschean philosophy, has not yet seen all its fruits ripen.

Certainly the edition alone cannot prevent a distorted reading of Nietzsche, just as the old incomplete editions have not prevented the production of significant and still relevant Nietzsche studies (Löwith, Jaspers, Heidegger, Fink, Andler, Salin). Many current works (such as those of Wolfgang Müller-Lauter) point out a deep-reaching philosophical and historical renewal of Nietzsche studies; important new building blocks for the reconstruction of Nietzsche's predecessors, immediate intellectual circles, and posterity have been supplied. That everything happened in part with, and by means of, the new collected edition cannot avert the fact that in Germany, too (as already in France and Italy), a new Nietzscheanism is forming (several signs of which have been visible for some time), and indeed, for the simple reason that popular demand and the phenomena of fashion develop in our time according to their own laws and causes, of which—so long as they are at work—the critical intellect and the historical sense remain unconscious.

2

As far as my personal reading of Nietzsche is concerned, it happened shortly before my collaborative work with my friend and teacher, Giorgio Colli, from which, at the beginning of the sixties, the project of a new collected works of Nietzsche originated. The personal, philosophical, and political disillusionment of the troubled end of the fifties allowed me again to pick up Nietzsche, whom I had not read since my days in secondary school. Without becoming a Nietzschean, I read freely through Nietzsche. This happened, mind you, after the fashion of Thomas Mann, who wrote, "Who takes Nietzsche at face value, takes him literally, believes him, is lost."[1]

In fact Nietzsche, more than any other author, becomes a personal experience for his readers; he challenges us to pose radical questions, to engage in argumentation about his thoughts, to expose our own moral Tartufferies, to let go of dearly held prejudices, but also to formulate resolute contradictions. In this sense, reading his writings works a liberating effect. Precisely those of his readers who are not prepared to confess themselves as his admirers confirm the radicality and honesty of his thinking, as with Nietzsche's unique and intellectually equal friend Franz Overbeck in Basel, the freethinker and theologian who never condescended to discipleship during the course of showing him all sorts of personal affection and attention. On the occasion of Nietzsche's death, this friend wrote: "Nietzsche was the man in whose proximity I breathed most freely, and accordingly I exercised my lungs in their most joyous use granted to me in the realm of human existence by engaging him in conversation. His friendship has been of too much value for me in life to still have any desire to ruin it for myself by some posthumous passion."[2] Whoever cannot breath more freely in Nietzsche's proximity should be discouraged from reading Nietzsche. In other words, Nietzsche must not be dogmatized, since if it were permitted to serve any old dogmatism, such as that of Buddhism, Christianity, Marxism, Freudianism, and so forth, then it would not be allowed—indeed, it would be nearly indecent—to be a Nietzschean, or as Jaspers put it, "Even those who hold fast to outmoded dogmas are closer to the truth than those who turn Nietzsche's thoughts into dogmas."[3] In fact, there is no reading of an author like Nietzsche, who called convictions "more dangerous enemies of truth than lies" and "prisons,"[4] worse than one presenting his violent and unsettling stream of thought as a rigid dogma. This is true, mind you, for both the Nietzschean literati at the turn of the century and the Brownshirts of the thirties, as well as for the ideologically dull anti-Nietzscheans à la Rudolf Augstein, to mention by name one of the most recent and most awful of this sort.

3

But if reading Nietzsche is—according to Thomas Mann, once again—an art, "and nothing clumsy and straightforward is admissible, <so that> every kind of artfulness, irony, reserve is required in reading him,"[5] then emancipation via Nietzsche must not be understood in the sense of an arrogant and contented abruptness in our intellectual attitude toward everything and everyone. Reading Nietzsche and reading him well, accordingly, means not constraining him by isolated catchphrases, by radicalism, by taking his pronouncements literally, but at the same time, as Jaspers reminds us, by not becoming sophistical and narrow ourselves.[6] After these general premises, the question arises: in what ways may the new critical edition help us toward a proper reading of Nietzsche? In these three respects, by

1. presenting each of Nietzsche's works as the respective philosophical and artistic shaping of definite paths of thought from a definite time in his life and creativity,
2. setting his works in an internal relation to his notebooks and thereby to Nietzsche's own development as a whole, and
3. bringing Nietzsche into a fruitful connection with his historical predecessors, immediate intellectual circles, and posterity, above all through reconstruction of his sources.

In other words, the critical collection of his works renders possible a philological-historical basis for reading Nietzsche's works, which must count as the presupposition of any philosophical interpretation.

4

The three points I have mentioned may best be verified by concrete examples.

Concerning number 1: In particular, this point concerns the developmental history of Nietzsche's works; this results from reading the critical apparatus. So it is of no small significance to learn through the preliminary material listed in the commentary that Zarathustra was the original protagonist in an entire series of aphorisms that Nietzsche wrote in 1881 for *Gay Science,* long before the creation of *Thus Spoke Zarathustra* (1883).[7] Among these we find the significant aphorism 125 concerning the death of God. In the final version the speech announcing God's death is delivered by a "madman"; in the preliminary material it is Zarathustra. Zarathustra is superseded <*aufgehoben*>, so to speak, by the later work of the same name in which the thought of eternal recurrence, in whose immediate vicinity the figure of Zarathustra arose (August 1881), achieved its complete artistic and philosophical expression. In general the less meaningful variations also demonstrate how serious Nietzsche was in the choice of words, accentuation, and rendering of nuances for his ideas. No image, word, or even punctuation mark was accidental with Nietzsche. Patiently taking this into consideration makes the reader richer; it makes him deeper, more observant, more suspicious (toward Nietzsche and himself).

Concerning number 2: We will leave the uninteresting question, Which is more important for Nietzsche, his works or his notebooks? to speculators and those obsessed with generalizations. And we will calmly establish instead that the works and notebooks stand in a supplementary and explanatory relation to each other—assuming, of course, that the notebooks are read chronologically, as in the new critical collected edition.[8] Concerning this I provide three examples here:

I. In *The Birth of Tragedy* we are able to trace two separate lines of thought: on one side, the exposition concerning the paired opposites "Apollonian-Dionysian"; on the other side, that concerning the death of tragedy from Socratism and from the "conscious aesthetics" of Euripides. If we include the preliminary material for *The Birth of Tragedy,* we discover that the subject of the decline of Greek tragedy and the conflict with so-called Socratism was the earlier core of the book on tragedy (back into the year 1868) and that the famous pair Apollonian-Dionysian appears for the first time in "The Dionysian Worldview," from summer 1870. The blending of the two lines of reasoning in the final version was not entirely successful for Nietzsche. Yet I do not wish to conceal that the entire problem of interpretation of Nietzsche's philosophical firstling is still wide open. Perhaps an attentive, slow reading of the super-rich notebook materials will bear some fruit in this connection, in particular, important sources for Nietzsche who are mentioned in the fragments but who have received no consideration whatsoever in the research.

II. The notebooks from autumn 1882 to winter 1884–85 constitute the absolutely necessary supplementary background of the four parts of *Thus Spoke Zarathustra.* Better than does any commentary to this work, the *Zarathustra* fragments and plans elucidate Nietzsche's intentions, as, for example, with the figures of the fourth part. And that is no accident. When in *Ecce Homo* Nietzsche speaks of the four parts of his work as "ten-day compositions" <"Books" §5>, that is not true for the appearance of the basic ideas and their exposition, of the various parables, metaphors, proverbs, of the poetic ideas and narrative framework, of the individual characters, and so on, which are present in the notebooks long before the writing of the respective parts of *Zarathustra*. Nietzsche entered sketchy notes into small notebooks continually, almost daily (often during his hikes); he then wrote them down in larger notebooks without orienting them, for the time being, according to a definite plan—that is to say, without looking for an arrangement of his material or altering a previously outlined order. (Incidentally, as Nietzsche's thought in the process of becoming, this is true of the entirety of the notebooks). Then, when he came to the composition of a part of *Thus Spoke Zarathustra,* he could complete it quickly, because he had already prepared for it, without knowing the literary outcome of his work in advance.[9]

III. If one had read Nietzsche's last writings, *Twilight of the Idols* and *Antichrist,* together with the chronological background of the notebook fragments from 1887–88, as is possible today, then the even less interesting discussion concerning the "Will to Power" would never have arisen; I would certainly like to add nothing to it!

Concerning number 3: We should never forget that our reading of Nietzsche is a "postponed, delayed reading."[10] That is, the questions Nietzsche answered through his writings and meditations are not identical to our questions. To really understand him, one must consequently make the attempt to understand those questions (and the ones posing the questions). We must be able to understand Nietzsche historically *also* (not *only:* a note for the speculative). As a result, it is the necessary task of Nietzsche research to seek his sources, to reconstruct his ideal library, to become acquainted with those contemporaries with whom he had argued, along with Nietzsche's real bonds to individuals and circles of his time who would become decisive for his later impact: Nietzsche's predecessors, immediate intellectual circles, and posterity. This historical work—be it through commentaries of the *Kritische Studienausgabe,* through the publication of Nietzsche's correspondence, through the gradual knowledge of important documents from Nietzsche's time (such as Cosima Wagner's diaries), or finally, through research in monographs, along with biographical works such as those by Curt Paul Janz, Werner Ross, or the Wagner biography of Martin Gregor-Dellin—has been only partially accomplished.[11] In these ways the good reader of Nietzsche becomes aware that an "edifying" <*erbaulich*> reading of his author is scarcely possible. By "historicizing" Nietzsche, the good reader places him in the grand tradition of German classicism and romanticism, of the European, above all, French, culture; he concretely participates in his confrontation with Stendhal, Emerson, Dostoyevsky, and Tolstoy; he learns that Nietzsche's conversational partners in Paris from the eighties to the close of his intellectual productivity were the Goncourt brothers, Turgenev, Sainte-Beuve, Renan, Baudelaire, Astolphe de Custine, Balzac, Flaubert, Georges Sand, Maupassant, Paul Albert, Ferdinand Brunetière, Edouard Scherer, Paul Bourget, and many more or less significant others; and he establishes that Nietzsche's readings of natural science is of great significance, for example, for his meditations concerning the doctrine of eternal return of the same and concerning the will to power as a philosophical principle.

5

Perhaps Nietzsche scholars and readers will reproach me that such a reading as I present here amounts to a historical and philological interpretation of his philosophy. I would like to remind them, on the first count, what Nietzsche wrote concerning the "historical sense," and on the second count—and by way of conclusion—that he wished for a philological reading of his own writings.

His confrontation with the historical sense amounts to more than just what he had written in the second of his *Unfashionable Observations* (1874). He himself said this twelve years later in the preface to the second volume of *Human, All Too Human:* "What I had to say against the 'historical sickness' I said as one who had slowly and toilsomely learned to recover from it and was in no way prepared to give up 'history' thereafter because he had once suffered from it" <Hollingdale translation>. But by 1878 at the latest, Nietzsche believed it necessary to claim in aphorism 10 of *Assorted Opinions and Maxims* that the philosophy of history had deteriorated: "The veil-philosophers and world-obscurers, that is to say all metaphysicians of finer or coarser grain, are seized with eye-, ear- and toothache when they begin to suspect that the proposition 'The whole of philosophy is henceforth forfeit to history' is quite true. On account of the *pain* they feel, they must be forgiven for throwing stones and dirt at him who speaks thus: the proposition itself, however, can thereby become dirty and unsightly for a time, and its effectiveness be diminished."[12]

In 1882 Nietzsche once again spoke of the historical sense in aphorism 337 of *Gay Science.* This is the "distinctive virtue and disease" of contemporary humanity: "This is the beginning of something altogether new and strange in history: If this seed should be given a few centuries and more, it might ultimately become a marvelous growth with an equally marvelous scent that might make our old earth more agreeable to live on. We of the present day are only just beginning to form the chain of a very powerful future feeling, link for link—we scarcely know what we are doing" <Kaufmann translation>.

In this thoroughly honest aphorism, the finest quality of Nietzsche's thinking is expressed, his openness toward the not yet conceived possibilities for humanity in the world of immanent eternal recurrence after the death of God. The godlike feeling of being able to assimilate the entirety of history in oneself finally becomes the sign of the "future humanity."

I return now to my main topic—reading Nietzsche—and do so by allowing Nietzsche himself to address the question of a philological reading of his writings.

In *Ecce Homo* he wishes for himself a good reader, "a reader as I deserve him, who reads me the way good old philologists read their Horace" <"Books" §5, Kaufmann translation>. The year before, 1887, he had expressed it still more clearly and unmistakably in the preface to *Daybreak:*

> This preface is late but not too late—what, after all, do five or six years matter? A book like this, a problem like this, is in no hurry; we both, I just as much as my book, are friends of *lento.* It is not for nothing that I have been a philologist, perhaps I am a philologist still, that is to say, a teacher of slow reading:—in the end I also write slowly. Nowadays it is not only my habit, it is also to my taste—a malicious taste, perhaps?—no longer to write anything which does not reduce to despair every sort of man who is "in a hurry." For philology is that venerable art which demands of its votaries one thing above all: to go aside, to take time, to become still, to become slow—it is a goldsmith's art and connoisseurship of the word which has nothing but delicate, cautious work to do and achieves nothing if it does not achieve it *lento.* But for precisely this reason it is more necessary than ever today, by precisely this means does it entice and enchant us the most, in the midst of an age of "work," that is to say, of hurry, of indecent and perspiring haste, which wants to "get everything done" at once, including every old or new book:—this art does not so easily get anything done, it teaches to read *well,* that is to say, to read slowly, deeply, looking cautiously before and aft, with reservations, with doors left open, with delicate eyes and fingers. . . . My patient friends, this book desires for itself only perfect readers and philologists: *learn* to read me well!" <Hollingdale translation>

Notes

1. Thomas Mann, *Addresses Delivered at the Library of Congress, 1942–1949* (Washington D.C.: Library of Congress, 1963), 99 <LOC document 834M31L1963>.

2. Carl Albert Bernoulli, *Franz Overbeck und Friedrich Nietzsche: Eine Freundschaft* (Jena: Eugen Diedericks, 1908), vol. 2, p. 423.

3. Karl Jaspers, *Nietzsche: An Introduction to the Understanding of His Philosophical Ac-*

tivity, trans. Charles F. Walraff and Frederick J. Schmitz (Chicago: Henry Regnery, 1965), 455.

4. Compare *Human, All Too Human* 1:483; *Antichrist,* sec. 54.

5. Mann, <*Addresses,*> 99.

6. Jaspers, <*Nietzsche,*> 455.

7. See pages 70–71 of this volume.

8. See page 80 of this volume.

9. See KGW VII₁, p. viff. (editor's preliminary remarks).

10. See Mazzino Montinari, *Su Nietzsche* (Rome, 1981), 106ff.

11. Concerning the history of Nietzsche scholarship after 1945, see Jörg Salaquarda, ed., *Nietzsche* (Darmstadt, 1980), esp. Salaquarda's introduction. Concerning the present situation, see Bernhard Lypp, "Nietzsche: ein Literaturbericht," *Philosophische Rundschau,* issue 1–2 (1982).

12. See page 38 in this volume. <Quotation is from Nietzsche, *Human, All Too Human,* trans. R. J. Hollingdale (Cambridge: Cambridge University Press, 1986).>

2   The New Critical Edition of Nietzsche's Collected Works

Our edition has a previous history. It was in the small medieval Italian town of Lucca when we—a small group of secondary school students—first heard the name "Nietzsche" from the mouth of our admired philosophy teacher, Giorgio Colli. At that time—1943—he was twenty-six years old and sought to lead us through the "stubble field" of philology to facilitate an image of classical Greek philosophy. But we also learned opposition to Fascism from him. The best among us became freedom fighters then. The rest of us were expelled from school because of an anti-Fascist demonstration. Our teacher Colli was forced to flee to Switzerland. In the darkest hours of 1943 to 1944, the "expelled" students usually assembled at my apartment; there, to the anger of the Fascists, new strikes were prepared. By our own means and with the help of other anti-Fascist teachers, some studying was done; there we discussed and read aloud from Plato, Kant, and—*Thus Spoke Zarathustra*. Why am I narrating this? To make clear that the defective (because ideological) equation "Nietzsche = Fascism" was not true for us Italian anti-Fascist secondary school students at that time. Our relation to Nietzsche also remained essentially uncompromising when the war was at an end and Nietzsche fell victim to denazification in Germany.

After many years, a period of widely divergent personal experiences, we—my former philosophy instructor, Giorgio Colli (who now taught the history of Greek philosophy at the University of Pisa), and I—met again in Florence for a collaborative work in 1958. My friend wanted to make a new Italian translation of Nietzsche's writings, as complete as possible (works and notebooks), for the Turin publisher Einaudi; in doing so, we would reopen the 1956 discussion begun by Richard Roos in France[1] and revived by Karl Schlechta in Germany[2] concerning the trustworthiness of previous publications of Nietzsche's last writings, in particular, the question of the so-called "philosophical prose magnum opus" (as Elisabeth Förster-Nietzsche denominated it), the "Will to Power."

2

What was the situation surrounding editions of Nietzsche before Schlechta's much-discussed undertaking?

After Elisabeth Förster-Nietzsche had halted Peter Gast's attempted start at a complete edition of Nietzsche's works (1892 to 1893), she founded the so-called Nietzsche Archive, first in Naumburg (1894) and later in Weimar (1897); the grand archive of the classics inspired her in the choice of a new location in the city of classics. The so-called *Großoktavausgabe* (GOA) of Nietzsche's works was the most significant achievement of the collective editorial activity of the Nietzsche Archive; it appeared in Leipzig in the years 1894 until 1926, published first by C. G. Naumann and then by Kröner. It was organized in the following fashion:

Part 1, volumes 1–8: works edited by Nietzsche himself, along with, in the eighth volume, *Antichrist,* "Dionysian Dithyrambs," poems, proverbs, and fragments of poetry from the unpublished writings.

Part 2, volumes 9–16: unpublished writings. Volume 15 contains *Ecce Homo* and the first two books of the so-called "Will to Power." Volume 16 contains books 3 and 4 of "The Will to Power" along with a philological commentary by Otto Weiss. Volumes 15–16 appeared for the first time in 1911; they were to replace volume 15 (1901), which contained a shorter version of "The Will to Power." In like fashion, the definitive volumes 9–12 were to take the place of volumes 9–12 (1896–97) prepared under the care of Fritz Koegel.

Part 3, volumes 17–19: philologica, containing Nietzsche's philological publications as well as (selected) Basel lectures.

Volume 20: an index by Richard Oehler.[3]

The GOA became the foundation for *all* later editions, including the Musarion edition. The latter distinguished itself from the GOA exclusively by the publication in the first volume of a number of youthful writings from the years 1858 to 1868 not yet known at that time (1922), by a new collation of the philological writings with the manuscripts, and finally by the publication of the "preface" "Über das Pathos der Wahrheit" <"On the Pathos of Truth">, not yet known as such.[4] Otherwise the Musarion edition takes its material, without reworking, entirely from the GOA, albeit in a different, more chronological arrangement. As far as the genuinely philosophical unpublished works are concerned, the Musarion edition is identical to the GOA and exactly as incomplete and untrustworthy as it. Its monumentality is inversely proportional to its scholarly significance.

3

The GOA appeared in Leipzig beginning in 1894. Editors relieved one another, each in his turn having fallen into the bad graces of Frau Förster-Nietzsche. But that is a chapter in itself—even if not the least interesting in the long story of Nietzsche editions. The first part of the GOA, by the way, shows no serious textual alteration, despite the change of editors responsible over the course of the years; volume 8 alone appeared in three distinct versions.[5]

The situation is entirely different with the second part, that is, with the publication of Nietzsche's unpublished philosophical works. This appeared in its final form between 1901 and 1911. This most important editorial accomplishment of the Nietzsche Archive appeared in detail as follows:

Volumes 9–10 (1903), edited by Ernst Holzer. These volumes contained unpublished writings and fragments from 1869 until 1876. The arrangement of the fragments is predominantly chronological. A table of manuscripts, along with the philological evaluative report by Ernst Holzer, provides insight into the chronology of the edited texts.

Volumes 11–12 (1901), edited by Ernst and August Horneffer. They contain unpublished fragments from the period of *Human, All Too Human* until *Thus Spoke Zarathustra,* hence from 1875–76 until 1886 (addenda to *Zarathustra*). To the extent that the manuscripts from which the fragments were published originate in one definite, not overly long period of time, chronology is respected here to a certain degree. However, they were ripped out of their special chronological and intellectual context through a categorizing, purportedly neutral arrangement according to key terms such as philosophy in general, metaphysics, morality, woman and child, and so on. Consequently, one is unable to follow, for example, the creation of Nietzsche's simultaneous works.

Volume 13 (1903), edited by Peter Gast and August Horneffer, contains "unpublished material from the period of the revaluation," thus forming a sort of warehouse for the philosophical Nietzsche rejects, meaning that it contains fragments that were not taken for the "Will to Power," although they come from precisely the same manuscripts and plans that were used for the "Will to Power." The fragments are consequently ordered not chronologically (which, with a time span of six years, is serious) but instead according to systematic, categorizing keywords.

Volume 14 (1904), edited by Peter Gast and Elisabeth Förster-Nietzsche, is, so to speak, an extension of the warehouse for philosophical rejects from the period of the revaluation. The years of the origin for the fragments range from approximately 1882–83 to 1888. Fragments of this volume are also ripped from the same manuscripts and plans that served for the compilation of the "Will to Power" and ordered not chronologically but rather according to systematic, categorizing keywords. In the second half of the volumes one occasionally finds several chronologically connected fragments, even under the category "From the Prefaces Material" (that is, Nietzsche's prefaces to the new printing of his works in the years 1886 and 1887).

Both volumes 13 and 14 conclude with an index to the locations of the fragments in the handwritten texts with citations for manuscript page numbers.

Volumes 15–16 (1911), edited by Otto Weiss, contain, along with *Ecce Homo,* the "Will to Power" in its expanded and final form as it was first published by Peter Gast and Elisabeth Förster-Nietzsche in the pocketbook edition.[6] To this Otto Weiss appended the following: (1) the plans, arrangements, and outlines from 1882 to 1888 (the multifariousness of these plans is the best refutation of the selection in preference to *one* plan from the year 1887, on which foundation Peter Gast and Elisabeth Förster-Nietzsche based their compilation—but there is more!); (2) notes to the text that, as Richard Roos has noted, betray a certain cynicism for an edition that had otherwise proved itself philologically, as had Otto Weiss himself. In fact, they record an indeterminate number of deletions, interpolations, and willful partitioning of unified texts. But there is still more! Here, the remarks contradict the text. The index of locations for the so-called aphorisms of the "Will to Power" in the manuscripts and a chronological chart of the handwritten notes at the end unintentionally expose the entire scale of the actual compilation. Here we must not forget that fragments of volumes 13 and 14 come from precisely the same manuscripts from which those of volumes 15 and 16 were taken. The selection of texts for the construction of a Nietzsche system in the "Will to Power," of such consequence to Nietzsche studies for decades, must be completely and fully attributed to the two philosophical (and philological) nullities, Heinrich Köselitz (alias Peter Gast) and Elisabeth Förster-Nietzsche.[7]

But there is even more! The new "Will to Power," from 1906/11, was supposedly to replace the old volume 15, that is, the first "Will to Power." Edited by Peter Gast and Ernst and August Horneffer, this first version of "Will to Power" appeared in the year 1901. It contained only 483 aphorisms, not the 1,067 of the final edition. In this one, however, 17 of the 483 from the first vanished. Otto Weiss gives only 5 in the appendix to his edition as "doubtful texts," although they are genuine Nietzsche texts. In comparison to the first edition, the new one was inferior, too, because they took 25 continuous and often very important texts, ripped them apart, and increased their number to 55, as, for example, with the significant fragment concerning "European nihilism" (dated by Nietzsche, Lenzer-Heide, June 10, 1887).[8] This and other fragments are better read in the edition from 1901 than in the one from 1906/11, which has become canonical. It should finally be remarked that Elisabeth Förster-Nietzsche acknowledged several unpublished fragments—also from notebooks from the so-called period of revaluation—only in her biographical publications.

4

That the epoch-making compilation "Will to Power" was untenable as Nietzsche's main philosophical work was proven in 1906–7 by Ernst and August Horneffer,[9] as well as fifty years later by Karl Schlechta. Elsewhere I have indicated the noteworthy resistance of Nietzsche enthusiasts and scholars against what was really at stake.[10] Here I want only to emphasize once more that this commonplace—namely, that Nietzsche wrote no work under this title, yet *in the end wanted to*—was utter "fact" when, at the beginning of the thirties, a new beginning came to the Nietzsche Archive itself. <Montinari sarcastically refers to the nazification of the archive.> For example, Walter Otto, a member of the academic committee for the new edition, may be heard in this way on December 5, 1934: "A tremendously important, but just as difficult, task stands before the editors of the notebooks from the last years. Because what is incumbent on them is nothing less than that they produce Nietzsche's writings, from the area of thought of 'will to power,' for the first time without conventional editing, precisely such as they are found in the extraordinarily difficult to read, and now newly decoded, manuscript notebooks."[11]

Hans Joachim Mette, who in his preliminary report as editor of the 1932 edition[12] had taken stock of the editorial activity of the Nietzsche Archive, expressed himself in this fashion:

> The result is . . . , seen from a scholarly standpoint, not entirely satisfactory . . . to the . . . ideas. To destroy the essential form of Nietzsche's thoughts in the unconnected aphoristic writings in the individual notebooks, and

to arrange the individual sentences of the notebooks according to a systematic interpretation, was not very fortunate, even if certainly justified
at the time; the decision of the Nietzsche Archive foundation to restore this
unpublished writing to its original form in the critical edition of the works
signifies in this regard a liberating act.

At that time Elisabeth Förster-Nietzsche was still alive; she toned down
Mette's statements in the final version of the preliminary report (1933),[13] so
much so that the cautious criticism of the earlier systematic arrangement disappeared completely, and there was no longer any talk of a "liberating act" but
rather only mention of a "printing in the original sequence, as unabridged as
possible." And in spite of this, one year later—and still in Elisabeth Förster-
Nietzsche's lifetime—the call was raised by Walter Otto to eliminate any conventional editing of "Nietzsche's writings, from the area of thought of 'will
to power,' for the first time"! The crux of the issue was finally and unambigu-
ously clarified.

5

The entire argument surrounding the Schlechta edition appeared all the more
curious to those of us who were obscure and uninvolved at that time (the beginning of the sixties). We just could not see, for example, that such a solemn
notion as an "unwritten law" according to which no one may organize an
edition of Nietzsche who does not honor him (thus Pannwitz)[14] would be tak-
en as a serious objection to Schlechta's undertaking, let alone as a solution
superior to it. For we were faced with a very simple question: "According to
which text should our translation be produced?" On the other side, we also
could make no proper use of the Schlechta edition for our purposes. In his first
two volumes we had before us a mostly faithful rendition of the first printing
of Nietzsche. In his third volume, however—under the title "From the Unpublished Writings of the Eighties"—we had precisely the same material that had
become known through the publication of the second (and canonical) "Will
to Power" of 1906 and 1911, although arranged somewhat chronologically. In
Florence we were certainly able to eliminate several incomprehensible omissions for which, curiously enough, none of his opponents (Löwith, von den
Steinen, Pannwitz, and so on) had reproached him. Specifically, with the help
of Otto Weiss's apparatus to the "Will to Power," we were able to undo many
crude mutilations and dismemberments of the fragments; in addition, we
were also able to consult the first one-volume "Will to Power" (1901) and thereby recover those important fragments that had otherwise vanished from the

second, final, yet much more extensive "Will to Power" of 1906/11; finally, we were able (in agreement with Schlechta's call for a restoration of the manuscripts) to supplement the manuscripts used for the "Will to Power" (hence, those that were also indexed in volumes 15 and 16) on the basis of the manuscript indexes in volumes 13 and 14 of the GOA. In these ways we were able to produce a more extensive edition of unpublished writings from the eighties, to some extent chronologically ordered according to the manuscripts. In spite of this, new difficulties arose:

1. For a good half of the unpublished writings (from the period of *The Birth of Tragedy* until approximately *Thus Spoke Zarathustra:* 1869 to 1885), we in Florence had no choice other than to translate the texts as they were published in volumes 9–12 of the GOA—systematically, not ordered chronologically and according to manuscript, because we had no page index for the manuscripts to them.

2. Volumes 9–12 of the GOA were published in two different versions: the one by Fritz Koegel, from the years 1896–97, had been replaced with the later one by Peter Gast, August and Ernst Horneffer and Ernst Holzer, from the years 1901–3, but many important things that could be read in the Koegel edition were no longer found in the later one, and vice versa.

3. Our hair stood on end when we came again and again to decisive passages from Nietzsche cited in the text of the lesser Nietzsche biography (1912–14) by Förster-Nietzsche, only to read remarks by Richard Oehler such as: "apparently [!] not printed in the Works," "quoted from the manuscripts, not printed in the published works," or "apparently not published in the *Nachlaß.*" Were not all these also texts that we ought to translate? Did not the same issues arise in view of the earlier so-called greater biography by his sister,[15] where one likewise can read many texts that were otherwise unknown (at least without "scholarly" concessions to the remarks)? Or as regards the pocketbook edition, too, which also has texts not contained in the GOA?

4. For a large number of fragments that are found in the so-called folders <*Mappen*>, no chronological arrangement was possible on the basis of the index in volumes 13–16 of the GOA.

5. If we also had the manuscript page numbers where the fragments could be found, what would be the sequence according to which we should translate the fragments having the same page number?

6. What lay dormant in the manuscripts for more than seventy years that we—in Florence—could never come to know at all?

We had a trustworthy text for only the juvenilia and philologica, which may be found in the unfinished historical-critical edition (volumes 1–4, 1933–40), hence, for the writings from 1854 until spring-summer 1869 (the earliest Basel period); however, from that we could understandably use only a small portion for an Italian translation. The genuinely philosophical unpublished writings, from the preliminary studies for *The Birth of Tragedy* to the last Turin period, had not yet been reconstructed by scholars. Twenty years' worth of Nietzsche's intellectual creativity, from the summer of 1869 to January 2, 1889, presented itself to us in an extremely unsatisfactory and incomplete form.

What were we to do? We decided then and there to check the condition of the Nietzsche manuscripts. In the first days of April 1961, I went to Weimar. There I found Nietzsche's manuscripts carefully stored in the Goethe-Schiller Archive; there I was able—thanks to the friendly kindness of Helmut Holtzhauer, general director of the Nationale Forschungs- und Gedenkstätte der klassischen deutschen Literatur,[16] which supports the Goethe-Schiller Archive, and of Karl-Heinz Hahn, director of the archive—to take an initial fourteen-day inventory, whose outcome read: we require a completely new text of Nietzsche's unpublished works. My friend Colli drew the single correct conclusion from this: since no one else has had the idea to produce it, we ourselves would edit the entire unpublished writings; moreover, since the one also conditions the other, we would prepare a critical collected edition of Nietzsche's works. With this, our plan exceeded its original framework. However, our publisher, Einaudi, no longer appeared to be interested in so grand an undertaking. Happily we soon won over to our bold adventure an old friend who had founded a small publishing house: Luciano Foà, the manager of Adelphi Edizioni in Milan. But we also had to have a German publisher. They were not to be found at that time, however; none of the German publishers to whom we presented our proposal appeared to trust the somewhat risky matter. At the crucial moment, however, Foà succeeded in winning over the great Parisian publisher Gallimard. In this way our work was financially secured; moreover, we could wait for a German publisher with confidence. The first Italian volumes appeared in 1964 on the basis of a recent solid advance from German philologists. In the same year, we—Giorgio Colli and I—met Karl Löwith at an international discussion on Nietzsche in Paris. Because of this meeting Heinz Wenzel, manager of the humanities division at the Walter de Gruyter publishers, Berlin, became aware of our work in Weimar, for Wenzel, who wanted to produce a Nietzsche edition at his publishing house, had consulted with him <Löwith> in February 1965. Shortly thereafter, the *German* publisher Walter de Gruyter bought the rights to publish the new critical edition of the collected works of the *German* philosopher Friedrich Nietzsche in the original language from the *French* publisher Gallimard and the *Italian* Adelphi. The German edition has appeared since autumn 1967. It encompasses thirty-three volumes in eight parts. To this point in time <1981>, twenty volumes have appeared. The most important outcome of these fourteen years is that Nietzsche's unpublished philosophical works, from 1869 to 1889 (hence from the preliminary studies for *The Birth of Tragedy* to Nietzsche's psychological breakdown), are henceforth complete: approximately 5,000 pages rather than the 3,500 of the previously most comprehensive edition, the GOA.

6

The completion of the Nietzsche edition will claim many more years of my life. Whether such a completion shall be granted me, I do not know. I know one thing with certainty, though; without having met my friend and teacher, Giorgio Colli, *I* would never have begun it. Without Giorgio Colli there would not be *the* new edition of Nietzsche, about which I have reported.

Notes

1. Richard Roos, "Les Derniers Écrits de Nietzsche et leur publication," *Revue de Philosophie* 146 (1956): 262–87.

2. Friedrich Nietzsche, *Werke in drei Bänden,* ed. Karl Schlechta (Munich, 1956–58); see, in particular, Schlechta's appendix to the third volume, pp. 1383–1432 ("Philological Evaluative Report").

3. Richard Oehler gives an overview of the Nietzsche editions produced by the Nietzsche Archive in HKG 1, pp. xxviii–xxix.

4. From the Basel unpublished writings: "Five Prefaces to Five Unwritten Books," from 1872.

5. In 1894, edited by Fritz Koegel; in 1899, edited by Arthur Seidl; and in 1906, edited by the Nietzsche Archive (Peter Gast).

6. *Nietzsches Werke,* pocketbook edition: vol. 9, "The Will to Power" (1884–88), "Attempt at a Revaluation of All Values"; vol. 10, "The Will to Power" (1884–88, continuation), *Twilight of the Idols* (1888), *The Antichrist* (1888), "Dionysian Dithyrambs" (orig. 1888) (Leipzig: C. G. Naumann, 1906).

7. Elisabeth Förster-Nietzsche wrote in her evaluative report concerning volume 9 of the pocketbook edition: "The first edition of the Will to Power appeared in the year 1901; the new edition before you has been completely reworked and assembled, the first and third books by Mr. Peter Gast, the second and fourth books by the undersigned."

8. See pages 90–91 in this volume.

9. See August Horneffer, *Nietzsche als Moralist und Schriftsteller* (Jena, 1906); Ernst Horneffer, *Nietzsches letztes Schaffen* (Jena, 1907).

10. See pages 145–47 in this volume.

11. In *Bericht über die neunte ordentliche Mitgliederversammlung der Gesellschaft der Freunde des Nietzsche-Archivs* (Weimar, 1935), 15.

12. First appeared as a special printing: H. J. Mette, *Der handschriftliche Nachlaß Friedrich Nietzsches* (Leipzig, 1932), 81–82.

13. See H. J. Mette, "Sachlicher Vorbericht zur Gesamtausgabe der Werke Friedrich Nietzsches," HKG 1, pp. cxxi–cxxii.

14. See R. Pannwitz, "Nietzsche-Philologie?" *Merkur* 2 (1957): 1073–87.

15. Elisabeth Förster-Nietzsche, *Das Leben Friedrich Nietzsches,* 2 vols. (Leipzig, 1895, 1897, 1904).

16. This same support was shown to our undertaking by Holzhauer's successor, General Director Professor Walter Dietze. I would like to expressly and cordially thank him at this time.

3   Nietzsche's Recollections from the Years 1875–79 Concerning His Childhood

At an age that we call, after Dante, "midlife," a personal dynamic came to its conclusion in Nietzsche, the beginnings of which lay in turn several years in the past; here we mean the year 1879, when Nietzsche turned thirty-five and left the University of Basel, and by extension the years leading from 1875 to 1879. In our considerations we will presuppose several things and, consequently, will intentionally *not* treat the crises in his relation with Richard Wagner, the worsening of his medical condition, or his own personal philosophical developments. We focus exclusively on Nietzsche's childhood memories from this period because they have not at all been noticed by Nietzsche scholarship up to this point, and we seek to construct from them an image Nietzsche painted at that time of the first years of his life. In aphorism 360 from *Assorted Opinions and Maxims,* he himself tells us that these memories are significant by placing dreams of the past in an explicit relation to "violent changes": "If we dream of people we have long since forgotten or who have for long been dead, it is a sign that we have gone through a violent change within ourself and that the ground upon which we live has been completely turned over: so that the dead rise up and our antiquity becomes our modernity" <Hollingdale translation>. We are able to better and more precisely define the chronology of the matter (dreams of the long forgotten or dead), which Nietzsche refers to in his aphorism, with the aid of a short note in a small notebook titled "Memorabilia" and coming from the summer of 1878, the time in which most of the aphorisms of *Assorted Opinions and Maxims* originated: "In Sorrento, I scraped off the accumulated moss of nine years. Dreaming of the dead."[1] During the winter of 1876–77, while in Sorrento, this "violent change" completed itself in relation to

Wagner and Schopenhauer's philosophy. The latter is the topic of discussion in a letter from Nietzsche to Cosima Wagner on December 19, 1876; moreover, Nietzsche tells his friend that he has been dreaming as of late: "The isolation of my current existence, forced by my illness, is so intense that the last eight years are almost entirely forgotten, and the earlier times of life, about which I had not at all thought in the like-natured concerns of these years, force themselves on me with violence. Almost every night I associate in my dreams with long-forgotten people, above all with the dead. Childhood, youth, and schools are all very much current to me."[2] The "violent change," the departure from the recent past, from Wagner and Schopenhauer, is accompanied by the scraping off of the "accumulated moss" of eight or nine years. The most distant past becomes the present. On the basis of the texts contained in the new critical collected edition, however, Nietzsche's personal crisis may be dated further back, indeed, to the summer of 1875, when he, far from the dress rehearsal of the *Ring* in Bayreuth, sojourned in Steinabad, near Bonndorf. In the middle of the composition of the fourth of the *Unfashionable Observations,* in a notebook that Nietzsche himself titled "Preliminary Studies for Richard Wagner in Bayreuth" and that he used in that summer of 1875, we read,

> The moon rose like it did for me at Nimsdorf in the golden meadow! In Plauen, at the stream among butterflies in the spring. In Pobles, when I wept over my lost childhood. In Röcken, when I discovered multicolored snail shells. At Naumburg, when I dug for limestone and gypsum. In Pforta, when the fields were barren and autumn came. When grandfather explained Hölty's "Wundseliger Mann" to me. At Bonn where the Wied (?) flows into the Rhine, the feelings of childhood overcame me once again. Then in the Neugasse, where I had always heard the admonishing voice of my father. The story that the housekeeper for Pastor Hochheim told me. Skating in the moonlight at Krummen Hufe. "What I earn by day on my lyre"—Ravaillac.[3]

Fragments of this sort are very rare with Nietzsche; the one just cited is the first trace of the mature man's personal reflection on childhood and youth; the last one is found four years later in a notebook from late summer 1879. In the following years Nietzsche returned to this sort of reminiscence only seldom, essentially twice and in entirely different circumstances, the final one being in *Ecce Homo,* where we read an allusion to his childhood, the total significance of which may be seen by means of the notes treated here for the first time. Of course, we may not exclude the possibility of there having been other such notes no longer extant, lost through the destruction of manuscripts. It is all the more important, then, that the "violent changes" were accompanied by such unambiguous memories and, indeed, not just from the summer of 1875 but also from the spring and summer of 1878. We have already mentioned the "Memorabilia" notebook; here one finds, along with notes concerning other later periods of his life, numerous notes illuminating and broadening the notes from the summer of 1875 in a most surprising way. The following juxtaposition is possible:

Summer 1875

The moon rose like it did for me at Nimsdorf in the golden meadow! In Plauen, at the stream among butterflies in the spring. In Pobles, when I wept over my lost childhood. In Röcken, when I discovered multicolored snail shells. At Naumburg, when I dug for limestone and gypsum. In Pforta, when the fields were barren and autumn came. When grandfather explained Hölty's "Wundseliger Mann" to me. At Bonn, where the Wied (?) flows into the Rhine, the feelings of childhood overcame me once again. Then in the Neugasse, where I had always heard the admonishing voice of my father. The story that the housekeeper for Pastor Hochheim told me. Skating in the moonlight at Krummen Hufe. "What I earn by day on my lyre" —Ravaillac.

Beginning of Year/Summer 1878 (Memorabilia)

Seven years old. Felt loss of childhood.
Wind erosions. Stones as signs of a prehistoric age.
Depressed afternoon—
Worship in the chapel at Pforta, distant organ notes.
But at twenty years of age at Bonn where the Lippe (?) flows into the Rhine,
felt as a child.
Daemons—warning voice of my father.
The housekeeper of the hermit parsonage.
Witness to my early seriousness.
Christ as child among the scholars.
Krummen Hufe moonlight skate
"What I earn by day with my lyre, by night is lost to the wind."
Happy days of life!
As a child, saw God in a glow.
First philosophical writing concerning
the origin of the devil (God can imagine himself only by means of representation of his opposite).
As a relative of pastors, earlier insight into the intellectual and spiritual limitations, abilities, arrogance, decorum.[4]

We will group our considerations around this important, unique biographical core to better investigate the function and significance of these acts of introspection. This shall proceed according to four main points.

1. Nietzsche's bond to his deceased relatives
2. The happiness of childhood

3. The loss of childhood
4. Nietzsche's childhood religious experience

1. Nietzsche's Bond to His Deceased Relatives

We return to the fragment from the summer of 1875. In what order did Nietzsche write down his memories? First, he names several places in Thüringia, the Prussian province of Saxony, and the kingdom of Saxony, which define the landscape of his childhood: Nirmsdorf (near Weimar), Plauen, Pobles (near Weißenfels), and Röcken (near Lützen).

The sentence concerning Nirmsdorf has no equivalent note from the early year/summer of 1878; however, it is supplemented by a composition of the fourteen-year-old Nietzsche, "From My Life," the first biographical sketch from the year 1858. There we read: "I also remember the stay in Nirmsdorf, where the dear late Uncle Pastor was. I still remember how the evening moon shone on my bed and how the golden meadow looked before me; then how Aunt Auguste spoke, 'The moon has risen / the golden little star is resplendent, and so on.' Oh, I shall never forget this time."[5]

Friedrich August Engelbert Nietzsche, the eldest stepbrother of Nietzsche's father, Carl Ludwig, lived in Nirmsdorf, near Weimar, until his death in 1858, shortly before the composition of the cited biographical note. He was born there in 1785, and his father, Friedrich August Ludwig, who was also the father of Carl Ludwig (born in 1813 from a second marriage) and therefore Nietzsche's paternal grandfather, died in 1826. Thus the pastor at Nirmsdorf was the sole surviving Nietzsche of an earlier generation; consider that Nietzsche's maternal grandfather, David Ernst Oehler, was two years younger than this stepuncle. Further, we should remember that Friedrich August Ludwig Nietzsche was born in 1756 and in this way realize that Nietzsche's living heritage—I know no other word for it—reaches back into the middle eighteenth century through his grandfather's generation, into the revolutionary period, into the Age of Enlightenment. In fact, both Friedrich August Ludwig, doctor of theology at the University of Königsberg, and his firstborn son, Friedrich August Engelbert, exercised a decisive influence on the intellectual development of their son and younger brother, respectively, Carl Ludwig, the prematurely deceased father of the philosopher. They were both representatives of a rationalistic Enlightenment orientation in theology influencing Nietzsche's father, too, in that he joined the so-called revival movement <*Erweckungsbewegung*> of the Lutheran church. According to Reiner Bohley, the foremost expert on the spiritual milieu in which Nietzsche grew up, "many of Carl Ludwig Nietzsche's sermons give one the impression that the orthodox and devotional-revivalist pastor was still held hostage to the rationalist generation."[6] Indeed, Bohley writes further that "the difference between rationalism and the revivalists remains intact in the quiet 'world of sentiment' <*Gemüthswelt*> of Nietzsche's father—his son, too, would grow up later in this contradiction both at Naumburg and at Pforta." Nietzsche's theological thinking has this as a not-to-be-underestimated premise.

Auguste Nietzsche, his aunt, who spoke (or sang?) Matthias Claudius's "Evening Song" to her little nephew on that unforgettable evening, was one of Carl Ludwig Nietzsche's two unmarried sisters. She and Rosalie (as the other sister was called) lived with their brother and his family in Röcken and later, from 1850, after the death of their brother (July 27, 1849), in Naumburg.

Auguste Nietzsche died on August 2, 1855; when the news reached him during the holidays, Nietzsche went "outside and wept bitterly." Eight months later his grandmother Erdmuthe Krause, his father's mother, also died. In this year (1856) the collective household with Rosalie Nietzsche, the surviving sister of Nietzsche's father, was broken up. She remained in Naumburg, where her two stepsisters also lived (Fredericke, married name "Daechsel," who lived together with the unmarried sister, Lina), but kept a distance from her sister-in-law and her two children, who, for their part, rented the first apartment on Neustrasse (which Nietzsche called Neugasse) in Naumburg.

His bond to his relatives named "Nietzsche," especially that to Rosalie Nietzsche, remained meaningful for the young Nietzsche; when she died on January 3, 1867, Nietzsche saw, in his own words, an entire piece of his past, and foremost of his childhood, fade away from him. Nietzsche's last aunt, Fredericke Daechsel, died at the age of eighty in September 1873. The letter Nietzsche wrote to his mother on this occasion is telling:

> So, then, our good aunt is gone, and again we are more lonesome. Growing old and growing more lonely appear to be the same, and at the very end one is together only with oneself, and our death makes others more lonely. Since I know little of my father and must conjecture about him from occasional stories, his closest relatives were more to me than aunts usually are. I am happy whenever I think of Aunt Riecken <Fredericke Daechsel>, as well as of the others in Plauen, that they maintained a special character into advanced age and had the self-control to depend less on the external world and on the dubious benevolence of humanity; I am happy about this, because in this I discover the lineal characteristic <*Raceeigenschaft*> of those named "Nietzsche," and I have it myself. Consequently, my good aunt was always most friendly in her disposition to me, because she sensed that we were related in this salient matter, that is, the matter of what it is to be a Nietzsche.

And so I honor her memory, by desiring in my heart, if I should grow old, at least to not fall short of myself, that is, of the spirit <*Geist*> of my forebears.[7]

We call this letter "telling" because, first of all, an unceasing desire for an image of his father is expressed in it. We learn from several suggestions in his sister's letters that Nietzsche had placed high hopes on the literary estate of his last aunt Nietzsche for elucidation of his own, and his father's, life story, but Fredericke Daechsel had already burned most of the important family papers in her own lifetime, "because in her letters, she had conjectured who ought to be granted a posterity."[8] Second, in these lines a secondary emphasis resonates indicating a contrast, conscious on Nietzsche's part, between those who "are named 'Nietzsche'" and those who—so we would add—"are named 'Oehler,'" whom we shall discuss later.

Continuing our commentary, in Plauen there was a whole series of relatives named "Nietzsche": three sisters and three sons of Friedrich August Engelbert Nietzsche, along with a brother of Erdmuthe Krause. Nietzsche himself wrote in his biographical note of 1858 concerning the rather bourgeois atmosphere reigning in Plauen: "Once . . . we fulfilled the wish of our dear aunt in Plauen and stayed there several weeks. Since the rich factory owners there are our very relatives, the visit was continually a truly pleasant one."[9]

Nietzsche was nine years old at the time of this stay, when he went to see a hermit's parsonage near Plauen, a visit of which we learn only in the notes of 1875 and 1878. In the notes Nietzsche's discusses his early seriousness, and he compares himself to "Christ as a child among the scholars." We see that Nietzsche's contemplation of the distant past, of the "forebears," is at the same time contemplation of the Christian religious roots of his own life. His father's voice spoke with admonition and warning to the small boy in Naumburg; it was the voice of a pious pastor. And so Nietzsche remembers it in 1875 and 1878 as in no way necessarily frightening; entirely the opposite, because it sincerely belonged to a happy time, for which the mature Nietzsche longed.

Finally, a cordial relation existed with his maternal grandfather, the pastor David Oehler in Pobles, whom Nietzsche mentions in connection with an early, perhaps very first literary-poetic impression, Hölty's poem "The Country Life." God, living nature, and death are the motifs explained by the country pastor of Pobles, and the impression would never fade away.

The Country Life
Marvelously blessed man who left the city
Every rustle of the trees, every babble of the brook
Every gleaming pebble
Preaches virtue and wisdom to him!

Each cloud thicket is, in his eyes, a divine
Temple, where his God more closely prevails,
Each grassy patch an altar
Where he kneels before the sublime.

His nightingale casts a light sleep on him.
His nightingale wakes him again with her warble
When the precious break of day
Shines through the trees upon his bed.

Then he contemplates Thee, God, in the morning mead,
In the mounting splendor of thy evangelist,
The all-ruling sun,
Thee in the worm and budding branch.

He lies in the fluttering grass, when cool breezes blow
Or directs the well water to the flowers
Drinks the breath of the blossoms
Drinks the mildness of evening air.

His straw-woven roof, where the pigeon populace
Sun themselves and play hopscotch, affords him sweet rest
Like treasure for a burgher
Like cushions for a fair lady.

And the hopscotch troops dive and whirl around him and back,
Coo and murmur at him, flutter to his basket
Peck, peck, peck at crumbs and peas
Peck, peck, peck the seed from his hand.

Oft would he walk alone, engrossed in thoughts of death,
Through the village graveyard
Sit down upon a tomb
And contemplate the crosses
And the swaying wreath of the dead.

Marvelously blessed man who left the city!
Angels above bestowed on him their blessings
When he was born, spread flowers
From Heaven upon the boy's crib.[10]

Yet Nietzsche remained fairly distant from his Oehler relatives—among them four uncles and three aunts who were pastors and pastors' wives, respectively. Also, the bond to Grandmother Oehler, who, as the last relative of her generation, died in 1876, was not as close as that to Grandmother Nietzsche. We have already alluded to a contrast between those "who are named 'Nietzsche'" and "those who are named 'Oehler.'" This contrast was even present to Nietzsche's sister as biographer: "The Nietzsche and Oehler families," she wrote, "were quite different." It was more than mere difference, because, as

Reiner Bohley has proved,[11] just a few months after his wedding, Nietzsche's father complained about his parents-in-law, "whom, the longer I get to know, the less and less I can respect. . . . It is such a different direction of life and faith between me and them, that I . . . fear a formal break with the parsonage of Pobles." Specifically, Carl Ludwig Nietzsche, in a letter to a friend, accused his mother-in-law of being "a completely worldly and common woman"! In this connection, we must think of Nietzsche's later conflict with his mother and sister up to the final "expectoration" in *Ecce Homo,* where Nietzsche plays off his supposedly Polish heritage on his father's side against his mother's Germanness: "I am a Polish nobleman *pur sang* <pure bred>, without a drop of bad blood mixed in, least of all German. When I look for the most profound antithesis to me, the incalculable commonality of the instincts, I always discover my mother and sister."[12] We certainly do not need to prove that his mother, but also his sister, was done a great injustice here or that, further, it is not Nietzsche's final definitive word concerning his difficult relations to his closest relatives. In spite of this, the rift symptomatically indicated here, the inner split in Nietzsche's nature in its entire scope, stands before our eyes. It should not be underestimated.

2. The Happiness of Childhood

In his notes from 1875 and 1878, Nietzsche recalled the happy days of childhood: "I shall never forget this time," the fourteen-year-old had already written. Happiness found him, we read further in his autobiography of 1858, "in the open temple of nature," where he found the "truest joy."

The colorful snail shells in Röcken; the golden meadow in the silver moonlight at Nimsdorf; the butterflies at the stream in the spring at Plauen; the excavated stones, limestone and gypsum, as signs of a prehistoric period at Windlücke, a hill between Naumburg and Bad Kösen; autumn in Pforta with the barren fields: these are deeply entrenched experiences of nature in Nietzsche's mind, which mean so much only to him, like a dream to a dreamer, and whose "virgin honey" <*Honigseim*> to use Nietzsche's word, he tasted for the first time as a child. In *Assorted Opinions and Maxims,* number 49, Nietzsche used these early experiences as characteristic of his person:

> *In the Mirror of Nature.*—Has a man not been fairly exactly described when one hears that he likes to wander between fields of tall yellow corn, that he prefers the colors of the woods and flowers in glowing and golden autumn because they intimate greater beauty than ever nature achieved, that he feels quite at home among great thick-leafed nut-trees as though among his blood relations, that in the mountains his greatest joy is to encounter

those remote little lakes out of which solitude itself seems to gaze up at him, that he loves that gray reposefulness of twilight mist that creeps up to the windows on autumn and early winter evenings and shuts out every soulless sound as though with velvet curtains, that he feels the unhewn rocks to be unwillingly mute witnesses to times primeval and has revered them from a child, and finally that the sea, with its rippling snake-skin and beast-of-prey beauty, is and remains alien to him? <Hollingdale translation>

That is Nietzsche's self-description, and it goes back—as we know now for the first time—to the happy days of his childhood. To the same belongs the exhilaration of ice skating. The notes of the youthful Nietzsche contain ideas concerning this physical exercise that bring to mind similar statements by Klopstock and Goethe. Nietzsche specified the location of this experience as a suburb of Naumburg, the "Krummen Hufe"; and both times, 1875 and 1878, he recited a folk proverb, "What I earn by day with my lyre, by night is lost to the wind" <Was ich des Tages verdient auf meiner Leyer, das geht des Abends wieder in den Wind>, about which we have no further information. Nietzsche returned once more to ice skating in autumn 1878, when he coined the concept of *bonheur de l'escalier* <*Treppen-Glück*> in an unpublished note. "*Bonheur de l'escalier.* Youths on the ice, an oil lamp on a moonlit night at the stream."

What is *bonheur de l'escalier*? Shortly afterward Nietzsche clarified it in an aphorism from *Assorted Opinions and Maxims:*

> 352. *Bonheur de l'escalier.*—Just as many people's wit fails to keep pace with the opportunity for it, so that the opportunity has already gone out of the door while the wit is still standing on the stairs: so others experience a kind of *Bonheur de l'escalier* which runs too slowly always to stay by the side of fleet-footed time: the best they get to enjoy of an event, or of an entire period of their life, falls to them only a long time afterwards, and then only as a feeble, spicy fragrance that awakens sorrow and longing—as though it had once been possible to imbibe this element to the full, though now it is too late. <Hollingdale translation>

The happiness of childhood, too, is a *bonheur de l'escalier,* a lost happiness. Childhood itself is necessarily lost.

3. The Loss of Childhood

Nietzsche made note of this loss both in 1875 and 1878 as a meaningful but, insofar as the outward connection concerns us, secretive event. At seven years of age, during a visit to Grandfather Oehler in Pobles, he experienced the loss of childhood and wept over it. "At an absurdly early age, at seven, I already knew that no human word would ever reach me," said Nietzsche ten years later, shortly before his mental breakdown, in *Ecce Homo*.[13] The dramatic attitude of this late statement should not be overlooked: Nietzsche was thankful for his fate, too, and precisely because of his solitude from an early age, he never suffered from solitude <*Einsamkeit*> but always only from "multitude" <*Vielsamkeit*>. The function of this recollection of the loss of childhood in *Ecce Homo* is entirely different from that at the time of the compositions from 1875 and 1878. Of course, *I myself* see no contradiction in this, for the reason that I have long been inclined to search for the alleged contradictions in Nietzsche's life and works within the understanding of Nietzsche scholars rather than with Nietzsche himself. *Ecce Homo*, it should be said again and again, remains the best and most trustworthy biography of Nietzsche. The unexpected confirmation, by unpublished notes written long, even ten years before, and in an entirely different atmosphere, of this interpretation in *Ecce Homo* concerning an event that happened to the seven-year-old strengthens my considered viewpoint. However, we must accept that this event of a "loss of childhood" is most closely bound with a new feeling, the feeling of loneliness; being a child means *not* being lonely.

The feeling of childhood, of not being alone, overcame Nietzsche once more, "near Bonn, where the Wied (?) flows into the Rhine," when he turned twenty years old. This was the journey from Naumburg to Bonn that Nietzsche then made with Paul Deussen, after the closing of school, to visit the university. Nietzsche traveled via Elberfeld to Oberdreis, in Westerwald, to Deussen's family home (Deussen's father was pastor there), and on October 16 (one day after his twentieth birthday) he and his friend walked from Oberdreis to Neuwied, where the Wied feeds into the Rhein. On October 11, 1866, Nietzsche wrote to Carl von Gersdorff: "Several afternoons were so mild and sunny that I incessantly reflected on that singular and irretrievable time when, free from the pressures of school for the first time, I saw the Rhine with the free, proud feeling of an inexhaustibly rich future." Not a word—how cheap!—to his friend Gersdorff about the feeling of childhood having overtaken him at that time. But Nietzsche speaks of a feeling of irretrievability in an aphorism from *The Wanderer* that we—or so I believe—are able to read differently and better and understand after everything said up to this point:

> 168. *Sentimentality in music.*—However favourably inclined we may be towards serious and opulent music, there are perhaps, and for that very reason, hours when we are overcome, enchanted and almost melted away by its opposite: I mean by those utterly simple Italian operatic melismas which, in spite of all their rhythmic monotony and harmonic childishness, sometimes seem to sing to us like the soul of music itself. Whether you admit it or not, you pharisees of good taste, it is so, and it is now my con-

cern to discuss the riddle presented by the fact that it is so and to offer a few guesses at its solution.—When we were still children we tasted the virgin honey of many things for the first time, and the honey never again tasted so good, it seduced us to life, to living as long as we could, in the shape of our first spring, our first flowers, our first butterflies, our first friendship. At that time—it was perhaps about the ninth year of our life—we heard the first music that we actually *understood,* the simplest and most childish music therefore, not much more than a spinning-out of our nurse's song or the organ-grinder's tune. (For one has first to be *prepared* and *instructed* even for the most trifling "revelations" of art: there is no such thing as a direct "effect" of art, however much the philosophers have fabled of it.) It is to these first musical delights—the strongest in our life—that our sensibilities connect when we hear those Italian melismas: childhood happiness and the loss of childhood, the feeling that what is most irrecoverable is our most precious possession—this too touches the strings of our soul and does so more powerfully than art alone, however serious and opulent, is able to do. <Hollingdale translation>

4. Nietzsche's Childhood Religious Experience

Being a child, *for Nietzsche, too,* means being secure in family and God. "As a child, saw God in a glow," he noted in 1878. The pious child, as Christ among the scholars, obtained an early "insight into the intellectual and spiritual limitations, abilities, arrogance," of his pastoral relatives. But that was not enough. He philosophized very freely concerning God. "First philosophical writing concerning the origin of the devil (God can imagine himself only by means of a representation of his opposite)."

At that time he was twelve or thirteen years old. He is said to have become an atheist a few years later, if we wish to believe—and why should we not?— an unpublished note that is the last of the sort of interest to us and that originated in the summer of 1879. "As an atheist I never said grace at Pforta and was never made weekly inspector by the teachers. Tact!"[14] We know of this early atheism from no source other than this note, which loses none of its value even when we learn that Nietzsche was indeed once made weekly inspector at Pforta.[15] Most certainly Nietzsche never conversed with his narrow relatives concerning what was occurring at the core of his being. When his uncle Edmund Oehler, in a letter to his nephew from November 1862, referred to him as "a searching, struggling, combative soul,"[16] we should sooner think of what Nietzsche had hidden from the pious uncle than what he had confided to him. Signs thereof are to be found in the unpublished writings from this early period, even if sparse and cautious: I am referring to the poem "Before the Crucifix" and the novella "Euphorion."

But now back to Nietzsche's first philosophical writing. It is mentioned twice in the later unpublished writings, the first time in 1884: "When I was twelve years old, I fabricated <*erdacten*> a marvelous trinity: specifically, God the Father, God the Son, and God the devil. My conclusion was that God, thinking of himself, created the second person, but that in order to think of himself, he had to conceive his own opposite, and thus had to create it as well. With this I began to philosophize."[17] The second time was in the summer of 1885:

> The first trace of philosophical reflection that I have for an overview of my life, I encounter in a short composition from my thirteenth year: it contains a scenario concerning the origin of evil. My presupposition was that for God to create something was the same thing as for God to conceive of it. Then I concluded: God thought of himself at the time he created the second person, but to be able to think of himself, he had to first conceive his opposite. The devil had the exact same age as the Son of God in my notion, and an even more clear origin—and the same *origin*. Concerning the question whether it would be possible for God to conceive his opposite, I supported myself by saying that for him, everything is possible. And second, *that* he has done it is a fact, in the case where the existence of God is a fact; consequently, it is also possible for him.[18]

Unfortunately, this composition has been lost. In 1887 Nietzsche speaks of it once again, this time in a published work, *On a Genealogy of Morals,* preface 3:

> Because of a scruple peculiar to me that I am loth to admit to—for it is concerned with *morality,* with all that has hitherto been celebrated on earth as morality—a scruple that entered my life so early, so uninvited, so irresistibly, so much in conflict with my environment, age, precedents, and descent that I might almost have the right to call it my *"a priori"*—my curiosity as well as my suspicions were bound to halt quite soon at the question of where our good and evil really *originated.* In fact, the problem of the origin of evil pursued me even as a boy of thirteen: at an age in which you have "half childish trifles, half God in your heart," I devoted to it my first childish literary trifle, my first philosophical effort—and as for the "solution" of the problem I posed at that time, well, I gave the honor to God, as was only fair, and made him the *father* of evil. <Kaufmann translation>

The tendency toward free-spiritedness was given to the young Nietzsche very early; it comported all too well with his religiosity. In fact, as he himself said repeatedly, it was the logical conclusion to his inherited Christianity. It was not in vain that Nietzsche grew up in the "most dangerous region of Germany": "The most dangerous region of Germany was Saxony and Thüringia: nowhere else was there more intellectual activity and knowledge of human nature, together with free-spiritedness, and yet it was all so modestly concealed by the ugly dialect of the populace and their eagerness to be of service that you hardly noticed that what you were dealing with was the intellectual sergeant-majors of Germany and its instructors in good and evil."[19]

Notes

1. KGW IV₃ 28[33], p. 366.

2. Compare to pages 36–37 in this volume.

3. KGW IV₁ 11[11], p. 270.

4. Fragments from "Memorabilia": KGW IV₃, the series after 28[8.6.7.8.9.13.6.7], pp. 362ff.

5. HKG I, p. 15.

6. Reiner Bohley, "Nietzsches Taufe: Was, meinst du, will aus diesem Kindlein werden?" *Nietzsche-Studien*, vol. 9 (1980), 393.

7. Nietzsche to Franziska Nietzsche, September 21, 1873, KGB II₃, pp. 159f.

8. Elisabeth Nietzsche to Nietzsche, November 29, 1873, KGB II₄, p. 352.

9. HKG I, p. 15.

10. Hölty's poem is quoted here according to L. Chr. H. Hölty, *Werke und Briefe,* ed. U. Berger (Berlin and Weimar, 1956), 165. <Montinari offered only the final two stanzas. I have given the poem in full.>

11. Bohley, "Nietzsches Taufe," 389f.

12. Compare page 103 in this volume.

13. KGW VI₃, p. 295 (*Ecce Homo,* "Wise," 10).

14. KGW IV₃ 42[68], p. 466.

15. See Nietzsche to Franziska and Elisabeth Nietzsche, March 13 and May 28, 1864, KGB I₁, pp. 274 and 279.

16. Edmund Oehler to Nietzsche, November 17, 1862, KGB I₁, p.391.

17. KGW VII₂, 26[390], p. 251. Goethe reported something similar to this of himself in *Dichtung und Wahrheit,* vol. 8, bk. 7 (conclusion).

18. KGW VII₃, 38[19], p. 344.

19. KGW IV₃, p. 149 (*Assorted Opinions and Maxims,* aphorism 324) <Hollingdale translation>.

4   Nietzsche and Wagner One Hundred Years Ago

1

Exactly one hundred years ago today—on March 26, 1877—Nietzsche wrote to his friend Franz Overbeck in Basel, "From various perspectives, I have pondered what I shall discuss first with you, when we reunite."[1] In this letter written from Sorrento, Nietzsche reported on his eye ailments and the life of the small society surrounding Malwida von Meysenbug in Sorrento, to which he, along with Paul Rée and Albert Brenner, belonged. Death was also a topic of discussion in this letter; Overbeck's mother had died, and in Wilhelmine Hahn-Oehler, his own grandmother, Nietzsche had lost the final piece of childhood. Almost simultaneously, he was painfully affected by the passing of his "greatly beloved teacher," Friedrich Ritschl. Letters from this time period and unpublished notes regarding it allow us to detect a mood of wise resignation and of reflection on the past, respectively—and of a slow departure.

Slow departure, above all, from the most recent past, from Wagner and Schopenhauer, from all the illusions of an entire period of life, of youth. One of the most important pieces of evidence for this is Nietzsche's letter of December 19, 1876, to Cosima Wagner, written for her birthday. It is scarcely known, since it was not included in the *Historische-Kritische Gesamtausgabe* at the time of its termination. The crucial passages read:

> A person grows more quiet year after year and finally no longer has a word to say concerning personal matters. The isolation of my current existence, forced by my illness, is so intense that the last eight years are almost entirely forgotten, and the earlier times of life, about which I had not thought at all

during the like-natured concerns of these years, force themselves on me with violence. Almost every night I associate in my dreams with long-forgotten people, above all with the dead. Childhood, youth, and schools are all very much current to me; in the light of earlier goals and actual achievements, it occurs to me that I have, in everything that I have in fact done, exceeded the hopes and general wishes of youth by a wide margin and that in contrast to everything that I have consciously planned for myself since, I had been able to achieve on the average still only one-third. And so it shall probably remain into the future. If I were completely well, who knows how far into adventure my tasks would have taken me? In the meantime, I am compelled to lower the sails somewhat. For the next few years in Basel, I plan to complete several philological works. [. . .] Once I have brought the philologica into order, something still more difficult awaits me: would you be interested in a difference with Schopenhauer's doctrines, brewing for some time but only now coming to consciousness? I oppose him on practically all matters of general principle: since I am removed from all dogmatic principles, the entire affair concerned only the human being, as I have already written concerning Schopenhauer. For the time being, my "reason" <Vernunft> has been quite active—as a result, then, my life has become a degree more difficult, the burden greater! How is one supposed to hold out till the end? Do you know that my instructor Ritschl has died? This very year I found confirmation, in a letter from Ritschl, of a touching impression that I had gotten from his earlier association with me; he remained confident and loyal toward me, though he thought a temporary suspension of the association, indeed, a cautious separation, to be necessary. I have him to thank for the single genuine act of benevolence in my life; I owe my position as professor of philology at Basel to his open-mindedness, his keen insight, and his willingness to help young men. With him, the last great philologist died; he left behind approximately 2,000 students who call themselves his own, among them some thirty university professors.[2]

2

There is hardly another letter from Nietzsche's Sorrentine period as meaningful as the one to Cosima Wagner just quoted. In it I even hear resonance of *Ecce Homo,* such as the "unintentionality of what has actually been achieved" in Nietzsche's life. This—if I may say—reminds me of the rigorousness of all the autobiographical statements of this philosopher up to, and in, *Ecce Homo*— of course with imprecision in the details, about which Nietzsche scholars must rightfully concern themselves without losing sight of this great rigor.

This letter seems meaningful to me in three aspects.

1. It registers the deep breach that this period directly after Bayreuth represents in Nietzsche's life. Eight years at the Basel position, but also eight years of friendship and comradery with Wagner, lay between "earlier periods of

life" and this Sorrentine present. Nietzsche looked back on the pre-Wagnerian period, certainly not only on childhood and school years but also on specific figures and ideas that he had never forgotten but that lay buried alive, so to speak, in him. I am thinking, for example, of Democritus, who in conjunction with the reading of Lange's *History of Materialism* stimulated important lines of thought for him in 1868. In fact, in his notes from 1873 concerning the Greek philosophers, Nietzsche recalled Democritus's world "without moral and aesthetic significance," his "pessimism of chance," and his "rigorous natural science" and "refutation of the mythological," but Democritus seems to become quite topical for Nietzsche again in the summer of 1875 (we will say more about this summer later).[3]

2. The manner whereby Nietzsche remembered his instructor Ritschl for Cosima Wagner is worth pondering, specifically when he writes, "he remained confident and loyal toward me, though he thought a temporary suspension of the association, indeed, a cautious separation, to be necessary." Cosima Wagner knew, just as we too know, the precise reason for this difficulty and separation: Nietzsche's "Wagnerian" book, *The Birth of Tragedy.* "With every fiber of my being, I belong so decisively . . . to the *historical* orientation and historical consideration of human matters that for me the solution to the world never seemed be in one or another philosophical system. [. . .] You cannot ask an 'Alexandrian' and scholar to condemn *knowledge* and find the world-shaping, redeeming, and liberating power in art *alone.*" Thus had Ritschl written his student, who had prompted him to a judgment on the latter's book on tragedy at that time (1872). And five years later these words must have held a new significance for Nietzsche, for he had by then come to this expression concerning philosophy and history: "The veil-philosophers and world-obscurers, that is to say all metaphysicians of finer or coarser grain, are seized with eye-, ear- and toothache when they begin to suspect that the proposition 'The whole of philosophy is henceforth forfeit to history' is quite true."[4] And he wrote specially to Sophie Ritschl, the widow of his instructor, "I am happy [. . .] to think that he [Ritschl], when he could not agree with me, still regarded me confidently. I believed he would still see the day when I would be able to publicly thank and honor him, as I have wished with all my heart for so long, and in a way that perhaps he, too, could have enjoyed."[5] It would be a mistake to interpret these words from Nietzsche as dictated solely by the wish to speak comfortingly to an old friend: they indicate, on the contrary, a more profound change in his stance toward the deceased teacher and toward his own book on Greek tragedy.

3. The philologica under discussion in the letter to Cosima would have included the "Democritea." <This philologica would have also included his lecture series on the pre-Platonic philosophers, including a lengthy one on Democritus, which Nietzsche at this time intended to publish.> Nietzsche does not get around to it, but he does mention his "difference with Schopenhauer's doctrines"—for example, by quoting this sentence from his friend Paul Rée, "The moral person does not stand any nearer to the intelligible (metaphysical) world than the physical person," and then commenting, "This

proposition, hardened and sharpened by the hammer blows of historical knowledge, can perhaps someday, at some future time, serve as the ax that gets laid to the root of the 'metaphysical need' of human beings."[6] Ten years later, when Nietzsche philosophized with a hammer, this passage from *Human, All Too Human* became in *Ecce Homo* a sort of advance announcement for the "revaluation of all values," which Nietzsche equated with this hammer blow of *historical* knowledge. I have the impression that even today people have not entirely believed him.

We now know what Nietzsche "pondered" at that time and to what purpose he had employed his reason: his book *Human, All Too Human,* which took on its provocative form in the Sorrentine papers. Statements from this letter must have raised worries for Cosima and Richard Wagner. In Cosima's reply they remain unstated: "But, of course, it would interest me to hear what arguments you have against our philosopher," wrote Cosima on January 1, 1877.[7] A few weeks thereafter her thoughts and those of Richard Wagner regarding Nietzsche were expressed in a letter to Malwida von Meysenbug, in which we read, among other things:

> I believe that there is a dark, productive fundament in Nietzsche, of which he himself is not conscious; from this comes what is of significance about him, what shocked even himself. Whereas everything that he thinks and says, what is seen in the light, is really not worth much. The telluric in him is important, the solar meaningless and, by means of its struggle with the telluric, even frightening and unproductive. [. . .] "Great thoughts come from the heart," says Vauvenargües, a phrase that may be applied to Nietzsche, since his great thoughts come to him certainly not from his head . . . but from where? Indeed, who can say?[8]

3

At the end of October 1876, Nietzsche was in Sorrento, where he met with Wagner for the last time: the Wagner family had already departed for Italy at the beginning of September. Little is known from documents concerning Nietzsche's meetings with Wagner in Sorrento. Paul Rée was also with them. According to Nietzsche's later statements, Wagner warned him at that time about Rée; also, Wagner's conversation with Nietzsche concerning *Parsifal* would perhaps be misplaced in these days. In an unpublished note from 1886, Nietzsche wrote: "Wagner speaking of raptures, which he would attribute to the Christian sacrament. That was decisive for me; I considered him *conquered.*"[9] The fact is that after his return from Italy, Wagner set about the composition of *Parsifal.* It concerned, as is well known, an earlier inspiration on Good Friday 1857, in Zurich, which served as its outline in the year 1865—with the ponderable date of August 25—and with which, according to Cosima's entry in her diaries, Nietzsche became familiar on December 25, 1869: "Read *Parsifal* with Professor Nietzsche, a renewed horrible impression."[10] The composition of *Parsifal* was completed at the end of 1877, at the same time that Nietzsche finished his work on the printer's draft of *Human, All Too Human.* On January 3 a copy of *Parsifal* with Wagner's dedication came to Nietzsche in Basel; a few days later the printer's manuscript of the book for free spirits arrived at the printers. In this sense, the ominous crossing of the two books, "as if swords had crossed,"[11] of which Nietzsche speaks in *Ecce Homo,* rings true. The Wagner of *Parsifal* and the Nietzsche of *Human, All Too Human* were truly antipodes. The year 1878 signifies the end of a friendship and an alliance. The pinnacle of the friendship was reached in 1872, when, at the beginning of January, Wagner wrote to the author of *The Birth of Tragedy:* "I have never read anything more beautiful than your book! It is simply glorious! [. . .] I have just said to Cosima that you stand second only to her, then, for a long time, there is no one until we reach *Lenbach,* who has painted such a striking portrait of me!"[12] And in June of the same year: "Strictly speaking, you are the one and only gain life has brought me so far, aside from my beloved wife."[13] One year thereafter, the alliance no longer seemed so secure to Wagner: "As far as you are concerned," he wrote on September 21, 1873, "I shall repeat the conceit, which I recently expressed to my family, namely, that I foresee the time when I shall be obliged to defend your book against you, yourself. I have been reading it again and I swear to you, by God, that I consider you the only person who knows what I am driving at."[14]

The quiet war between Nietzsche and Wagner began five years later, in 1878 ("both of us remained silent," said Nietzsche in *Ecce Homo*): each attacked the other openly, yet not by name. Richard Wagner died after another five years, in 1883. A contemptuous word regarding his rebellious friend comes down to us from his last hours in Venice. An essay in the *Internationale Monatsschrift* concerning *Gay Science* provided the occasion for it. Cosima noted in her diary: "I spoke of it; R[ichard] looked at it to make known his complete antipathy to it. Everything of value in it being borrowed from Schopenhauer, and the 'person being entirely loathsome to him.'"[15]

It was Nietzsche who had created a Wagnerian and Schopenhauerian book in his philosophical firstling, *The Birth of Tragedy.* It was Nietzsche, again, who departed from Wagner and Schopenhauer to seize possession of himself once more. The irresistible single-mindedness of Nietzsche's intellectual development clarifies the personal schism, not vice versa. Wagnerians and Nietzscheans have overvalued the selection of biographical epiphenomena. Scholarly biographical research should be employed with historical and philological meticulousness here, too. Yet the historical sense also requires that one remain conscious of the decisive fact that Nietzsche's schism with Wagner was an intellectual act, a philosophical act clarifying every previous biographical discovery, and bringing details—*edita, inedita,* or entirely *inaudita*—to light, too.

4

Now back to Nietzsche and Wagner one hundred years ago and to the portrait that Nietzsche painted—with means other than Lenbach's—of the Bayreuth maestro in the summer of 1876. Wagner considered the portrait not "striking" but instead "incredible." "Where did you learn so much about me?" he asked his friend.[16] The uncanniness of the fourth of the *Unfashionable Observations, Richard Wagner in Bayreuth,* still remains, in both Nietzsche and Wagner scholarship and elsewhere, as a fairly overlooked fact, in that it is an extremely adroit mosaic of quotations from Wagner's writings, such as *Art and Revolution, Artwork of the Future, Opera and Drama, An Announcement to My Friends,* and others. Wagner was presented and explained by Wagner. In this manner it became a type of mirror for Wagner in Bayreuth, as if Nietzsche were to have asked his friend: "You were that, you wished to be that, are you still that today?" It is a sort of manifesto, then, of the Wagnerian party, which was still viable at that time before the festival: an interpretation before the fact of the event at Bayreuth, the most magnificent act of a modern artist; a challenge to Wagner, to whom Nietzsche suggests a certain interpretation of his life and works. Loyalty distinguishes all Wagner's artworks, according to the fourth of Nietzsche's *Unfashionable Observations.* Would Wagner remain loyal to himself? A reform of the theater means a reform and change of the entirety of modern man in our modern world, in which there is a necessary dependence of "everything <...> on everything else." "It is absolutely impossible," wrote Nietzsche in the fourth section of this text, "to produce the highest and purest effect of performing art without at the same time introducing innovation everywhere, in mores and government, in education and commerce. Having become powerful in one area—in this instance, in the realm of art—love and justice expand further in accordance with the law of their inner necessity and not fall back to the emotionlessness of their former chrysalis."[17] The revolutionary effect of a reformed art is emphasized in an unpublished fragment from the first preliminary work for *Richard Wagner in Bayreuth* (summer 1875): "We—those who know all the things that once came with art properly understood, the network of duties—most deeply despise all existing institutions for the preservation of art." Today art is "an activity of an opulent and self-serving class [...] far from the needs of the nation and basically a means to 'distinguish' themselves from the rest of the nation. Down with art that does not advance revolution in society, does not advance the rejuvenation and unification of the nation!"[18] Here we are completely in the conceptual sphere of Wagner's work *Art and Revolution,* in which the revolutionary mentality of the Wagner of 1848 still prevailed. This cast of mind certainly originates in the sentimental utopian notion of so-called true socialism, a quite German variation on socialism: Feuerbach + Proudhon + (in Wagner's case) Bakunin, that is, left-wing Hegelianism and French socialism. The vague "folk" <*Volk*> and even vaguer "human being" <*Mensch*> are the protagonists of this utopia, which knows no classes and even less a class struggle. Yet Nietzsche radicalized precisely this utopia. It is a "dangerous radicalization," as Hans Meyer has already noted, because it led *ad absurdum* the Bayreuth reflections, concerning whose groundlessness and instability Nietzsche, at least at that time, still deluded himself.

Now here are the main features of that radicalization. It begins with the question concerning the task of history and philosophy for Wagner. "If history were no longer simply a disguised Christian theodicy [*which is, incidentally, a variation on a theme from Ludwig Feuerbach*], if it were written with more justice and passion, then it would truly be least capable of serving the function it serves today: as an opiate against everything subversive and revitalizing." For Nietzsche, it is similar with philosophy: the most important question of all philosophy is, namely, the "extent to which things possess unalterable nature and form, so that once this question has been answered, we can with relentless courage set about the *improvement of that aspect of the world recognized as being alterable.*" But the "insights of human beings" are "very alterable." True philosophers, "instead of keeping their wisdom to themselves," work for the improvement of human judgment. Wagner—as the true disciple of true philosophy—knows how to "imbibe" from philosophy "enhanced resolution and determinacy" for his will, but no "sleeping potions." Bayreuth signifies, in Nietzsche's estimation, the defeat of contemporary society as the pillar of the entire educational structure, of the repellent structure "that now derives its strengths from its reliance on the spheres of power and injustice, from the state and society, and sees its advantage in making these more and more evil and ruthless. [. . .] Anyone who fights for love and justice among human beings has little to fear from it, for his actual enemies will stand before him only when he has concluded his battle against their vanguard, present-day culture." Nietzsche's strategy aims at separating true scholars from contemporary education by means of the Bayreuth reform: without their "tacit contribution," the modern educational structure must collapse, since in this way, only support from the state and society ("the spheres of power and injustice") would remain for it. Expressed in different, perhaps more timely, terms, when scholars and educators leave the "rotting structure" of education, the educational entity will show its repressive character. Nevertheless, the struggle against contemporary culture is only a vanguard skirmish; the real enemy, "who fights for love and justice among human beings," will stand before them for the first time only after the victory won here. Thus, it concerns far more than a "mere" reform of the theater, according to Nietzsche; indeed, "the time is rife <*sic*> for those who wish to conquer and triumph powerfully; the greatest empires stand waiting, a question mark has been added to the names of the property holders." For the supporters of the ideas out of Bayreuth, consequently, art is not a "medicine and narcotic with which we could cure ourselves of all other miserable conditions." And further:

> In the image of the tragic work of art at Bayreuth, we witness precisely this struggle of these individuals against everything that confronts them as a seemingly invincible necessity: against power, rule of law, tradition, convention, and the whole order of things. These individuals can live in no more beautiful way than by preparing themselves to die and sacrificing themselves in the battle for justice and love. [. . .] Art does not exist only for the purpose of the battle itself, but also for the intervals of quiet before and during the battle, for those moments when looking backward and ahead we understand the symbolic. . . .[19]

We would like to learn more about that greatest domain, which lies open and about that question mark, which is set against the name of the possessor. Nietzsche speaks of a struggle for justice and love among men, a struggle led by individuals. And the individual suffers from the following deficiencies <*Mißstanden*>:

1. One cannot be happy as long as everyone around one suffers and creates sorrow;
2. one cannot be moral as long as the course of human events is determined by violence, deception, and injustice; and
3. one cannot even be wise as long as the entirety of humanity has not struggled in competitive zeal for wisdom and has not led individuals to the wisest sort of life and knowledge.

The revolutionary and innovative in the ideas out of Bayreuth, according to Nietzsche's notion, has no relation to historical reality. We hear compelling exhortations; everything appears to fall: educational structures, the state, society. Yet individuals who struggle for justice and love are destined for self-sacrifice. Every concrete consequence of their struggle fails to materialize.

5

Toward the conclusion of his observation, in the tenth section, Nietzsche speaks of an altered future "in which the only supreme blessings and joys that exist are those common to the hearts of all people. [. . .] When presentiment ventures into the distant future in this manner, conscious insight will examine the dismal social insecurity of our present age and will not conceal from itself the danger threatening an art that appears to have no roots at all except in that distant future."[20] Wagnerian art lacks a home in the present; it does not itself give rise (as at the beginning of the observation) to the revolution. On the contrary, Nietzsche wonders, "How can we rescue this homeless art for that future; how can we dam up the flood of the revolution that everywhere appears inevitable so that the blissful anticipation and guarantee of a better future, of a freer humanity, will not be swept away with the many things that are doomed and deserve to be doomed?"

I believe that the role of (Wagnerian) art in the strategy of Nietzsche's writing gradually changed. He had begun to work on it in the summer of 1875; the first eight sections were finished at the end of September, but Nietzsche wrote the three final sections for the first time between the end of May and June 11, 1876 (one year later). Whoever reads the final report to the fourth part of the critical collected works edition will be able to form a rough notion of the great trouble Nietzsche had in reaching the conclusion. In a letter to Erwin Rohde he opined, "Concerning the work itself not one word, at most a sigh of relief."[21]

6

A peculiar relation between art and the future, German spirit and humanity, reformation and revolution, finds expression in those final pages with which Nietzsche chose to conclude his "Bayreuth festival lecture." Something not too far removed from the present, that is, the present reality of the Bayreuth festival, needed to be said. Only with great effort and difficulty did Nietzsche succeed in discovering a bond between *his own* vision of the future and Wagner's artwork. Wagner's concessions to the realities of the German *Reich* in the 1870s were thus reinterpreted as an act of confidence "placed in the German spirit, even with regard to its political aims."[22] This would be, for instance, the "symbolism" of Wagner's *Imperial March*. The people < *Volk* > of the reformation have been destined to "channel the sea of revolution into the placidly flowing stream of humanity" (after a phrase by Carlyle that Wagner also used). Yet Wagner's ideas—as with those of every good and great German—"are *supra-*German, and the language of his art speaks not to nations but rather to human beings. But to *human beings of the future.*" In the eleventh and last section of his observation, Nietzsche states his own interpretation. Here he rejects any utopian explanation of Wagner's ideas. "May good sense preserve us from the belief that someday or other humanity will discover an ultimate, ideal order." And further: "No golden age, no cloudless sky is allotted to these coming generations [. . .] whose approximate features can be divined from the hieroglyphics of his art—to the extent that it is possible to infer the type of need from the type of satisfaction. [. . .] Perhaps this generation will seem on the whole even more evil than the present one—for it will be *more open,* in evil as in good; indeed, it is possible that if its soul were ever to speak out in full, free voice, it would shake up and terrify our soul in much the same way as if it had heard the voice of some previously hidden evil spirit of nature."

That is Nietzsche's vision of the future, not Wagner's. The latter's art shall be an interpretation and clarification of the past for this future, a future whose epitome will be "those among you who are free and fearless, who evolve out of themselves and flourish in innocent egotism, the Siegfrieds among you"— and not the Parsifals, I would add. "The idea of Bayreuth" had "transformed into something that should not puzzle those who know my *Zarathustra:* into that great noon at which the most elect consecrate themselves for the greatest of all tasks":[23] thus Nietzsche in *Ecce Homo* concerning the fourth of the *Unfashionable Observations,* and I believe him on this matter.

This change into something non-Christian, indeed anti-Christian, was still compatible with the Wagner of his revolutionary writings, for example *Art and Revolution,* but not with the religious Christian, Schopenhauerian, Buddhistic development culminating in *Parsifal.* And I once again remind you that Nietzsche had been familiar with the outline of *Parsifal* since Christmas 1869. Certainly he was not surprised by a Wagner allegedly turning pious. With the fourth of the *Unfashionable Observations* Nietzsche still sought to present himself as a sort of Wagnerian provocateur, so to speak. In reality he was at the most extreme point of that crisis, that rediscovery of himself about which he later wrote: "Around 1876 I was terrified to see all I had desired hitherto *compromised,* as I grasped which way Wagner was going now: and I was bound very closely to him by all the bonds of a profound identity of needs, by gratitude, by his irreplaceability and the absolute privation I saw before me."[24]

7

In many of its passages, *Human, All Too Human* harks back to the summer of 1875. From that period originates Nietzsche's program for the emancipation of the spirit. He wrote at that time, one year before Bayreuth: "It still awaits me to express perspectives that are *considered shameful* by the one who entertains them, since friends and acquaintances, too, shall become cautious and frightened. Through this fire I must go. Then I shall belong to myself evermore" (compare aphorism 619). Also: "If I were already *free,* I would have nothing to do with this struggle but rather turn to a work or task on which I could expend my entire energy. Currently, I may only hope to become free gradually, and I intuitively grasp that so far, it is occurring ever more."[25] But what do we read in the best and most trustworthy Nietzsche biography ever written, that is, *Ecce Homo? "Human, All-Too-Human* is the monument of a crisis. It is subtitled 'A Book for *Free* Spirits': almost every sentence marks some victory—here I liberated myself from what in my nature did not belong to me. [. . .] The term 'free spirit' here is not to be understood in any other sense; it means a spirit that has *become* free, that has again taken possession of itself."[26]

We will do well to take Nietzsche's departure from Wagner, his break with Wagnerism, in earnest, at least as earnestly as he himself took it. As a free spirit Nietzsche decided in favor of history and science against metaphysics and religion, in favor of skeptical wisdom versus "convictions," versus belief in general, and in favor of cool reason over the impure thinking of poets and artists such as Wagner. In this way Nietzsche became Nietzsche for the very first time, by means of "the heroic, awe-inspiring achievement and drama of German intellectual history [. . .], the self-overcoming of romanticism in Nietzsche and through him,"[27] as one of the philosopher's best readers, Thomas Mann, proclaimed in the face of Nietzsche's irrational, antihumanistic interpreters of the thirties.

The antinationalism, anti-Germanism, antiromanticism, anti-anti-Semitism, anti-obscurantism, antimetaphysics, anti-irrationalism, and antimyth (i.e., anti-Jesuitism) of Nietzsche's anti-Wagnerian struggle must never be forgotten. I even believe that we have not yet grasped the gravity and significance of the defeat of this anti-Wagnerian, Nietzschean tendency in relation to what was inflicted on the history of German culture in 1933—as representatives of national socialist ideology claimed—when the German people decisively chose instinct over reason, myth to the disadvantage of history, Germanism in favor of Europeanism and—we rightfully add—against Nietzsche, against Goethe, against genuine German culture.

8

All that having been established, we permit ourselves to go into Nietzsche's remaining proximity to, and affinities with, his great antipode. This should occur from three perspectives: first, music, second, the phenomenon of artistic inspiration, and third, aspects of friendship itself.

Music. In July 1882 Nietzsche sojourned in Naumburg to—or so he said—prepare his sister (but in reality, Lou Salomé) for *Parsifal.* He picked up old scores and played them again after so long an interval. "Several passages," wrote Nietzsche to Gast, "appeared to us both [. . .] entirely Parsifalesque! I confess: I am struck with genuine horror at becoming aware again as to *how closely related* I truly am to Wagner."[28] We may well forget my gloss here on their close relation, but not the horror. . . .

Inspiration. Concerning the fourth of his *Unfashionable Observations,* Nietzsche wrote in *Ecce Homo,* "The entire picture of the dithyrambic artist is a picture of the pre-existent poet of *Zarathustra,* sketched with abysmal profundity and without touching even for a moment the Wagnerian reality."[29] *Thus Spoke Zarathustra* was, for Nietzsche, the epitome of poetic inspiration, the highest point of his creativity. The demanding grandeur and beauty of this poem consist precisely in that combination of the "greatest intellect" with the "warmest heart" which appeared impossible to Nietzsche in the summer of 1875 (as he outlined the program of the free spirit). *Zarathustra* is poetry and philosophy (not to be forgotten, nonetheless: "the poets lie too much" for Zarathustra and the Greeks). But how is the dithyrambic artist portrayed in the fourth of the *Unfashionable Observations?* As "yearning to descend out of the heights into the depths," as "longing to return to earth, to the happiness of community."[30] Has anyone among Nietzsche's interpreters had a clear concept of the extent to which Nietzsche, along with Wagner, is portrayed by way of Wagner in this text? More evidence (and in fact some concerning that decisive passage about the dithyrambic artist): in 1851 Wagner wrote in his *Announcement to My Friends* concerning *Lohengrin:* "Precisely this sacred solitude awakened in me . . . a new, unspeakable yearning to overcome myself, *the yearning out of the heights for the depths,* out of the solar brilliance of the most chaste purity for the cozy shadows of loving human embraces."[31] Further, if the essence of the dithyrambic dramatist is to be conceptually comprehended, it would have to be—in Nietzsche's estimation—at the creative moment in his art, when its "uncanny, arrogant amazement and surprise at the world is coupled with the ardent longing to approach this same world with love" "in order finally to find love and not just devotion."[32] In the previously mentioned *Announcement,* Wagner says of Lohengrin that "he yearns not after awe and devotion but rather [. . .] after *love,* after *being loved,* after *being understood in terms of love.*"[33] This proximity of Zarathustra to Lohengrin, unconscious even to Nietzsche in 1888, seems worthy enough of consideration to me.

Friendship. The separation from Wagner had to be final, irreversible. All the more did Nietzsche remain loyal to the memory of the blessed isle, Tribschen. He himself expressed this more precisely, better, and more profoundly than any commentator on "Nietzsche and Wagner at the time of their friendship." I am thinking above all of that aphorism from *Gay Science* in which Nietzsche speaks of the sublime possibility of a "star friendship" with a friend turned stranger (precisely Wagner). I would like to conclude this discussion of Wagner and Nietzsche one hundred years ago with the finale of that aphorism: "That we have to become estranged is the law *above* us; by the same token we should also become more venerable for each other—and the memory of our former friendship more sacred. There is probably a tremendous but invisible stellar orbit in which our very different ways and goals may be *included* as small parts of this path; let us rise up to this thought. But our life is too short and our power of vision too small for us to be more than friends in the sense of this sublime possibility,—Let us then *believe* in our star friendship even if we should be compelled to be earth enemies."[34]

Notes

1. KGB II$_5$, p. 226.

2. First published by Joachim Bergfeld, "Drei Briefe Nietzsches an Cosima Wagner," *Maske und Kothurn,* vol. 10 (Graz-Köln, 1964), 597–602. See KGB II$_5$, p. 209.

3. See KGW III$_4$, 23[8], p. 136; 23[14], p. 140; 23[35], p. 151; IV$_1$, 6[12], p. 177; 6[18], p. 180; 6[21], p. 182; 6[25], p. 183; 6[48], sec. 2, p. 192; 6[50], p. 195. Democritus's "world without moral and aesthetic meaning," which is "irrational, also neither objective nor beautiful, but rather only necessary," anticipates in a very striking fashion the Nietzschean world of "eternal recurrence of the same" from summer 1881.

4. Friedrich Ritschl to Nietzsche, February 14, 1872, KGB II$_2$, p. 541; KGW IV$_3$, p. 20 (*Assorted Opinions and Maxims,* aphorism 10 <Hollingdale translation>). Also see page 10 in this volume.

5. Nietzsche to Sophie Ritschl, January 1877, KGB II$_5$, p. 213.

6. KGW IV$_2$, p. 59; *Human, All Too Human,* aphorism 37 <CWFN, vol. 3, p. 46>.

7. KGB II$_6$, p. 473.

8. Cited by R. Du Moulin Eckart, *Cosima Wagner: Ein Lebens- und Characterbild* (Berlin, 1929), vol. 3, pp. 794ff.

9. KGW VIII$_1$, p. 109; see VII$_3$, pp. 257, 411; VII$_2$, p. 248. Compare also IV$_4$, p. 254, variations to the preface of *Human, All Too Human,* 2 (summer 1886).

10. Cosima Wagner, *Die Tagebücher,* vol. 1, 1869–77 (Munich and Zurich, 1976), 182.

11. KGW VI$_3$, p. 325 <*Ecce Homo,* Kaufmann translation>.

12. KGB II$_2$, pp. 493f. <*The Nietzsche-Wagner Correspondence,* ed. Elisabeth Förster-Nietzsche, trans. Caroline V. Kerr (New York: Liveright, 1921), 94–95>.

13. KGB II$_4$, p. 29 <*Nietzsche-Wagner Correspondence,* 134>.

14. KGB II$_4$, p. 294; Wagner's letter concerning the first of the *Unfashionable Observations: David Strauss, Writer and Confessor* <*Nietzsche-Wagner Correspondence,* 179>.

15. C. Wagner, *Tagebücher,* vol. 2, 1878–83 (Munich and Zurich, 1977), 1105. The *Internationale Monatsschrift* appeared in Chemnitz from Nietzsche's publisher, Ernst Schmeitzner.

16. KGB II$_6$, p. 362 <*Nietzsche-Wagner Correspondence,* 267>.

17. KGW IV$_1$, p. 20; *Richard Wagner in Bayreuth* <hereinafter RWB>, sec. 4<CWFN 2, p. 275>.

18. KGW IV$_1$, 11[28], pp. 293f.

19. KGW IV$_1$, pp. 17–23; RWB, secs. 3 and 4 <CWFN 2, pp. 272, 277, 278>.

20. KGW IV$_1$, pp. 75f.; RWB, sec. 4 <CWFN 2, p. 325>.

21. KGW IV$_4$, p. 23, July 7, 1876.

22. KGW IV$_1$, pp. 76–81; RWB, secs. 10 and 11 <CWFN 2, pp. 326, 327, 330>.

23. KGW VI$_3$, p. 312 <*Ecce Homo,* "Books," RWB, Kaufmann translation>.

24. KGW VIII$_2$, p. 18 <*Will to Power,* 1005, Kaufmann translation>.

25. KGW IV$_1$, p. 170; KSA 8, 5[190, 189].

26. KGW VI$_3$, p. 320 <*Ecce Homo,* "Books," *Human, All Too Human,* Kaufmann translation>.

27. Thomas Mann, "Pariser Rechenschaft," *Gesammelten Werke,* vol. 11, p. 50.

28. KGB III$_1$, p. 000 <*sic*>.

29. KGW IV$_3$, p. 312 <*sic*>; VI$_3$, p. 312 <*Ecce Homo,* "Books," *Birth of Tragedy,* sec. 4, Kaufmann translation>.

30. KGW IV$_1$, p. 42; RWB, sec. 7 <CWFN 2, p. 295>.

31. <Richard Wagner>, *Gesammelten Schriften und Dichtungen,* 4th ed. (Leipzig), vol. 4, p. 295.

32. KGW IV$_1$, p. 43; RWB, sec. 7 <CWFN 2, p. 295>.

33. <R. Wagner>, *Gesammelten Schriften,* vol. 1, p. 296.

34. KGW V$_2$, pp. 203f., aphorism 279 <*Gay Science,* sec. 279, Kaufmann translation>.

5 Enlightenment and Revolution: Nietzsche and the Later Goethe

1

It stands to reason that we now pose several questions regarding a certain well-established historical-political-literary model held by Nietzsche. The Nietzsche with whom we concern ourselves here is the one "genuine" Nietzsche—hence, the antimythical, antiromantic, anti-Wagnerian Nietzsche—who, having returned to himself after a prolonged crisis in the second half of the seventies, wrote a "book for free spirits" and published it (exactly one hundred years ago), dedicating it "to the memory of Voltaire," "as a memorial celebration on the anniversary of his death, May 30, 1778." The book is called *Human, All Too Human.* As the points of departure for the first part of my remarks, I will take up two lengthy aphorisms: first aphorism 197 from *Daybreak* (1881), titled "German hostility to the Enlightenment," and then aphorism 26 from *Human, All Too Human,* titled "Reaction as progress." The focus of the second, final part of this essay shall be the position Goethe occupied within Nietzsche's historical model, in conjunction with aphorism 221, "The revolution in poetry," once again from *Human, All Too Human.*

2

Nietzsche's train of thought finds its best expression in the aphorism from *Daybreak* regarding "German hostility to the Enlightenment." He discovered among the Germans a tendency contrary to the Enlightenment; German philosophy had retreated to a prescientific species of philosophy, beginning with

Kant, who saw as its purpose to "make way again for faith, setting knowledge outside its boundaries." Historians and the romantics turned toward folk spirit, folk wisdom, toward the Middle Ages, the Orient.[1] German natural scientists, Nietzsche wrote further, revolted against Newton and Voltaire. From a piety toward all things existent developed a piety toward all things ever in existence, replacing a cult of reason with a cult of feeling, until the danger of "setting knowledge in general below feeling" arose.

Still, Nietzsche believed that this danger had already passed. Why? Since *history,* "as a reactionary power undertaken after the <French> Revolution" and "as a counterwill to reason," had produced an unwanted result—so we read from this circle of ideas in concurrent unpublished notes (summer-autumn 1880).[2] And still more clearly in the aphorism from *Daybreak:* "The study of history [. . .] <and a> newly aroused passion for feeling and knowledge,[3] one day assumed a new nature and now fly on the broadest wings above and beyond their former conjurers as new and stronger genii of *that very Enlightenment* against which they were first conjured up. This Enlightenment we must now carry further forward" <Hollingdale translation>. Thus concludes Nietzsche, unconcerned that there has been, and *still exists,* a "great Revolution." The pair revolution-reaction exists as a negation consisting of two aspects, two complementary moments (to wit: revolution and reaction). The Revolution, in Nietzsche's estimation, came to be misunderstood as the consequence of the Enlightenment, and the reaction consisted of this misunderstanding.

An unpublished fragment from spring 1881—hence, shortly before publication of *Daybreak*—provides us with additional keys for the decipherment and interpretation of the aphorism.[4] The nineteenth century is therein portrayed as reactionary: in that century a conservative frame of mind rules, searching after the fundamental principle of everything that has ever existed, while the "egoism of the owners" counts as the strongest argument against eighteenth-century philosophy, against the Enlightenment. Those who own nothing and the discontents are mollified with "church and the arts"; the gifted, when they serve conservative interests, receive rewards in honor as geniuses (perhaps we may think of Carlyle's hero cult in this connection). History, however, has been transformed into the most certain means of annihilating precisely this conservative principle. In Nietzsche's note history includes Darwin's idea of evolution. From it we learn to recognize in history forces *in motion* and not our "beautiful" notions. Socialism—finally—plants its own foundations in history, and modern national wars as well.

Let us return to the aphorism from *Daybreak.* What did we achieve from our consultation with the unpublished fragment? What is the meaning of the Enlightenment, which we must forward still further, unconcerned that a revolution and a great reaction have occurred and—do not forget—*are still occurring*? I believe Nietzsche may be understood as saying that the enlightenment we are to forward makes its claim not *against* but rather beyond a great revolution (socialism) and a great reaction, *beyond* the conservative frame of mind. In Nietzsche's estimation, to conceive the Enlightenment as the cause of the Revolution was an error (this misunderstanding was the reaction itself); it would be an equally great error to conceive the continuing enlightenment, the "new" enlightenment, as the cause of socialism (the new great reaction, the conservative frame of mind itself, consists in this error). History itself, however, becomes an integral part of the new enlightenment. This is evident from aphorism 26 of *Human, All Too Human,* where Nietzsche speaks of reaction as progress. Again, at the time of the Renaissance, there was a first springtime of freedom for the spirit and for the sciences, a prior form of the Enlightenment "cut off" by Luther's Reformation, just as in our century the Enlightenment spirit was held in check by romanticism and Schopenhauer's metaphysics.

A bygone phase of humanity was conjured again by these "brusque, powerful, and impassioned, but nonetheless backward spirits." Only afterward, with Schopenhauer's "assistance," "could we do justice to Christianity and its Asian relatives; only after we have corrected in so essential a point the way of viewing history that the Age of Enlightenment brought with it can we once more bear the flag of the Enlightenment farther—the flag with the three names: Petrarch, Erasmus, Voltaire. We have made reaction into progress."

We may distinguish the following three phases within Nietzsche's historical model, each of which is characterized by an enlightenment and a paired revolution and reaction:

1. Italian and European humanism, the Renaissance (Petrarch, Erasmus) as an early enlightenment; the German Reformation (Luther) as progress and emancipation but also as regression into the religiosity of the Middle Ages and as the direct cause of the Counter-Reformation, hence revolution and reaction;
2. the French Enlightenment (Voltaire), conceived by Nietzsche as the continuation of the *grand siècle* of French culture, the seventeenth century, with the French Revolution and German romanticism as the corresponding revolution and reaction; and
3. the enlightenment to be further advanced, which several years later Nietzsche designated as the "new" enlightenment and which contrasts itself to the continuing "great revolution" and "great reaction," socialism and conservatism.

With regard to the first and second phases of this model, hence the Reformation and French Revolution as Nietzsche understood them at that time, we find an exceedingly interesting analogue to them in the distich from Goethe's "Four Seasons" (1799), specifically that for "Autumn," in which—as Werner Krauss notes—Lutheranism and the French Revolution are portrayed as forces hostile to education:

> The Frenchman does in these uncertain days,
> What the Lutheran did
> In his own ways,
> Oppressing calm learning.

Oppressed "calm learning"—doubtless meaning, in the first instance, the Enlightenment but also, in the second, humanism: hence, once more, Voltaire and Petrarch-Erasmus. We must not forget here that Nietzsche's educator in matters of the Renaissance was his Basel colleague Jakob Burckhardt, who was rightfully once called "a man of the Weimar classics."[5] From this point onward, that is, 1878 to 1888, Nietzsche considered the third phase of enlightenment as the sole noble task for the free spirit of his own times. His later explanations and extrapolations on the model we have presented belong to this period. Thus Germans come to represent the holding action par excellence to every cultural advance in Europe. Ancient culture[6] was annihilated by the Christians in league with Germans and "other lead boots." Likewise, German crusader knights destroyed, or at least drove from Europe, "Moorish" culture, also an early form of enlightenment. Finally, the so-called wars of liberation thwarted the unification of Europe under Napoleon, to whom only one German was equal by birth: Goethe.[7] Assessment of the French eighteenth century was (under Taine's influence) altered, in that Nietzsche came to identify it more and more with Rousseau, the sentimental plebeian, and with the "tragic farce" of the Revolution; remaining as its opponent was the noble culture of the seventeenth century and Voltaire's Enlightenment, with classicism as their continuation. A polarity of the following sort was construed: on one side, the classical ideal, presented through French Classicism, the Enlightenment, the national bourgeoisie of Europe, Voltaire, Napoleon, and Goethe; on the other side, the Christian ideal in its various incarnations: Rousseau, the Revolution, romanticism, nationalism, and socialism.

3

Now, finally, to the aphorism with regard to revolution in poetry, allowing us to more precisely determine Goethe's place in Nietzsche's historical scheme.

Revolution in poetry, the subject of aphorism 221 from *Human, All Too Hu-*

man, begins before the political revolution with Lessing and is completed as the inexorable dissolution of all form and bonds in modern times, which was introduced through the political revolution. The revolution in poetry—in France as in Germany—means a break with a tradition that has been lost to European culture once and for all. The grand antagonists in Nietzsche's remarks in this regard are Voltaire and Goethe. Voltaire was, in Nietzsche's assessment, "the last of the great dramatists who used Greek moderation to restrain a polymorphic soul that could encompass the greatest tragic thunderstorms—he was able to do what no German was yet capable of doing because the French are by nature much more closely related to the Greeks than are the Germans." "Simply read Voltaire's *Mahomet* from time to time," opined Nietzsche, "in order to perceive clearly what was lost once and for all to European culture by that break from tradition." Since that break, Nietzsche continues, "the modern spirit, with its restlessness, its hatred of moderation and restraint, has come to dominate in every area, first unleashed by the fever of revolution, and then reining itself in again when seized by fear and dread of itself" <CWFN 3:148>. For his part, Goethe sought to rescue himself from naturalism, that is, to rescue himself from a retreat into the "beginnings of art," always intentionally binding himself anew to various sorts thereof. He also successfully put the "barbaric advantages" of our times to use in his *Faust*.[8] Yet art moves from this point toward its dissolution and consequently touches—in a way Nietzsche admits to finding very instructive—"every phase of its beginnings, its childhood, its incompletion, its one-time gambles and extravagancies: it interprets, as it descends toward destruction, its emergence, its becoming" <CWFN 3:150>.

Lord Byron once wrote, "We are all upon an inwardly wrong revolutionary system."[9] His insight, in Nietzsche's assessment, is also that of the mature Goethe, "precisely because his nature held him for a long time firmly within the path of the poetic revolution, precisely because he savored most deeply all the discoveries, prospects, and resources that were indirectly uncovered by that break from tradition and had been unearthed, as it were, from beneath the ruins of art." "Therefore his later transformation and conversion carries so much weight: it means that he felt the deepest desire to regain the artistic tradition. [. . .] Thus he lived in art as though in recollection of true art: his writing became a means of recollecting, of understanding ancient, long-departed artistic eras" <CWFN 3:150>. With his insight, however, the elder Goethe attained a leap beyond a series of generations, such that we must agree with Nietzsche: "Goethe has not yet had his effect and <. . .> his time is still to come." The time will come for a Goethe for whom fulfillment of his artistic demands would be possible only in reverse, that is, in the past, by means of art "as the Greeks and the French, too, *practiced* it."[10]

The enlightenment that we are to continue may be found beyond religion and art. It can give support to only the historical understanding of religion and art, insofar as history belongs to enlightenment in the Nietzschean sense. Nonetheless, Goethe's classical ideal continued to take its exemplar from the Greeks (and French), particularly since what counts as the modern artistic drive is nothing more than the *inexorable* dissolution of art, its end. Thus, Goethe's "mature aesthetic insight from the second half of his life" takes on its pronounced fatalistic and resigned, even if historically enlightening, character: the demands of Goethe, *this* Goethe, were genuinely unattainable, in Nietzsche's estimation, precisely *in the light of the modern era's power.*

After 1878, of course, Nietzsche did not remain with the Goethean search for the classical ideal: the free spirit's contemplative behavior gave way more and more to Zarathustra's attempt, "relying on nothing," to become a "new legislator." Nevertheless, it is a fact that, in Goethe's wake, Nietzsche maintained the classical ideal along with both antirevolutionary and antiromantic, even antireactionary, polemics as demands placed on himself until his last writings. Did Nietzsche consequently embrace an antiquated Goethe, exploitable by bourgeois education in the Age of Reason and by epigones of later periods? I believe not, because the new restraints and constraints that Nietzsche appeared to demand include that we—like Goethe—must become aware of the process of modern art in all its implications. But is the decline of values in the bourgeois era, in the words of Hermann Broch, a Nietzschean illusion? Is the desolate landscape where Nietzsche's *enlightenment* lands on its final voyage representative of the entire miserable history of the modern bourgeois soul, itself an argument against the classical Goethean ideal? Probably not. It remains appropriate to inquire—and this will be my concluding question—whether that "classical ideal" as such *can* or cannot continue to persist even *today.*

Notes

1. Werner Krauss remarks in his essay "Goethe und die französischen Revolution," *Goethe Jahrbuch* 94 (1977): 127: "The particular aversion of the historical school belongs more to the French Enlightenment than to the French Revolution." Krauss means the "romantic historical school under the direction of Sauvigny."

2. KGW V$_1$, 4[86], p. 451; 6[428], p. 638.

3. Concerning the "passion for knowledge" see chapter 6 in this volume.

4. KGW V$_1$, 10[D88], pp. 763f. <KSA 9, 10[D88]>.

5. See Curt Paul Janz, *Friedrich Nietzsche: Biographie* (Munich, 1978), vol. 1, p. 325. (Janz cites Alfred Martin's book on Burckhardt and Nietzsche.) Continuing Burckhardt's (and Jansen's) historical notion, Nietzsche speaks, in *Human, All Too Human,* aphorism 237, of "Renaissance and Reformation." In accordance with the historical model described, he characterizes the Renaissance as follows: "The Italian Renaissance contained within

itself all the positive forces to which we owe modern culture: that is, liberation of thought, disdain for authorities, the triumph of cultivation over the arrogance of lineage, an enthusiasm for science and the scientific past of humanity, an unfettering of the individual, an ardor for veracity and an aversion against appearance and mere effect. . . . Indeed, the Renaissance had positive forces that, *up until now,* have never since become as powerful in our modern culture. . . . The great task of the Renaissance," however, "could not be brought to completion<;> the protest of a German nature that had meanwhile remained backward . . . hindered this." The German Reformation compelled the Counter-Reformation, a Catholic Christianity on the defense. Had Luther been defeated, Nietzsche concludes, "the Enlightenment would perhaps have dawned somewhat earlier and with more beautiful luster than we can now conceive."

6. The concept of "culture" in Burckhardt's sense coincides in many ways with Nietzsche's concept of enlightenment.

7. See in particular Nietzsche's invectives against "the Germans" in *Antichrist* and *Ecce Homo.*

8. Here Nietzsche combines the quotation from *Anmerkungen zu Rameau's Neffen des Diderot* (1805) with a letter from Goethe to Schiller on June 27, 1797.

9. Nietzsche quotes from a letter by Byron to Murray on September 19, 1817—specifically, from Byron, *Vermischte Schriften, Briefwechsel und Lebensgeschichte,* vol. 2, ed. E. Ortlepp (Stuttgart), 360 <Handwerk translation; CWFN 3:150>.

10. The conclusion of the aphorism runs: "To be sure, his demands were unable to be fulfilled, considering the strength of the new age; the pain of this was, however, amply compensated by his joy in the fact that they once had been fulfilled, and that we, too, can still participate in this fulfillment. Not individuals, but more or less ideal masks; no reality, but an allegorical generality; historical types, local color attenuated almost to invisibility and made mythic; contemporary society compressed to the simplest forms, stripped of their stimulating, absorbing, pathological characteristics, made ineffectual in any sense other than an artistic one; no new materials and characters, but the ancient, long-familiar ones in everlasting reanimation and transformation: that is art as Goethe later *understood* it, as the Greeks and the French, too, *practiced* it."

6 Nietzsche's Philosophy as the "Passion for Knowledge"

1

Looking back on his first winter in Genoa, Nietzsche noted to himself one year later:

> The genuine pathos in each of my life's phases has never become clear as such; rather, I have always believed each to be the sole possible and reasonable situation for me at the time and—to speak with the Greeks and share their distinction—an *ethos,* not a *pathos.* I went astray when, for instance, in the winter of 1880 to 1881, I worked on *Daybreak* in Genoa (via Palestro 18, no. 13 interno)—this extremely hermitlike, austere life was entirely *pathos,* and yet now, in the feelings of completely different circumstances, I hear again a few musical chords made in that house as something so good, so courageous in the face of pain, and so trustworthy that no one ought possess such comforting things over a period of years. One would become too rich, too overly proud—yes, it was the spirit of Columbus in me.[1]

The pathos that for Nietzsche did not become clear as such in those months was nevertheless already called "passion" at that time: certainly an "entirely new" passion—the "passion for knowledge." This will be the object of our considerations.

2

We must devote our attention, consequently, to an aphorism from *Daybreak* in which the new passion is described: number 429, bearing the title "The new passion." We juxtapose each passage of the aphorism next to some of the corresponding preliminary material that we find in a small notebook. Nietzsche used this forty-two-page notebook at the end of 1880 in Genoa; *Daybreak*'s aphorism 429 was also conceived during this time, when Nietzsche—after a year of collecting and drafting his ideas in Venice, Marienbad, Stresa, and other locations—prepared himself "to write a book from the heart."[2] The juxtaposition appears as follows.

Daybreak 429, "The new passion"

Why do we fear and hate a possible reversion to barbarism? Because it would make people even unhappier than they are? Oh no! The barbarians of every age were *happier:* let us not deceive ourselves!—The reason is that our drive to knowledge has become too strong for us to be able to want happiness without knowledge or the happiness of a strong, firmly rooted delusion; even to imagine such a state of things is painful to us! Restless discovering and divining has such an attraction for us, and has grown as indispensable to us as is to the lover his unrequited love, which he would at no price relinquish for a state of indifference—perhaps, indeed, we too are *unrequited* lovers! Knowledge has in us been transformed into a passion which shrinks at no sacrifice and at bottom fears nothing but its own extinction; we believe in all honesty that all mankind must believe itself more exalted and comforted under the compulsion and suffering of *this* passion than it did formerly, when envy of the coarser contentment that follows in the train of barbarism had not yet been overcome. Perhaps mankind will even perish of this passion for knowledge!—even this thought has no power over us! But did Christianity ever shun such a thought? Are love and death not brothers? Yes, we hate barbarism—we would all prefer the

Preliminary Material (KSA 14, p. 221), Untitled

Fear of barbarism—why?
Does it make one unhappy?

No, our drives for knowledge are too strong, such that we consider happiness *without* knowledge as being *unacceptable* to us.

The restlessness of knowledge is so attractive to us as the unhappiness of love (which no one would trade for a condition of indifference).

Were we to press knowledge to the point of a passion, we would be content if *for its sake humanity were to perish: it is not impossible to think in this manner.*

Christianity, too, did not shrink before such ideas. All loving things wish to perish.

We prefer destruction to regression.

But how! If the passion for knowledge were, in general, to lead necessarily to a regressive path, a weakness! It is good that the other drives claim just as much, each creating its own ideal.

Finally: if humanity does not decline from its passions, it perishes from its weaknesses. Which does one prefer!! This is the main question.

destruction of mankind to a regression of knowledge! And finally: if
mankind does not perish of a *passion*
it will perish of a *weakness:* which do
you prefer? This is the main question.
Do we desire for mankind an end in
fire and light or one in the sand?
<Hollingdale translation, p. 184>

The comparison demonstrates (1) that the title of the aphorism, as well as
the notion "new passion," is not contained in the preliminary material—not
even *implicitly*—and (2) that with a few not inessential nuances, the preliminary material nonetheless contains all the paths of thought and formulations
of the final draft, with the exception of two sentences dropped by Nietzsche.

3

We come across the concept of a "new passion" at the end of another notebook
from the same period and strangely enough in one of those provisional titles
that occasionally interrupt Nietzsche's meditations and serve him, so to speak,
as both an attempted summary of previous notes and a guidepost for what
remains to be written. On the last pages of his notebook, Nietzsche wrote three
titles next to one another, presenting a sort of progression: first "On the History of Honesty"; then "The Passion for Honesty"; and finally, "Passio nova,
or, On the Passion for Honesty."[3] In *Daybreak* "honesty" becomes a virtue and,
in fact, the most recent of virtues, the primary virtue of the man of knowledge.[4] It has not yet "become clear"; it is still "becoming something." In *Zarathustra,* part I ("On the Afterworldly"), we read, "Many sick people have always
been among the poetizers and God-cravers; furiously they hate the lover of
knowledge and that youngest among the virtues, which is called 'honesty'"
<Kaufmann translation>. In the note for *Daybreak,* honesty is also the virtue
distinguishing the man of knowledge from the artist—Wagner is in the vicinity! ("I am not disposed to entertain any sort of greatness which is not allied
with honesty," begins a well-known fragment concerning Wagner.) Honesty,
as the "most recent virtue," would be suitable for that which has in itself the
"new passion" for knowledge. Karl Jaspers also understood it in this sense.[5]

4

The theme of barbarism is only intimated in the preliminary material, albeit
with all the essential motifs exhibited in the aphorism—there being two of

them: (1) the "fear of barbarism" and (2) the question, "Does barbarism create unhappiness?" Yet in the final analysis, the problem of happiness is decisive. To hold happiness—in all its meanings relevant to the "happiness of barbarians"—in contempt is one of the continual characteristic features of Nietzsche's philosophizing. We know that Nietzsche also spoke of another happiness, for instance, in the Markusplatz poem "My Happiness" or the section "At Noon" in *Zarathustra,* part 4—happiness as instantaneous, personal. Another sort of happiness may be found at the end of the entire misadventure of humanity, as in *Antichrist:* "Beyond the north, ice, and death—our life, our happiness. We have discovered happiness, we know the way, we have found the exit out of the labyrinth of thousands of years. [. . .] Formula for our happiness: a Yes, a No, a straight line, a goal. [. . .] What is happiness? The feeling that power is growing, that resistance is overcome."[6] Otherwise Nietzsche remained opposed to "odious pretensions to happiness," both in 1875, when he noted this Schopenhauerian-inspired expression from Goethe's friend Merck,[7] and in *Twilight of the Idols* (1888), where we read: "If we have our own *why* of life, we shall get along with almost any *how.* Man does not strive for pleasure; only the Englishman does."[8]

Now concerning happiness in barbarism, Nietzsche describes it as a "coarser contentment that follows in the train of barbarism," as a "happiness without knowledge." Knowledge is, nonetheless, "unhappy"; the trail of thoughts in our aphorism tends in this direction. "Sorrow is knowledge," Nietzsche said with Byron in *Human, All Too Human.*

What is knowledge for Nietzsche? "Knowledge is essentially appearance"— that is the primary definition we find specified in the Marienbad notebook.[9] Knowledge is also constraint, since necessity demands limitations in its sphere for it to be able to exist at all. The world is the sum of relations of a limited sphere to its mistaken suppositions. That is knowledge as "knowing and sensing" from the perspective of gnoseology/epistemology, in contrast to knowledge as the object of passion, which is principally knowledge of all that and something yet different; it is, so to speak, knowledge of knowing—in short, philosophy, theoretical activity *prior to* every judgment about experience. This philosophy has modern science as the model for its method. "I know so little about the achievements of science," Nietzsche noted during this period, "and yet this little seems to be inexhaustibly rich for the elimination of earlier ways of thinking and behaving."[10] Nietzsche constantly protested against those who struggle to uncover the limits of human knowledge only to gain free rein for their own metaphysics at the same time. That is precisely what Nietzsche detested, what he called "Jesuitism." "After my first phase," he wrote in a notebook from autumn 1883, "smirks the face of Jesuitism: I mean, the conscious holding fast to an illusion and the compulsory application of the same as the basis of culture. [. . .] Wagner was bagged by this very hazard."[11] In relation to the illusions of his youth, he committed "suicide," in Nietzsche's words, as Paul had done in the face of his entire pre-Christian period. That is the meaning of the free-spirited books, above all of *Human, All Too Human;* again and again we come across polemics against sudden enlightenment, "intuitive" knowledge. In fact, while living out the "passion of knowledge," Nietzsche also wanted nothing to do with flashes of inspiration: "Bits of knowledge with one stroke, intuitions, are not knowledge but rather notions of a greater vividness and as little reality as is an hallucination," he wrote in his Marienbad notebook. And further: "This burning hot feeling of the enraptured, this is 'truth,' this laying-on-of-hands and seeing-with-one's-eyes, for those overcome by fantasies, these gropers for a new afterlife—is an illness of the intellect, not a path to knowledge."[12] It is one of the alluring qualities of Nietzsche's philosophizing that he does not for an instant abandon the knowledge given solid ground by historical and scientific standards and at the same time draws the limits of this sort of knowledge. "To the position of philosopher, I would raise the free spirit," we read in the previously cited notebook from autumn 1883, "who, *without turning Jesuit,* nonetheless penetrates the irrational constitution of existence."[13] So we understand why he also said in his Genoa notebook, "An overflowing of the human, as if it were all old comedy, is possible; for a creature of knowledge it is always a horrific constraint, forced forever to acknowledge oneself as man; it could create a nausea at humanity."[14] Thus we also understand the meaning of the "great silence" described by Nietzsche in *Daybreak,* aphorism 423: at "the crossroads of day and night," before the sea, where we may forget the city, come conflicting voices: "I pity you, nature, that you have to be silent," but then, "I begin to hate speech, to hate even thinking; for do I not hear behind every word the laughter of error, of imagination, of the spirit of delusion? [. . .]—O sea, O evening! You are evil instructors! You teach man to cease to be man!" All the same, man can never cease "being human," meaning to speak, to think, if he remains "honest." Religious, mystical experience takes place only as a limiting boundary from this point onward, in the same vein as a <very rough> note from summer 1878: "Knowing *Petrifaction*—Behavior Epilepsy involuntary. Like a curare arrow of knowledge am I shot, seeing all."[15]

5

Knowledge is further, in Nietzsche's words, pleasure, desire, and intoxication, but it is also unhappiness. An unhappiness compared in our aphorism with that of the unlucky lover: "perhaps, indeed, we too are *unrequited* lovers!"

In his notebook sketches Nietzsche expressed himself approximately thus:

we live for knowledge not for the sake of a goal but instead for the sake of the astonishing and frequent pleasures "in seeking and finding the same." Sight of the world becomes bearable for the first time when we see through the soft, smoky fire of pleasurable passions. "Without our passions, the world is quantity and line and law and nonsense; in all that, the most repulsive and presumptuous paradox."[16] And just as he said that Plato described the drive for knowledge as an idealized aphrodisiac, so for Nietzsche, by evidence from 1885, "abstract thinking, on a good day" is "a festival and an intoxication."[17] Ultimately Nietzsche hoped science would satisfy his urges "for brightness, cleanliness, cheerfulness, soberness, rationality."[18] But wherein lies the misfortune of knowledge? "Sometimes the peaceful happiness of knowledge played a tune for me—but I never found it, indeed I loathe it, now that I know the *blessedness of unhappiness in knowledge.* Am I ever bored? Always concerned, always a heart palpitation in expectation or disappointment, I bless this misery! The world is rich for it! I pass by it with my slowest stride and slurp these bitter sweets."[19]

6

As Nietzsche's aphorism has it, "Knowledge has in us been transformed into a passion"; the preliminary material reads, "We press knowledge to the point of a passion." The aphorism's established fact, the preliminary material's hesitant hypothesis, was the "task" of all the preceding aphorisms. The drive for knowledge is still youthful and crude; Nietzsche wants to treat it as a passion; he wants to so powerfully "sublimate" the drive for "honesty" toward oneself and "justice" toward all things—both belong to his new notion of knowledge—that its joy outweighs the value of the other sorts of desires.[20] The goal is to conduct ourselves toward distant things as toward the most immediate (here we recall the "love of the farthest" in *Zarathustra*), because passion for abstractions (as in the case of Plato) and the incapacity to remain distant and objective toward an abstraction constitute a thinker.

Scientific men, in contrast, are incapable of comprehending the entirely new position of science itself, in Nietzsche's assessment. "They are unconcerned about science—this gives them the right to it!" The scientific type's science, that is, "a struggle after knowledge without heroism," is the sole sort of science previously promoted by the state. "It is an entirely new situation," he wrote in autumn 1881; science, too, "has its sublimity, it may also be seen heroically, though none has done so yet."[21] Since 1875 consciousness of modern man's entirely new situation vis-à-vis the world and history has been awakened: "Our fundament differs from all previous ages, for we may learn something of man as a species," says a fragment from the unfinished "unfashionable observation" on philologists. "That we ultimately prefer to live in this over any other age," it continues, "is basically the service of science. [. . .] We have excelled the Greeks in *explanation* of the world, in natural history and anthropology; our knowledge is much greater, our judgments more measured and exact."[22]

"We are allowed our taste"—it is now claimed—"but it is no longer *the* eternal, mandatory taste! And every age *believes* that of its own! We are not permitted such! An entirely new situation!" The essential characteristic of this new situation—the passion for knowledge—is pointed out in a fragment from autumn 1881. "My brothers! Let us not deceive ourselves! Science—or more honestly put, the *passion for knowledge*—stands before us, an uncanny, *new,* growing force, the likes of which have never yet been seen, with eagle's flight, owl's eyes, and dragon's feet—truly, it is already so powerful that it grasps itself as a problem and asks, 'How on earth am *I* even possible among *human beings?! How is a future with me even possible for humanity?!*'"[23] We find the fragment in a small notebook containing thoughts on the eternal recurrence of the same and the death of God, as well.

The final question marks of that later fragment build to the culmination point of *Daybreak* aphorism 429, where the genuine pathos for knowledge has its day with its extreme consequence. "Knowledge has in us been transformed into a passion that shrinks at no sacrifice and at bottom fears nothing but its own extinction; we believe in all honesty that all mankind must believe itself more exalted and comforted under the compulsion and suffering of *this* passion than it did formerly, when envy of the coarser contentment that follows in the train of barbarism had not yet been overcome. Perhaps mankind will even perish of this passion for knowledge! [. . .] Yes, we hate barbarism—we would all prefer the destruction of mankind to a regression of knowledge!" This consequence is conditioned by Nietzsche's earlier development. He himself said it in a fragment from 1885: "One day—it was during the summer of 1876—a disgust and insight suddenly came to me: I have mercilessly surpassed the beautiful objects of desire and dreams as I had loved them in my youth; mercilessly I continued on my way, a path of 'knowledge at any cost.'" The same motif exists in the sketches for *Daybreak*. Only one among many examples: "Falsification of the truth in favor of those things we love, [. . .] the most execrable nonentity to the enlightened spirit, who is used to trusting men and who *consequently* corrupts the same, holds one fast in delusion. And it is often a heavy sacrifice for you, *sacrificum intellectus propter amorem*! Oh, even I have praised it! Richard Wagner in Bayreuth."[24] The demise of humanity is the topic of discussion precisely there in the fourth of the *Unfashionable Observations,* cited by the fragment. There we read: "And if humanity must perish at some time—who may doubt it!—so the goal for all subsequent ages has been set as the highest task, to develop together into a unity and community, such that it would, *as a whole,* face its imminent demise with a *sense of the tragic.* [. . .] There is only one hope and one guarantee for the future of humanity: it consists in his *retention of the sense for the tragic.*"[25] The "sense for the tragic" in the parting work that Nietzsche devoted to Wagner and to the wishes of his youth—"happiness without knowledge"—has transformed itself into the sacrifice of humanity for knowledge of the truth, because—as we read at the outset of *Daybreak's* aphorism 45—this is "*one* tremendous idea [. . .] self-sacrificing mankind." Not only the metaphysics of art but also the vital connection with humanity as a whole—what Nietzsche called "pity"—is lost in *Daybreak.* "Honesty" forbids him any retreat into that colorful social utopia, toward which the fourth of the *Unfashionable Observations* represents the final and most risky attempt.

"Indeed, we are perishing from this passion for knowledge! But that is no argument against it. Otherwise, death would be an argument against the life of the individual. We *must* perish, as individuals and as humanity! Christianity showed such by extermination and renunciation of all crude drives. With renunciation, we arrive at precisely the behavior, hate, love, on the path of the passion for knowledge. Contented *observer*—until there is nothing more to see! For that reason you hate us, you actors! We shall see your disgust: *away* from us, from humanity, from existence, from all becoming!" As we see from this fragment, the going under of the contemplative individual is something other than that of humanity. Still, Nietzsche will also think through the purpose of mortal mankind—because "this task shall come to be concentrated upon."[26] And this mortal goal is, according to aphorism 45 of *Daybreak,* "knowledge of the truth." It may even be thought of as a sort of cosmic sacrifice: "Perhaps, if one day an alliance has been established with the inhabitants of other stars for the purpose of knowledge, and knowledge has been communicated from star to star for a few millennia, perhaps enthusiasm for knowledge may then rise to such a high-water mark!"

7

As we have already remarked, two sentences were deleted before the final draft. The first one expresses doubt whether the passion for knowledge might, "in general, <. . .> lead necessarily to a regressive path, a weakness!"; the other one contains the judgment that "it is good that the other drives <those other than the drive for knowledge> claim just as much, each creating its own ideal." We find similar expressions in other unpublished notes of this time and in the further progression of Nietzsche's thinking.

The problem of humanity's weakening from knowledge is not new for Nietzsche; we read, for example, in the previously mentioned notes to *We Philologists,* "a milder humanity has been prepared, thanks to the age of enlightenment, which has *weakened* man."[27] The chance for a *future* strengthening of mankind appears to be given precisely in the passion for knowledge: "I believed that knowledge kills energy, the instincts, that it allows no activity to develop out of itself. Only the truth is that a new knowledge stands at the ready, not a rehearsed mechanism, still less a pleasant passionate habit. Rather, *everything* capable of growth! regardless whether it means waiting on trees that later generations—not us—shall *harvest!* That is the resignation of the one who knows! He has become less empowered, awkward in acting, robbed of his members, so to speak—he has become a *seer,* blind and deaf."[28]

Meanwhile, modern man has weakened, too, in comparison with the Christian period. "Our standards *after* Christianity: after that unheard-of exercise of all the muscles and abilities in extreme pride, we are all condemned to play the ones who are weaker than the weakened: let it be, then, that we attain an unheard-of sort of *manliness* bearing this condition of human abasement still more proudly than Christianity. Cannot *science* be of help here? We must contrast something unsurpassable for the noble-minded type—a renunciation and a strength!—to the fantasy-effect of Christianity."[29] And once again occupying himself with the same problem one year later: "I do not fully know how courage and justice and hard, patient rationality shall be validated, when everything is so transitory, so fantastic, so uncertain for us. As men we wish to speak precisely *this truth,* if it is truth at all, and not one hiding from us! To the anatomist, too, a cadaver is often repulsive—but his manliness proves itself in his perseverance. *I yearn to know.*"[30]

The second sentence deleted from the preliminary material to *Daybreak* 429 concerns the relation between the drive for knowledge and the other drives in man: "It is good that the other drives claim just as much, each creating its own ideal." Each drive should derive its own ideal, meaning that along with the man of knowledge, having devoted himself to *knowledge,* the other human types—artists, warriors, and so forth—should create their own ideals. A half-year later, in summer 1881, as Nietzsche asked "how science is even possible among *human beings,*" he emphasized the inevitability of error precisely in the passion for knowledge:

> Life conditions knowledge. Error conditions life, and at the most fundamental level, actual error. [. . .] We must love and nurture error; it is the

womb of knowledge. Art as the nurturing of illusions—*our* cult. To love and promote life for the sake of knowledge, to love and promote illusion for the sake of life. The fundamental condition of all passion for knowledge is *to give existence an aesthetic meaning, to augment our taste for it.* Thus, we discover here, too, a night and a day as the conditions for *our* lives: desiring knowledge and desiring error are ebb and flow. Ruled by *one* absolute, mankind would perish and *with it its capacities.*[31]

8

From this moment onward, Nietzsche considered the passion for knowledge in the light of a new knowledge—that of the eternal recurrence of the same. In the notebook where this knowledge was sketched for the first time, summer 1881, we also find the previously quoted fragment. Now his own philosophy appeared to him as one of "indifference." We close our commentary to aphorism 429 from *Daybreak* with the following fragment, in which we find eternal recurrence of the same in a reciprocal relation to the passion for knowledge:

> To see the world with *many* eyes, [. . .] to *wait,* to know how far knowledge and the truth are able to embody themselves—and to what extent a transformation of mankind occurs when he finally lives out his life only *in order to know*—this is the result of the passion for knowledge: as the source and power of knowledge, error, and passions, out of whose struggles it takes its power of perseverance, *there is no means for its existence.* [. . .] But now comes the most burdensome knowledge <that of eternal recurrence>, making all life terribly questionable: an absolute excess of desire *must* be displayed, or our very annihilation would be preferable. Sooner this: we must place the past—ours and that of mankind—on the scales and predominate, too. No! This piece of human history *shall* and must eternally return. Whether we may ignore that, since we have no influence thereupon, or if it impedes our pity and takes over life in general. That it not disrupt us, our pity must not be too great. Indifference must have worked itself into us deeply and into our enjoyment of looking, too. The misery of future mankind, too, shall *not at all* concern us. But *whether we would still desire to live,* that is the question, and how![32]

9

As the "will to truth," the passion for knowledge becomes "the will to thinkability for all things"—the "will to power"—in *Zarathustra.* It preserves "sorrow" as the distinguishing trait of its "spirit." "Spirit is life that cuts into itself." By the way, *Daybreak*'s aphorism 460 already says, "As long as truths do not cut into our flesh with knives, we retain a secret contempt for them." The passion for knowledge as science leads to the idea of eternal recurrence of the same insofar as this is the "mechanical worldview, thought through to its conclusion."

Nietzsche's later thinking revolved around the illusory consciousness of being the possessor of a "cultivating" idea resulting from the store of previous scientific knowledge. The few whom Nietzsche trusted were never able to shake his confidence in the communicable meaning of this idea—the eternal banishment of mankind into the contingency of the known world after the death of God. He allowed Zarathustra to speak (entirely in the spirit of the conclusion to *Daybreak* 429) for himself: "May the world break apart upon our truths! There are so many worlds to create! For if truth does not allow us to create a new world, what, then, would truth matter?"[33]

Notes

1. This note is preliminary material for *Gay Science,* aphorism 317, which is retained in somewhat less personal form: see KSA 14, p. 269.

2. KGW V$_1$, 7[117], p. 672: "I do not find sufficient joy in anything—hence I began to write a book from the heart."

3. KGW V$_1$, 6[457.459.461], p. 646.

4. See *Daybreak,* aphorism 456.

5. See Karl Jaspers, *Nietzsche: Einführung in das Verständnis seines Philosophierens* (Berlin, 1947), esp. 184–213 <English edition, *Nietzsche: An Introduction to the Understanding of His Philosophizing,* trans. Charles F. Wallraff and Frederick J. Schmitz (Chicago: Henry Regnery, 1965), 184–211>.

6. *Antichrist,* secs. 1–2 <Kaufmann translation>.

7. KGW IV$_1$, 6[14], p. 178.

8. *Twilight of the Idols,* "Maxims and Arrows," sec. 12 <Kaufmann translation>.

9. Nietzsche was in Marienbad in July-August 1880; see KSA 15, pp. 113f.

10. KGW V$_1$, 4[290], p. 501.

11. KGW VII$_1$, 16[23], p. 533; see also in this volume pages 160–61.

12. KGW V$_1$, 4[321], p. 510; 4[152], p. 470.

13. KGW VII$_1$, 16[14], p. 529.

14. KGW V$_1$, 4[150], p. 469; see *Daybreak,* aphorism 483.

15. KGW IV$_3$, 28[18], p. 364.

16. KGW V$_1$, 7[122], p. 673; 7[226], p. 694.

17. KGW V$_1$, 7[242], p. 697; VII$_3$, 34[130], p. 183.

18. KGW V$_1$, 7[182], p. 684.

19. KGW V$_1$, 7[165], pp. 680f.

20. KGW V$_1$, 7[197], p. 697.

21. KGW V$_2$, 14[3], p. 521.

22. KGW IV$_1$, 3[76], p. 113.

23. KGW V$_1$, 7[5], p. 647; V$_2$, 12[96], p. 492.

24. KGW VIII₁, 2[9], p. 68 (first version); V₁, p. 514. See here pages 160–61.

25. Compare *Richard Wagner in Bayreuth,* sec. 4; KGW IV₁, p. 25 <Hollingdale translation; Hollingdale mysteriously drops the first half of the quotation from his translation>.

26. KGW V₁, 7[171], p. 682; 6[281], p. 600.

27. Compare KGW IV₁, 3[76], p. 113.

28. KGW V₁, 7[172], p. 682.

29. KGW V₁, 7[281], pp. 705f.

30. KGW V₂, 15[2], p. 532.

31. KGW V₂, 11[162], p. 402.

32. KGW V₂, 11[141], p. 392 <KSA 9, 11[141]>.

33. Variation on the chapter "On Self-Overcoming," *Thus Spoke Zarathustra,* pt. 2; see KSA 14, p. 302.

1

We come across the name "Zoroaster" (also known as "Zarathustra") for the first time in Nietzsche's unpublished fragments from September 1870 to January 1871. There we read: "The religion of Zoroaster would have ruled Greece, had Darius not been defeated."[1] This is a short excerpt from the orientalist Max Müller's *Essays*,[2] which Nietzsche avidly read at that time. The counterfactual victory of the Persians over the Greeks—especially in view of their religious development—appears to have fascinated Nietzsche. This counterfactual remained undeveloped, though; it relates, rather, to Nietzsche's ruminations over the Greeks in the decisive periods before and after the Persian wars. According to Friedrich August Wolf's schema,[3] the Persians, with their grand empire, were not a people of culture, but in Nietzsche's estimation, it would have been much more fortunate had the Persians, and not the mere Romans, become masters over Greece. Heraclitus, with his transnational thinking, had in any case torn down every barrier between barbarian and Hellenic, between Persian and Greek.[4] In his *Philosophy in the Tragic Age of the Greeks*, Nietzsche tolerated the notion that Heraclitus was influenced by certain ideas of Zoroastrianism, "if only its exponents did not burden us with their conclusion that philosophy was thus merely imported into Greece rather than having grown and developed there in a soil natural and native to it." "Nothing would be sillier," continues Nietzsche's characterization of this historical question, "than to claim an autochthonous development for the Greeks. On the contrary, they invariably absorbed other living cultures.

The very reason they got so far is that they knew how to pick up the spear and throw it onward from the point where others had left it."[5] We may complete this overview-inventory with two other fragments from early 1874: "Persians: shoot well, ride well, do not borrow, and do not lie"; "How the Persians were educated: to shoot with a bow and to tell the truth."[6] We do not know by what source Nietzsche wrote both times about the Persians; in any case, he remembered this nine years later in *Thus Spoke Zarathustra,* part 1: "To speak the truth and to handle the bow and arrow well—that seemed both dear and difficult to the people who gave me my name—the name which is both dear and difficult to me."[7]

2

In *Gay Science,* aphorism 342, that is, in the last aphorism of the first edition from the year 1882, the figure of the Nietzschean Zarathustra makes his public debut; this aphorism is nearly identical to the beginning of the prologue to *Zarathustra,* which appeared the following year, 1883. However, we find Zarathustra in Nietzsche's sketches a full year before the appearance of *Gay Science.* At the beginning of August 1881, Nietzsche wrote an outline concerning the "eternal recurrence of the same"; three weeks later, on a day precisely given as "Sils-Maria, August 26, 1881," the name Zarathustra turns up for the first time and, further, with a title—recurring in the unpublished fragments from this point on—to a new work, "Noon and Eternity."

There are three fragments. In the first we read: "Noon and Eternity. Signposts to a New Life. Zarathustra, born at Lake Urmi, left his home in his thirtieth year and went into the province of Arya and composed the *Zend-Avesta* in the ten years of his solitude."[8] This begs comparison with the opening of *Thus Spoke Zarathustra,* as well as with the beginning of aphorism 342 in *Gay Science:* "When Zarathustra was thirty years old, he left his home and Lake Urmi and went into the mountains. There he enjoyed his spirit and his solitude, and for ten years did not tire of that."

The subsequent fragment bears a close relation to the title "Noon and Eternity": "The sun of knowledge once again stands at noon, and coiled, the serpent of knowledge lies in its light—it is *our* time, you noontime brothers!"[9] But what does it mean that the sun of knowledge once again stands at noon? In each sphere of human existence, there is always the hour when, first for one, then for many, and then for all, the most powerful thought emerges, that of the eternal recurrence of all things—for humanity, it is always noon, according to Nietzsche. The idea itself says, "Your whole life is turned over like an hourglass, again and again—a great moment of time between them, until all those conditions from which you have become yourself once again come together in the course of the universe. And then you will find every pain and every desire and every joy and foe and every hope, and every error and every blade of grass and every beam of light, the entire interconnection of all things, once more. This ring, of which you are a speck, shines evermore."[10] In the third fragment Nietzsche describes the work "Noon and Eternity" as an outline to a new way of life. It encompasses four books:

> BOOK ONE. In the style of the first movement of the Ninth Symphony. *Chaos or nature:* "On the Dehumanization of Nature." Prometheus is shackled to the Caucasus. Written with the cruelty of CRATOS, "power."

> BOOK TWO. Fleeting-skeptical-Mephistophelean. "On the Embodiment of Experience." Knowledge = error that becomes organic and organized.

> BOOK THREE. The most intimate, supercelestial thing ever written: "On the Final Happiness of the Solitary One"—what comes to the "unified self" of the highest order from out of its "belongings": the perfect ego; only then does *this* ego have *love:* at the earlier stages, where the greatest solitude and self-mastery have not been achieved, there is something other than love.

> BOOK FOUR. Completely dithyrambic. "Annulus aeternitatus." The drive to experience everything once more and forever.[11]

Then the date at the conclusion of this outline: Sils-Maria, August 26, 1881.

3

The sole connections between this Zarathustra fragment and the two subsequent ones are the title ("Noon and Eternity") and the subtitle ("Signs of a New Life"); otherwise the name "Zarathustra" does not turn up again in this extensive notebook. For this reason, it is difficult—or more accurately, impossible—to imagine in what ways he would have connected "Zarathustra" to the cited four-part work, which had not been composed at that time. For the time being, it is advisable to think of *Zarathustra* as one possible execution of that work, about which we know scarcely more than the name.

But why exactly "Zarathustra"? The definite source from which Nietzsche took up this name must go unknown to this day. I cite as the most proximal stimulus to his use of this name a passage from Emerson's *Essays,* which Nietzsche read especially intensively at that time ("I have never felt so at home in a book and in my own home. . . . I may not praise it; it stands too near to me," he noted shortly after the cited fragments). The page in Nietzsche's own copy of the *Essays* is heavily underlined and marked, and in the margin we can still read his gloss, *"This is it!"* Emerson wrote:

We require that a man should be so large and columnar in the landscape, that it should deserve to be recorded, that he arose, and girded his loins, and departed to such a place. The most credible pictures are those of majestic men who prevailed at their entrance, and convinced the senses; as happened to the eastern magian who was sent to test the merits of Zertusht or Zoroaster. When the Yunani sage arrived at the Balkh, the Persians tell us, Gushtasp appointed a day on which the mobeds of every country should assemble, and a golden chair was placed for the Yunani sage. Then . . . Zertusht advanced into the midst of the assembly. The Yunani sage, on seeing that chief, said, "This form and this gait cannot lie, and nothing but truth can proceed from them."[12]

But now back to the three aphorisms. They indicate, especially the first and third, two different possible literary conceptions for Nietzsche's newly planned work, a work that under both conceptions was to be devoted to teaching the eternal recurrence of the same.

That the first and third fragments are incompatible as literary conceptions already becomes evident with the naming of Prometheus in the third fragment; this classical motif would not have been appropriate for the figure Zarathustra. I describe the two different conceptions in this way. One has as its subject the life of a wise man, the Persian Zarathustra, who will cautiously proclaim the teaching (compare to fragment 2); the other, cosmic and systematic, presents an architectonic structure of a work that in the fourth book culminates in the teaching of the *annulus aeternitatis*. The one is conceived as an epic narrative, perhaps even as marginal narratives to the orations and prophecies of Zarathustra (compare once again the second fragment); the other is a philosophical-symphonic poem with movement designations for the books: first, chaos or nature, in the style of the first movement of Beethoven's Ninth Symphony; second, fleeting-skeptical-Mephistophelean; third, intimate, supercelestial; and fourth, entirely in the dithyrambic style. The grand themes of the four books or movements are given in the preceding note: dehumanization of nature (book 1), embodiment of experience (book 2), self-mastery of the ego in the greatest solitude (book 3), eternal recurrence of the same and its affirmation (book 4).

4

Both conceptions, both possibilities for literary execution, retain their own self-same contents and thus exist side by side. We will follow the trail of the first, namely, the epic exposition, which Nietzsche left behind in his later notebooks. After Nietzsche took leave of Sils-Maria, Zarathustra became a protagonist from anecdotes (such as those from the lives of the ancient wise men or also from the lives of Jesus in the Gospels) in two notebooks from autumn 1881, written in Genoa. For a better overview, I will number these anecdotes and proverbs.

1. Two youths were brought to Zarathustra. "This one makes everything mediocre—this one does not wish to do harm; he is not heroic-cruel enough."

2. A youth was presented to Zarathustra. "Behold!" someone said. "That is one who has been corrupted by women!" Zarathustra shook his head and smiled. "It is men who corrupt women," he called back, "and everything that women lack should be atoned for and improved on by men—then man creates an image of woman, and woman fashions herself after his image." "You are too charitable toward women," said the bystanders; "You know them not!" Zarathustra answered, "Man's element is the will; woman's element, willingness—this is the law of the sexes; verily, it is a hard law for woman! All human beings are innocent in their existence, but women are innocent to a second degree; who could have oil and kindness enough for them?" Another in the crowd yelled, "What oil! What kindness! Women need to be better educated!" "Men must be better educated," said Zarathustra and then winked for the youth to follow him.

3. "I thirst after a master of the musical arts," said Zarathustra, "that he might teach me to forget my ideas, teach me to speak them from now on in his language; in this way I shall better lead mankind to ear and heart. With sound one may lead mankind to every error and every truth; who would be able to *refute* a sound?" One of his other students queried, "So you would like to be considered irrefutable?" "I would like the seed to become a tree. For a teaching to become a tree, it must be believed for a long time; for that it must be believed to be irrefutable. The tree needs storms, challenges, worms, and malice to make known the sort and strength of its seed; may it break, if it is not strong enough! But a seed is only annihilated, not refuted. ~~"I thirst for music that speaks the language of daybreak!" Here one of his students hugged him and cried.~~ As he said this, the youth he had questioned cried with fervor, "Oh, you are my true teacher! I believe your teachings so strongly that I shall tell everyone everything I feel about them." Zarathustra laughed to himself and pointed his finger toward that one. "This type of following," he said, "is the best, but it is dangerous, and not every type of teaching could tolerate it."

4. After Zarathustra had looked about the city's estates and delightful gardens and heights and terraced slopes, he exclaimed, "This region is resplendent with impressions of many bold men; their houses look at us like so many faces—they are *alive!*—they wish to live on! They were good for life, although they were often *evil* toward themselves."

5. "What do I matter," said Zarathustra, "if my bad arguments are not believed, too!"

6. "If Zarathustra wishes to motivate the masses, he must himself become an actor."

7. "Today you contradict what yesterday you professed." "But for all that, yesterday is not today," said Zarathustra.

8. "How *many* noble and fine goats have I met on my journeys!" said Zarathustra.

9. "Friends," said Zarathustra, "that is a new teaching and herbal medicine; it will not taste good to you. So prepare it as do the wise patients—drink it in one long gulp and follow it up with something sweet and spicy, that your palate may be refreshed and your memory purged. The effect will not fail to materialize in spite of this. Then you shall henceforth be "possessed by the devil," as the priests, who do not take kindly to me, will say to you."

10. "You come too soon! You come too late!" That is the cry heard around all those who come *for ever,* said Zarathustra.

11. Once Zarathustra lit a lantern in the morning, strode to the marketplace, and shouted: I seek God! I seek God! There, where many of those who stood about did not believe in God, he caused a great laughter. Has he become lost? asked one. Has he run away like some child? said another. Or has he hidden from us? Is he afraid of us? Has he set sail? Emigrated? Thus they cried and laughed among one another. Zarathustra leaped into their midst and bore through them with his gaze. Where has God gone? He called out. I will tell you! *We have killed him*—you and I! We are all his murderers. But how did we do this? How were we able to drain the sea? Who gave us the sponge to wipe away the entire horizon? Without this line—what would become of our ability to build? Will our houses stand firm in the future? Will we stand firm? Are we not continually tossed backward, sideways, forward, to and fro?! Does an Above and a Below still exist? Has it not become colder? Does not nighttime grow longer and longer? Must not lanterns be lit in the morning? Do we not yet hear the noise of the gravediggers who inter God? Do we not already reek of divine decomposition? Gods, too, decompose! How do we console ourselves, we murderers above all murderers? The holiest and mightiest this world has hitherto possessed—run through by our daggers— who would wash this blood off us? With what water would we wash ourselves clean? What redemptive ceremonies will we have to invent? Is not the immensity of the deed too grave for us? Must we not ourselves become gods, only to appear worthy of it? There has never been a greater deed! And whoever is born after us belongs to a higher history than any history hitherto, by the grace of this deed." Here Zarathustra fell silent and looked at his audience; they, too, fell silent and looked distantly at him. At last he threw his lantern to the ground, extinguishing it and breaking it to pieces. "I come too soon," he said; "it is not yet my time. This uncanny event is still underway and wanders—it has not yet found its way to the ears of humanity. Lightning and thunder require time, the light of the stars requires time, and deeds require time, too, after they have been performed. To them, this deed is still farther removed than the most distant star—*and yet they themselves have done it!*"[13]

This belongs with a note from another notebook.

12. Here Zarathustra fell silent again and sank deeply into thought. At last he said, as if in a trance, "Or has he killed himself? Were we but his hands?"

In conclusion, there is another title to mention that is contained in the final Zarathustra fragment from autumn 1881:

> 13. Zarathustra's Idlesse. By F.N. fluid fiery glowing—but light: the final book— it should unfold majestically and blissfully. So spoke Zarathustra, "I do not reproach; I will not even reproach the accuser."

5

The texts we have collected are Nietzsche's first attempts to give a literary shape to the figure he created in Sils-Maria. There is one more fragment from the unpublished writings of his autumn in Genoa in which Nietzsche draws a contrast involving Zarathustra; unfortunately, it was left incomplete. "I have an *origin;* that is the pride contrasted to *cupido gloriae.* It is not strange to me that Zarathustra. . . ."[14] This is preliminary material to a long-concluded text that is likewise found in an unpublished notebook from the same time period. However, the naming of Zarathustra there certainly loses its significance, since he is mentioned together with other historical greats:

> In antiquity every higher man felt the urge for fame [*cupido gloriae* in the preliminary material]—it came about that each believed humanity to begin with himself, that each understood to attribute sufficient breadth and duration to himself such that he included himself in any thoughts of an afterworld as a participating tragedian on the eternal stage. In contrast, my pride is that "I have an *origin*"—for this reason, I do not need fame. I, too, now live in that which moved Zarathustra, Moses, Mohammed, Jesus, Plato, Brutus, Spinoza, Mirabeau, and much that required a few millennia for its embryonic stage to come to light for the first time in me. We are the first aristocrats in the history of the spirit—the historical sense begins now for the first time.[15]

What is striking is the fact that in the finished fragment, "Zarathustra" remains the first name in the thoroughly *non*chronological series. It would be worth asking whether the (completed) preliminary material would have had Zarathustra as its sole subject matter, but for obvious reasons, no answer is possible.

The significance of the two fragments lies entirely in the proposition that "the historical sense begins now for the first time." In notebooks from autumn 1881 we find a chain of ideas concerning the historical sense, that characteristic virtue and illness of contemporary mankind; these culminate then in *Gay Science,* aphorism 337. Here the historical sense is elevated to a higher level as the possibility of an inexhaustible wealth, as the divine feeling finally accruing to the name "humanity." The man with this feeling is humanity "as the heir of all the old noblemen and at the same time the firstling of a new aristocracy, the likes of whom no era has ever seen or dreamed." Now the millennia before and after mankind, unknown to us, ineffable, are forged together in the thought of eternal recurrence: the soul in whom "what is most ancient and what is most recent—desires, hopes, achievements, victories for humanity," in Nietzsche's phrase—are forged together becomes possible for the first time in the noontime hour, the affirmation of the circular motion of history. So we should think of an embodiment of fundamental errors, of passions, of knowledge, which in the very first sketch for the eternal recurrence of the same Nietzsche postulates as the consequence of the passion for knowledge.[16] Beyond all this, there is another truth, or perhaps *the* truth. The truth, being grounded in the inorganic, in the dead, opposes the anthropomorphism of nature: life is indeed a special case of the dead, of the inorganic. The majestic attempt to describe *chaos or nature* finds expression in *Gay Science*, aphorism 109 (the same aphorism that fascinated Gottfried Benn in his time), and the notes for this aphorism are simultaneous with those giving rise to eternal recurrence. So it is here that "the total character of the world [. . .] is in all eternity chaos—in the sense not of a lack of necessity but of a lack of order, arrangement, form, beauty, wisdom, and whatever other names there are for our aesthetic anthropomorphisms." And if the subject for discussion is necessity, we need read only one of the next sentences: "The whole musical box repeats eternally its tune which may never be called a melody"—eternal repetition, eternal return: for the second time at a decisive passage, Nietzsche alludes to his premier Engadine conception. The teaching of return works on the world after God's death, on one side as the dehumanization of nature, as *chaos* (no longer *Deus* as with Spinoza!) *or nature,* but on the other side as the eternalization and naturalization of man in the "humanity" with a historical sense, the name for which shall later become "the overman." That is said very clearly in the *Nachlaß* from Sils-Maria, August–September 1881: in the course of the eternal recurrence of the same occurs "the greatest degree of unreason and likewise that of its opposite," yet "rationality and irrationality" are "not predicates of the universe" but rather are such for the human world.[17]

6

The collected Zarathustran anecdotes and proverbs from autumn 1881 did not become an epic narrative; shortly thereafter Nietzsche wrote a new book of aphorisms that he conceptualized as a continuation of *Daybreak* but then provided with an independent title, *Gay Science*. So the name "Zarathustra" was stricken from those notes that I have assembled and replaced with expressions such as "a sage" (GS 68), "an innovator" (GS 106), "every philosopher" (GS 332), "a philosopher who corrupted the youth as Socrates had once done" (GS 32), and "a madman" (GS 125). Otherwise the proverbs become anonymous. Consequently Nietzsche did without his "epic" project but also without his architectonic-symphonic work planned for four books, which he had outlined at the same time as the epic approach, August 26, 1881, in Sils-Maria. He wrote the fifth book of aphorisms in the series beginning with *Human, All Too Human,* that is, from 1876 to 1878, as the final one before the philosophical poem *Thus Spoke Zarathustra.* "With this book that series of writings beginning with *Human, All Too Human* comes to a close: in their totality, 'a new image and ideal of the freethinker' has been erected," wrote Nietzsche a few months later to his new friend, Lou von Salomé.[18]

From the standpoint of literary exposition, Nietzsche then chose the epic, very loose framework story as we know it in *Thus Spoke Zarathustra.*

It is doubtful whether the Zarathustra in *Thus Spoke Zarathustra* is the same as the one before it. The Zarathustra of Sils-Maria and Genoa arose during a time when Nietzsche—far from relatives, acquaintances, and friends from 1880 until January 1882—conquered a loneliness transfigured by physical pain and privation but also by a deep, uplifting experience of knowledge. What occurred in spring 1882 was his return to humanity, with a new exuberant hope for youth, for *the* young lady, Lou. The motto for *Gay Science,* taken from Emerson, is the humanistic, happy conclusion to that initial Zarathustra period: "To the poet, to the philosopher, to the saint, all things are friendly and sacred, all events profitable, all days holy, all men divine."[19]

This surrender of philosophical solitude had to end very soon—autumn and winter of 1882–83—in thoughts of doubt and, indeed, of suicide. We must believe his unambiguous statements that the all-important so-called Lou experience, with its never-to-heal wound from disappointment over himself and Lou, nonetheless ripened Nietzsche for his *Thus Spoke Zarathustra.* Whoever is familiar with the sublime, courageous mood of the passion for knowledge prevailing in the notes from Sils-Maria, summer 1881, and Genoa, autumn to winter 1881, becomes aware of an uncanny bitterness and darkness in reading the notebooks Nietzsche composed with the preliminary materials for *Thus Spoke Zarathustra.* Outlines for and fragments of correspondence to Frau Lou, Paul Rée, Overbeck, his relatives, and other acquaintances and friends, which soon sounded like pleas for help, like accusations, are mixed together with outlines for *Zarathustra.* Nietzsche attempted here to still make gold from the mire of his life.

This affected not the fundamental idea of his philosophy but certainly the manner and mode with which Nietzsche announced Zarathustra. The Zarathustra before that experience enjoyed his sublime, voluntary solitude; the Zarathustra afterward wanted to shout down from his newly forced loneliness.

Notes

1. KGW III₃, 5[54], p. 110.

2. Max Müller, *Beiträge:* Erster Band, *Beiträge zur vergleichenden Religionswissenschaft;* Zweiter Band, *Beiträge zur vergleichenden Mythologie und Ethologie* (Leipzig, 1869). See vol. 1, p. 145.

3. See KGW IV₁, 3[7], p. 92 (March 1875): "Wolf's reason why one may not place the Egyptians, Hebrews, Persians, and other oriental nations on the same line <of descent> as the Greeks and Romans: those have not lifted themselves at all, or at most only a few steps, above the sort of cultivation <*Bildung*> that one must rightly call *civil policing* or *civilization,* as opposed to *higher, genuine, spiritual culture.*" Nietzsche cites Friedrich August Wolf, *Kleine Schriften,* ed. G. Bernhardy (Halle, 1896), vol. 2 (paginated continuously), p. 817.

4. KGW IV₁, 5[15], p. 141; 6[49.50], pp. 194f. (spring–summer 1875).

5. KGW III₂, p. 300 <*Philosophy in the Tragic Age of the Greeks,* trans. Marianne Cowan (Chicago: Henry Regnery, 1962), p. 30>.

6. KGW III₄, 32[82], p. 399 (early 1874–spring 1874); 34[9], p. 413 (spring–summer 1874).

7. KGW VI₁, p. 71 ("On the Thousand and One Goals") <*Thus Spoke Zarathustra,* trans. Walter Kaufmann (New York: Penguin Books, 1954)>.

8. KGW V₂, 11[195], p. 417.

9. KGW V₂, 11[196], p. 417.

10. KGW V₂, 11[148], p. 396.

11. KGW V₂, 11[197], p. 417.

12. Ralph Waldo Emerson, *Versuche,* trans. G. Fabricius, (Hannover, 1858), 361 <*Essays,* Harvard Classic Library, deluxe ed., 193–94>.

13. These unpublished fragments all come from KGW V₂.

1. = 12 [131], preliminary material to *Gay Science,* aphorism 32.

2. = preliminary material to *Gay Science,* aphorism 68; see KSA 14, p. 246.

3. = preliminary material to *Gay Science,* aphorism 106; see KSA 14, p. 253.

4. = preliminary material to *Gay Science,* aphorism 291; KSA 14, p. 265.

5. = preliminary material to *Gay Science,* aphorism 332; see KSA 14, p. 270.

6. = 12 [112]; see *Gay Science,* aphorism 236, and *Twilight of the Idols,* "Maxims and Arrows," sec. 1.

7. = 12 [128].

8. = 12 [136].

9. = 15 [50].

10. = 15 [52]; see "Cunning Joke and Revenge," sec. 45.

11. = preliminary material to *Gay Science,* aphorism 125; see KSA 14, pp. 256f.

12. = 12 [157].

13. = 12 [225].

The preliminary material to *Gay Science,* aphorism 125, was first published and commented on by Eugen Biser in "Die Proklamation von Gottes Tode," *Hochland* 56 (1963): 137–52.

14. KGW V$_2$, 12[79], p. 488.

15. KGW V$_2$, 15[17], p. 540.

16. KGW V$_2$, 11[141], pp. 392ff.

17. KGW V$_2$, 11[157], p. 400.

18. To Lou von Salomé, KGB III$_1$, p. 213.

19. KGW V$_2$, p. 21 <sec. 8 of *Gay Science,* trans. Walter Kaufmann (New York: Vintage Books, 1974)>.

8   Nietzsche's Unpublished Writings from 1885 to 1888; or, Textual Criticism and the Will to Power

1

Two approaches to Nietzsche's unpublished writings are possible. One understands the totality of the handwritten notes—apart from their employment in the works—as the more or less unified expression of Nietzsche's thought in process. The other emphasizes Nietzsche's literary intentions, meaning his plans for publication insofar as we may detail them; consequently, it searches for the preliminary material to his works and concerns itself with the reconstruction of their composition process. What Nietzsche incorporated in his works, what was simply rejected or postponed for later use, what was ultimately unused and why—all this is the subject the second approach seeks to investigate. Each approach must complement the other in a complete interpretation of Nietzsche's thinking. Nevertheless, the second one is the distinctive modus operandi of the critical edition, whose purpose it is to mirror, in a "technical" manner, the subtle differentiations among the notes in their relations to the published works or extant finished works. This occurs through publication of the rejected or unused notes left in the literary remains and through evaluation, in the critical apparatus, of the preliminary material to the works.[1]

2

When we speak of the "will to power," we refer, first of all, to a philosophical theory and then to one of Nietzsche's literary projects, but also, finally, to the compilation of the unpublished writings with this famous title, which in 1906 appeared in its definitive—and in part still canonical—form, edited by Heinrich Köselitz (alias Peter Gast) and Elisabeth Förster-Nietzsche, the philosopher's sister. Reflections on the "feeling of power" that were committed to paper in *Daybreak* (spring 1881) and in the unpublished fragments from summer–autumn 1880 prepared the way for a conceptual determination of "will to power." We discover the first detailed description of "will to power" in *Thus Spoke Zarathustra*, part 2, specifically the chapter "On Self-Overcoming," written in the summer of 1883.

> Where I found the living, there I found will to power; and even in the will of those who serve I found the will to be master. [. . .] And life itself confided this secret to me: "Behold," it said, "I am *that which must always overcome itself*. [. . .] And you, too, lover of knowledge, are only a path and footprint of my will; verily, my will to power walks on the heels of your will to truth. Indeed, the truth was not hit by him who shot at it with the word of the 'will to existence': that will does not exist. For, what does not exist cannot will; but what is in existence, how could that still want existence? Only where there is life is there also will: not will to life but—thus I teach you—will to power. There is much that life esteems more highly than life itself; but out of the esteeming itself speaks the will to power."

As its initial adage, a notebook from autumn 1882 proffers, "The will to live? In its place I always found only the 'will to power.'"[2]

3

Let us examine the primary features of this characterization of will to power, which remained valid for Nietzsche until the end: the will to power is the "unexhausted, procreative will of life"; it is the "will to be master"; it is Nietzsche's "word concerning life and the nature of all the living"; it is life itself. This will to power is no metaphysical principle such as Schopenhauer's will to existence or will to live; it is not "appearance." It is simply another way of saying "life," of designating "life." Life is "*that which must always overcome itself,*" the tension between the stronger and the weaker; the smaller surrenders to the larger, "that it may have pleasure and power over the smallest," but the greatest, too, yields and "for the sake of power risks life." And the will to truth—what Nietzsche called "the passion for knowledge" in the period of *Daybreak*—as the "will to the thinkability of all beings," which is said to "yield and bend" for "you who are wisest," as "mirror and counterimage of the spirit," is the will to power. "What the people believe to be good and evil" betrays an "ancient will to power," the creator of values.

4

We now turn our attention to the emergence of Nietzsche's literary project of writing a work with the title "Will to Power." This title turns up for the first time in his manuscript from late summer 1885. The stage was set for it, so to speak, by a series of notes beginning in the spring of the same year. Of course, we find the theme of will to power in earlier manuscripts (from 1880),[3] just as this theme does not stand alone in the previously mentioned manuscript from the year 1885. The historical sense, knowledge as a falsification to make life possible, criticism of modern moral Tartuffery, the philosopher as legislator and the one who attempts new possibilities, so-called grand politics, the figure of the "good European": we find all these themes and others besides in the notebooks from this period. In their case, Nietzsche's unpublished writings reveal themselves for what they really are: an intellectual diary in which were written down all his attempts at theoretically working out intuitions and notions, his readings (frequently in the form of excerpts), his drafts of correspondence, and his plans and titles for intended works. In this regard, it proves important to keep in mind the character of these notes as experimental, their unity as a whole, and their complexity—above all, their complexity.

5

At this juncture a provisional title, which should be dated immediately before the composition of *Zarathustra,* part 4, is worth mentioning. We read in a notebook from summer–autumn 1884:

> *The Philosophy of Eternal Recurrence*
> *An Attempt at the Revaluation of All Values.*

The preface to this "Philosophy of Eternal Recurrence," with the title "The New Order of Rank," referring to "the order of rank of the intellect," is sketched "in contrast to the morality of equality." Here Nietzsche speaks of the "order of rank of value-creators (with regard to stipulating values)"—they are the artists, the philosophers, the legislators, the founders of religion, and the "highest man" (as "masters of the earth" and "creators of the future," who finally break apart on themselves). All are conceived of as "having not turned out well" (a leitmotif of *Zarathustra,* part 4, is almost imperceptibly anticipated here). This preface culminates in a depiction of "Dionysian wisdom": "To *feel* the highest power, everything imperfect, everything suffering as *necessary* (*worthy of eternal repetition*), out of a supercharged creative energy, which must break apart again and again and chooses the most high-spirited, difficult paths (principle of the greatest possible stupidity, God as the devil and symbol of pride). Mankind hitherto as an *embryo* in which all the form-giving powers *operate*—the reason for its profound *restlessness.*"

A few pages later Nietzsche develops a problematic in the will to power: the will to power as present in organic functions in relation to pain and pleasure, in so-called altruism (maternal love and philanthropy), and in the inorganic, too. A sketch of the authentic philosophy of eternal recurrence of the same follows, in which the successively ordered theories of eternal recurrence of the same, revaluation of all values, and the will to power are arranged. The idea of eternal recurrence of the same is the "weightiest idea": in order to bear it, a revaluation of all values is necessary—but of what does this consist? Nietzsche answers that we must desire not certainty but instead uncertainty; that we see not "cause and effect" but instead the "continually creative one"; that we replace the will to survival with the will to power; that we no longer humbly mumble, "Everything is just subjective" but rather, "It is our work; may we take pride in it!"

The title "Preface to the Philosophy of Eternal Recurrence" occurs again, among sundry others (the most important being "The New Enlightenment" and "Beyond Good and Evil"), until it becomes a subtitle and receives a new main title: "Noon and Eternity: A Philosophy of Eternal Recurrence." There would be no more said about a "Revaluation of All Values" in Nietzsche's notebooks for a long time. "New Enlightenment" and "Beyond Good and Evil" would become main components of a new plan a little later under the title "Eternal Recurrence: A Prophecy." At the end of this plan we find the main segment on recurrence, with the title, in fact, "Hammer and Great Noon."[4]

6

The completion of *Zarathustra,* by the publication of its fourth part early in 1885 at Nietzsche's own expense, was a thoroughly private affair. Only forty copies of this final part appeared, all going to a small number of close friends and acquaintances—it was growing ever quieter around Nietzsche. Since 1884 he had been embroiled in a prolonged dispute with the publisher Ernst Schmeitzner concerning his books and a portion of his small royalties. In the autumn of 1884 Nietzsche still fostered the plan to step before the public eye as a poet—proof of this: a previously unknown rough draft for correspondence to Julius Rodenberg, the editor of *Deutsche Rundschau.*[5] The years 1885 and 1886 were marked by Nietzsche's repeated attempts to find a publisher who would be prepared to purchase the remaining stock of his earlier works published by Schmeitzner and print his new writings. The solution was not found until summer 1886: his first publisher, Ernst Wilhelm Fritzsch, purchased the earlier writings, *Birth of Tragedy* to *Thus Spoke Zarathustra,* part 3, from Schmeitzner, and Nietzsche decided to publish his new writings at his own expense with the Leipzig printer Constantin Georg Naumann. We must not forget or even underestimate these matters in an evaluation of his various literary plans, which we come across so often in the manuscripts of this period. In our opinion, the extensively prepared experimental revision of *Human, All Too Human,* which Nietzsche undertook in spring and summer 1885, should be understood within the context of a return to the public eye. Outlines shortly before or concurrent with this, in which Nietzsche turned to the Germans with regard to the "good European," demonstrate this same movement toward renewed publicity. We should not overlook continuing plans for a new Zarathustra work (mostly with the title "Noon and Eternity"). Aside from the evident revision of aphorisms from *Human, All Too Human,* it would nevertheless be incorrect to parcel out and subsume the entirety of the notes under the relevant plans: the contrary is correct, meaning that in the course of his reflections, Nietzsche arrived at definitive titles and outlines, which now, with equal rights, so to speak, encompass the entirety of his notes, each from various literary (but also philosophical) standpoints. The plans reciprocally change, resolve themselves, and illuminate the entirety of his notes, each from a particular Nietzschean perspective. The unity (even if not "systematic" in the conventional sense) of Nietzsche's attempt is evident from the entirety of the unpublished writings that have already become well known in their actual, unsystematic form.

7

The fragments, read successively in their apparent chaos, just as Nietzsche committed them to paper, provide us with instructive glimpses into his thought processes: the plans strewn here and there serve him as a periodic respite, so to speak, as reflection amid that tension that overwhelms readers who want to follow Nietzsche's thoughts in process, his "labyrinthine body of ideas" (to use an appropriate phrase from Eckhard Heftrich). The idea that we may point out as the basis of the notes from this period is that of *eternal return,* and the frequency of *Zarathustra* plans (none of which is detailed) likewise signifies the central importance of that idea even before its spokesman stepped onto the stage of part 3 in early 1884. When we read in a notebook from summer 1885 that "Zarathustra can be made happy only after order of rank has been established. This is finally taught," we interpret the first sentence to mean that the idea of eternal recurrence of the same will bring happiness only when order of rank has been established; so we also understand why, in the previously mentioned outline from summer 1884, a preface concerning a new order of rank, that of the intellect, introduces "Philosophy of Eternal Recurrence" as an experimental revaluation of all values. In addition, during the revision of *Human, All Too Human,* we discover in the middle of the notes, as a further cipher for eternal recurrence, the provisional title "Philosophy of Dionysus." The experiment with his book for free spirits failed, but from the diligent labor of that summer sprang up numerous aphorisms for *Beyond Good and Evil*—in particular, those in which the experimental deity Dionysus announces his own arrival. From this same material comes—as we will remark in passing—the final aphorism, number 1067, of the compilation by Elisabeth Förster-Nietzsche and Heinrich Köselitz. However, we do *not* come across the outline in which will to power is used for the first time as a title planned by Nietzsche, within the context of a revaluation of all values and eternal return. This title, found in a notebook from August 1885, reads:

> "The Will to Power
> Attempt
> At a New Explanation of All Events."
> By
> Friedrich Nietzsche.

This is a shift of emphasis. In the subsequent aphorisms Nietzsche reduced nutrition, breeding, adaptation, heredity, and specialization to the will to power as a fixed, final fact. The will to truth is a form of will to power, just as are the will to justice, the will to beauty, and the will to help others. A preface and an introduction belong with this outline. His new theory is sketched in the preface:

> How naively we transfer our moral valuations into things, for example, when we speak of *laws of nature*! It would be useful to conduct the experiment for the first time in a *completely different* manner of interpretation: in this way, through bitter contradiction, it may be grasped how entirely unconsciously *our moral canon* (priority for truth, law, rationality, and so on) *rules over* our *entire so-called science.* Expressed in popular terms: God is refuted, but not the devil: all divine predicates belong to its essence, but the reverse is invalid! <Kaufmann translation>

And in the introduction we read ideas that anticipate the entire problematic of what Nietzsche would later call "nihilism":

> The great danger is not pessimism, a form of hedonism which calculates pains and pleasures to determine whether human life does not really deliver

a preponderance of pain with it. Rather, *the meaninglessness of all events!* Moral explanations fall at the same time as religious explanations: of course, the superficial do not know this! They hold on instinctively, the more pious they are, with their teeth clenched on their moral valuations. As an atheist, Schopenhauer had pronounced a curse on those who disguise the world with moral significance. In England they occupy themselves with turning morality and physics into brothers; <in Germany> Herr von Hartmann, morality and the irrationality of existence. But the genuinely great anxiety is that *the world no longer makes sense.* Insofar as God has fallen to the wayside, so too all morality: they reciprocally supported each other. Now I bring a new explanation, an "immoral" one, which appears as a special case relative to our previous morality. Popularly expressed: God is refuted, not the devil.

(We must remark with regard to these last two that neither fragment was selected for the compilation!)[6]

8

In the subsequent notebook we find a plan in which the motif of meaninglessness already emerges; it has a systematic, very general character, a style in which none of Nietzsche's books had ever been written:

> *Will to Power*
> Attempt at a New Explanation of All Events
> (Preface concerning the threatening "meaninglessness." Problem of pessimism.)
> Logic
> Physics
> Morality
> Art
> Politics

Worth noting here is the unconscious opposition to Schopenhauer's pessimistic metaphysics that had its origins in the *Zarathustra* passage at the beginning of our considerations, where Nietzsche contrasts the will to power to the will to live. Now the concern is an explanation that in Nietzsche's estimation is not really an explanation at all. His confrontation with Gustav Teichmüller and African Spir, by way of their books *Reality and the Apparent World* (1882) and *Thought and Reality* (1877), is an integral part of Nietzsche's epistemological meditations that unanimously condemn the degradation of the so-called phenomenal world as the root of all pessimism. "The world of thought is merely a second order of the phenomenal world," noted Nietzsche in an identically formulated outline to "Will to Power" as a "new explanation of all events." And concerning the word "appearance/phenomenon" itself, he took up the following position:

> *Appearance,* as I understand it, is the actual and singular reality of things—that to which all predicates obtain in the first instance. This phrase expresses nothing other than its *inaccessibility* for logical procedures and distinctions, hence, *appearance* in contrast to *logical truth*—which may be possible only in an imaginary world. Therefore, I do not contrast "appearance" to "reality," but instead conversely take appearance as that reality which opposes transformation into an imaginary "true world." A definitive name for this reality, that is, described from within and not from outside its inconceivable fluctuating Protean nature, would be "will to power."

(This fragment, too, was deemed insufficiently worthy to be selected by the compilers for their sorry effort!)[7]

9

A certain period of time lapsed before the title "Will to Power as a New Explanation of All Events" was granted equal rights to exist alongside other titles, the most significant (as a "Zarathustra work") of which remained "Noon and Eternity." Also, outlines to a prelude to the philosophy of the future emerged in this period (summer 1885 to summer 1886) as a work in progress. The frequent title for it was "Beyond Good and Evil," for which Nietzsche completed a printer's manuscript in winter 1885. Let us, then, insist on the fact that *Beyond Good and Evil* was conceived as a plan concurrent with other works ("Will to Power" and "Noon and Eternity"). In an important manuscript containing the lion's share of the fair copy for *Beyond Good and Evil,* we discover a plan with the heading "Titles for ten new books," dated by Nietzsche as "spring 1886." The titles in this series are recorded as

1. Thoughts on the Ancient Greeks
2. Will to Power. Attempt at a New Explanation of All Events
3. The Artist. Afterthoughts of a Psychologist
4. We Godless Ones
5. Noon and Eternity
6. Beyond Good and Evil. Prelude to the Philosophy of the Future
7. Gai saber. Songs of Prince Free-as-a-Bird
8. Music
9. Experiences of a Scholar
10. Nightfall on Modernity: A History

A detailed examination of these titles would lead us too far astray from our main concern; let us, then, remain content with the determination that for each of these titles there exists an extant, definite series of notes in the manuscripts and further, that with each of these titles, earlier notes are cast in a certain light, such that the titles themselves constitute a set of special themes as transitional points for further excursions. To offer but one example, Nietzsche describes the "history of a nightfall on modernity" several pages later: the decline of the family, the "good" man as a symptom of exhaustion, lewdness and neurosis, "black music," Nordic unnaturalness—keywords to a sketch of a darkening modernity. One of the titles even refers to a printer's manuscript already completed ("Beyond Good and Evil"), and the later "Songs of Prince Free-as-a-Bird" had been composed since autumn 1884 (in part since 1882). To give Nietzsche a dressing-down because he did not remain with this plan but instead "languished struggling with a systematic magnum opus"—as did Erich F. Podach in his *Blick in Nietzsches Notizbücher* (1963)—seems to us a remarkably unjust judgment on Nietzsche. First, Podach does not see the actual significance of the outlines, sketches, plans, and titles that we must view as thoroughly provisional, not intended as eternally binding over existing material, and as outlooks for future projects, especially since they themselves are mostly fragments that clarify certain statements by Nietzsche and are intelligible only within the entire massive procession of notes. (For this reason they belong in the text of a critical edition.) Second, Podach postulated a struggle with a magnum opus that never took place: Nietzsche's unpublished writings as a whole constitute an experiment; this experiment was broken off only by his illness. To claim from this that Nietzsche's lifework remained incomplete is, as we have already discovered, well nigh a naïveté caused by the more than dubious notion of a magnum opus.[8]

10

Several weeks later—*Beyond Good and Evil* appeared in the meantime—Nietzsche drew up a new sketch, dating it "Sils-Maria, summer 1886." The outline reads:

Will to Power
Attempt at a New Explanation of All Events.
In four books.

First Book:	The danger of all dangers (presentation of nihilism) (as the necessary consequence of all valuations hitherto)
Second Book:	Critique of values (of logic and so forth)
Third Book:	Problem for the legislator (in this the history of solitude). *How* must men be produced, who in turn create values? Men who have all the qualities of the modern soul but are strong enough to transform them into a sounder health
Fourth Book:	Hammer. Their means for their task.

Presentation of the danger of dangers, namely, "that everything is meaning-less," that is, nihilism; a critique of all values and culture hitherto; a revalua-tion of all values as the problem for legislators; finally, the eternal recurrence of the same as the hammer, as a teaching "that works a harvest of the most viable by an unleashing of the most death-addictive pessimism": Nietzsche varies these four moments in the numerous notes following the outline. Ni-hilism, critique of values, revaluation of all values in the sense of will to pow-er, eternal recurrence: here we discover once again motifs known to us from earlier notes. Of course, now they are clarified, in fact by the very quadripar-tite organization of the work, which for its part determined the course of sub-sequent reflections. We should also note that Nietzsche reached back to 1884 for the subtitle "Philosophy of Eternal Recurrence."

Beginning with this point, we are justified in speaking of a work planned in four books that Nietzsche wanted to publish with the title "The Will to Power: An Attempt at a New Explanation of All Events." He advertised it on the fourth dust-jacket page of *Beyond Good and Evil* (summer 1886), and a year after that he hinted of it in the text of *Genealogy of Morals* (summer 1887). *Beyond Good and Evil* cannot detach itself from "Will to Power"—as its compilers claimed—rather, it is nothing more than the assemblage of everything that Nietzsche considered worth communicating from the material of the *Zarathustra* period (1881–85) and the subsequent attempt to revise *Human, All Too Human* as a prelude to a philosophy of the future. This prelude was completed for the printer, as we have said, in winter 1885. Also, the prefaces and various supplements to the new edition of *Birth of Tragedy, Human, All Too Human, Daybreak,* and *Gay Science,* composed between summer 1886 and spring 1887, originate from the notes com-posed precisely for the literary purpose of a new edition. In any case, they do not emerge from a different set of notes allegedly selected for "Will to Power." We certainly ascertain reciprocal relations between this material and the out-line for "Will to Power": nonetheless, we must learn his specific literary inten-tions, just as here, in the case of the plan from summer 1886, we must be able to distinguish between all the previous notes and concurrent investigations of unrelated sorts. What Nietzsche chose to remember from his earlier material he noted to himself by a rubric of fifty-three numbers, which he appended in spring 1887. This rubric is neither a plan nor an outline but rather very simply an index of eventually usable notes. Remarkably, the famous final aphorism of the Köselitz–Förster-Nietzsche compilation, their number 1067, was *not* select-ed for the rubric. If Nietzsche's literary intentions are to have any value at all, we must decisively conclude from this fact that the aphorism had fulfilled its function in Nietzsche's eyes, another version of it having been published in

Beyond Good and Evil (aphorism 36). Obviously it possesses its own philosophical value, and it should appear in the *Nachlaß*, but it does not belong to those notes that Nietzsche wished to rescue in spring 1887. Another plan for the "Will to Power" originated from this period. That it belongs to the "Will to Power" we may only conjecture—although with the greatest probability—since the page has been cut at the upper edge, such that we read:

> [+++] of All Values
>
> First Book
> European Nihilism
>
> Second Book
> Critique of the Highest Values
>
> Third Book
> Principle of a New Valuation
>
> Fourth Book
> Discipline and Breeding
>
> Outlined March 17, 1887, Nice

This plan is important insofar as the compilers Köselitz and Förster-Nietzsche calculated it to be the most suitable for their sorry effort—how successfully will be illuminated by details yet to follow. It is scarcely distinguishable from the plan in summer 1886. Here, too, nihilism, a critique of values, a revaluation of all values, and eternal recurrence (as the hammer and thus the principle of discipline and breeding as we know it from the plan of summer 1886) constitute the four motifs of the four books.[9]

11

After Nietzsche had completed his work on the new edition of his previous works, he devoted himself with special intensity to reflections on the central problem of the plans from summer 1886 and spring 1887: the problem of nihilism, which he wanted as the theme of the first book of his work.

These reflections culminated in an impressive fragment with the title "European Nihilism," dated by him "Lenzer Heide, June 10, 1887." It is a brief essay in sixteen paragraphs. It is scarcely believable, but in the canonical compilation by Förster-Nietzsche and Köselitz, this text was cut up into segments (in the first "Will to Power" from 1901, in contrast, it was published in its entirety). Only the readers of Otto Weiss's scholarly apparatus in volume 16 of the GOA (1911) knew that the so-called aphorisms 4, 5, 114, and 55 (read in that order) constituted one organic essay.

Morality—if we may briefly summarize this text—has brought up truthfulness, but the latter knows the vacuity of morality, which leads to nihilism in the form of insight into the meaninglessness of events. That which is meaningless, eternally recurring, is now the most extreme form of nihilism. But if the fundamental character of events could be embraced, under the assumption that we can know their genuine fundamental character, then we could affirm their senseless recurrence. That occurs when the most hateful basic feature of life, the will to power, may be affirmed.

Now those who have not turned out well, those who *suffer* from the will to power and who consequently *hate* the will to power, too, can be persuaded that they are nothing other than their own oppressors, a will to power being disguised in their "will to morality" (because morality is a negation of will to power), and their hate being, therefore, the will to power. The phrase "those who have turned out badly" has no political connotation, those who have turned out badly finding themselves in every stratum of society.

The untenability of morality becomes, in turn, nihilism among those who have turned out badly. From them stems a crisis giving impetus to an order of rank from the perspective of healthy force: Nietzsche expressly remarked, "Letting the commanders command, the followers follow. Obviously remote from all existing social orders." The strongest in this crisis will be those who are most moderate, namely, those who do not require extreme articles of belief, those who not only acknowledge but also love a good portion of chance and irrationality: "men secure in their power, and those who represent the highest power achieved by mankind with a conscious pride."

The fragment concludes with a question: "What would such men think about eternal recurrence"; that is, what would the strongest think about eternal repetition of something meaningless?

12

After the publication of the *Genealogy,* Nietzsche worked from autumn 1887 onward in a concentrated fashion on the "Will to Power." This labor culminated around mid-February 1888 in the rubrication of 372 aphorisms that Nietzsche had written previously in two quarto notebooks and one folio notebook. For his rubrication he used an additional notebook in which he transferred the 372 fragments according to keywords (in reality there were 374 of them, because two numbers were used twice). The first three hundred keywords were partitioned between our books, Nietzsche writing the roman numerals *I, II, III,* or *IV* with a pencil alongside the keyword designation to the note. These numerals correspond to a plan without headings that we discover in the rubric notebook. It is divided into four books, but any heading to the four books is absent:

[For the first book]
1. Nihilism, thought through to its finale
2. Culture, civilization, the ambiguity of what is "modern"

[for the second book]
3. The Origin of the Ideal
4. Critique of Christian Ideals
5. How the Virtues Are Victorious
6. The Herd Instinct

[for the third book]
7. The "Will to Truth"
8. Morality as the Circe of Philosophers.
9. Psychology as the "Will to Power" (desire, will, concept, and so on)

[for the fourth book]
10. The "Eternal Recurrence."
11. Grand Politics.
12. A Life-Recipe for Us.[10]

Noteworthy in regard to this plan is the fact that the movement of the four primary motifs—nihilism, critique of values, revaluation of values, eternal recurrence—remains in force. The four books are divided into chapters that impart a special emphasis to the primary motif.

A closer examination of the rubricated fragments, above all in view of their fate in the compilation by Elisabeth Förster-Nietzsche and Heinrich Köselitz, serves here as an example of much of their editorial praxis. The four books of the plan according to which Nietzsche rubricated these fragments correspond precisely to the four books of the plan from March 17, 1887, chosen by the editors of the compilation. We should, therefore, expect that they would have followed Nietzsche's instructions—at least in this peculiar case in which he expressly left them behind. Köselitz often fancied himself a superior philosopher and writer to Nietzsche, however, and his sister even "studied philosophy" under Rudolf Steiner. . . . Here are the results:

1. Of the 374 fragments numbered by Nietzsche for the purpose of "Will to Power," 104 were not taken into in the compilation; of these, 84 were not published at all, and 20 were banished to volumes 13 and 14 of the GOA, as well as to the remarks by Otto Weiss in volume 16. In the foreword to volume 13 of the GOA, however, Elisabeth Förster-Nietzsche wrote, "Volumes 13 and 14 bring together the unpublished writings [. . .] with the exception of all those things that the author himself had unconditionally specified for the 'Will to Power.'"

2. Of the remaining 270 fragments, 137 are reproduced incompletely or with intentional alterations of the text (deletion of headings or often of whole sentences, dismemberment of texts that belong together, and so on).

a. Of these 137 fragments, 49 are corrected in the remarks by Otto Weiss, so that the general user of the "Will to Power," for example, the reader of the recently published Kröner edition (edited by Alfred Bäumler) will never learn of these corrections;

b. another 36 are only unsatisfactorily corrected in those remarks, in part because Weiss makes inexact statements about the texts, and he often errs in the decipherment of the excluded passages; and

c. the remaining 52 do without any comment, although they contain imperfections similar to those of the other fragments on which Otto Weiss deemed it necessary to comment.

3. The first 300 fragments, as has been said, are those that Nietzsche himself divided between the four books of his plan. This division was not upheld by the compilers in at least sixty-four instances.[11]

13

Nietzsche was in no way content with the results of his efforts. He wrote to Heinrich Köselitz on February 13, 1888, "I have finished the first draft of my 'Attempt at a Revaluation': it was, all things considered, torture; so far I totally lack the courage to go back to it. In another ten days I will make corrections to it." And thirteen days later: "You, too, should not think that I have created another work of 'literature' here: this composition was *for me;* from now on, for the duration of the winter, I will make one such composition after another *for myself*—the idea of 'going public with it' is completely out of the question." In this same letter Nietzsche told of his reading of Baudelaire's *œuvres posthumes,* which had recently appeared. In fact, we discover in the folio notebook—directly after the last numbered fragment (372)—a twenty-page excerpt from Baudelaire, after which—interrupted occasionally by various observations—follow other wide-ranging excerpts from Tolstoy's *Ma religion;* the Goncourt brothers' *Journal* (volume I); Benjamin Constant's introduction to his own translation of Schiller's *Wallenstein;* Dostoyevsky's novel *The Possessed* (in French translation); Julius Wellhausen's *Prolegomena to a History of the Israeli People;* and Renan's *Vie de Jésus.*[12] Important, partially hidden traces of these readings appearing in the writings of the year 1888 serve as proof.

Whereas until this time Nietzsche's confrontation with nihilism, foremost with Christianity, had led to historical and psychological ground (we mean, of course, in the mentioned notebooks with numbered fragments), from now on until the beginning of the subsequent folio notebook, whose first note is dated "Nice, March 25, 1888," the metaphysical aspect steps into the foreground, indeed, typically enough, in the form of a permanently fragmented but wide-ranging essay on art and truth in his *Birth of Tragedy.* This essay was horribly mutilated by the compilers Köselitz and Förster-Nietzsche; that is all the more regrettable since in it the important problem of the "true" and "apparent" world, which became one of the main points of the subsequent notes to "Will to Power," was attacked once more.

We discover the keywords "true and apparent world," in fact, as the first chapter in that plan to "Will to Power" according to whose headings Nietzsche himself classified the lion's share of notes in the important folio notebook.

Plans now take on a form rather different from those previously mentioned.

14

It is worth remarking that from autumn 1887 until summer 1888 provisional titles other than those for "Will to Power" scarcely occur in the manuscripts. And in addition to making this external observation, we remark that Nietzsche devoted himself to "Will to Power" with more fervor than he displayed at any previous period (with the exception, of course, of the composition *The Case of Wagner,* the pamphlet from spring 1888 in which Nietzsche treated a special case of modern decadence). Several plans show a certain compositional shift in emphasis: Nietzsche appears now to prefer a version in eight to twelve chapters over the quadripartite organization of a work in four books. Especially important is the following plan in eleven chapters:

1. The True and the Apparent World
2. The Philosopher as a Type of Decadent
3. The Religious Man as a Type of Decadent
4. The Good Man as a Type of Decadent
5. The Countermovement: *Art.* The Problem of the Tragic
6. Paganism in Religion
7. Science against Philosophy
8. Politics
9. Critique of the Present
10. Nihilism and Its Counterimage: Those Who Return
11. The Will to Power

Nietzsche classified the notes of the aforementioned wide-ranging folio notebook, beginning with the date March 25, 1888, according to these chapter designations. The connections between belief in a "true" world and decadence, as well as the countermovements—namely, the movements against those beliefs— are illustrated in the plan, such that Nietzsche, for example, provided the fragments of the previously cited essay on *Birth of Tragedy* with the keywords "Countermovement: *Art,*" which is also the fifth heading in this and one other similar plan. Nietzsche's experiment with an ordering of fragments according to this plan is just as significant as his experiment in February 1888; it is just as fragmentary, because it limited itself to the notes of one, albeit very wide-ranging, notebook. Obviously it received no consideration during the compilation. In Turin Nietzsche used two additional larger notebooks. In the meantime the many additions and reworking had made the notes confused. Nietzsche wrote them down in part on loose-leaf paper. Several constitute small self-contained essays; otherwise they were simply rendered into a fair copy, without any order. This copy originated in the last weeks of the spring in Turin. Nietzsche brought it with him to Sils-Maria, where he worked first on the printing of *The Case of Wagner* (this work took more time than expected, since Nietzsche had to complete a second fair copy, because the first one was illegible).[13]

15

In Sils-Maria Nietzsche made a fair copy of an additional portion of his notes. Nonetheless, he was still not satisfied with the experience or with what lay before him. Consequently, he wrote to Meta von Salis on August 22: "In comparison with last summer [. . .] this summer appears to have simply 'fallen through' <*ist ins Wasser gefallen*>. This makes me extraordinarily sorry, since compared to the first spring sojourn, which turned out so well, I brought even more energy in me this time than last year. Also, everything had been prepared for *one grand and very specific task*." Meta von Salis had offered Nietzsche a copy of his *Genealogy of Morals* (and he made mention of this work in his epilogue to *The Case of Wagner* during this very time): the renewed reading of his own work produced a peculiar impression in Nietzsche that would not remain without repercussions. In the same letter he wrote:

> The first look in it shocked me: I discovered a lengthy preface to the *Genealogy* whose existence I had *forgotten*. [. . .] Basically, I remembered merely the titles of the three essays; the rest, meaning the *contents,* had completely escaped me. This, the consequence of an extreme intellectual activity that consumed this winter and spring and that erected a *wall* between them, so to speak. Now the book has come alive for me again—and at the same time, the circumstances of the previous summer, from which it originated. Extremely difficult problems for which I had no language, no terminology, but I must have been in a nearly uninterrupted condition of inspiration, that this writing would come to me like the most natural thing in the world. It required no toil. The style is vehement and provocative, full of finesses as well, and pliant and painterly, prose the likes of which I had never composed before.

This serious assessment reflects the final phase of Nietzsche's lifework, although it gains its full significance when we compare its date—August 22—with two other dates: that of the final plan for "Will to Power" and that of the preface to a new work, "The Revaluation of All Values."

16

With regard to the final plan for "Will to Power," Erich F. Podach[14] merely published its date but not the plan drawn up on that date; Otto Weiss,[15] for his part, published the plan without its date. Podach later published the plan, although without connecting it to its date.[16] This is because the date and plan were written on separate sheets, but there can be no doubt that the two sheets belong together (they have the same paper and format, the ink and handwriting are identical on both sheets, and the edges of both sheets show that they lay together for an extended period of time). The plan reads:

> Outline of the plan for:
> Will to Power
> Attempt at a Revaluation of All Values.
> Sils-Maria
> On the last Sunday of the month
> August, 1888.
>
> We Hyperboreans—the Cornerstone of the Problem
>
> First Book: "What Is Truth?"
> First Chapter.   Psychology of Error.
> Second Chapter.   Value of Truth and Error
> Third Chapter.   The Will to Truth (justified for the first time in an affirmation of life)
>
> Second Book: Origin of Value
> First Chapter.   The Metaphysicians
> Second Chapter.   Religious Man (homines religiosi)
> Third Chapter.   The Good and the Improvers
>
> Third Book: Struggle of Values
> First Chapter.   Thoughts on Christianity
> Second Chapter.   Physiology of Art
> Third Chapter.   Toward a History of European Nihilism
>   Diversion for Psychologists
>
> Fourth Book: Great Noon
> First Chapter.   The Principle of Life ("Order of Rank")
> Second Chapter.   The Two Paths
> Third Chapter.   Eternal Recurrence.[17]

The problem of truth has gradually developed into the theme of the first book.

The second book remains, as with the previous quadripartite plans, reserved for the critique of values but in the sense of a history of this value itself, and of its proponents. In the third book Nietzsche treats the battle of values, and the headings of the chapters correspond exactly to notes on Christianity, the physiology of art, and the history of European nihilism. After an "intermezzo" (probably consisting of maxims, of which Nietzsche had committed an entire array to paper) comes the fourth book, which—as with all other plans—is devoted to eternal recurrence.

17

The final plan for "Will to Power" was committed to paper, then, as Nietzsche wrote, "on the last Sunday of the month August, 1888," meaning August 26, four days after his complaint about the unsuccessful summer in Sils-Maria. Nietzsche arranged a certain number of previous notes according to this plan, but he did not stay with that number. On August 30 he repeated his complaint in a letter to his mother: "I am now completely engaged in activity—hopefully it will last awhile, because a well- and long-prepared work, which should have been produced this summer, has literally 'fallen through.'" Yet in these lines the hope was expressed of achieving success at that time. In fact, the exposition of the "well- and long-prepared work" took a form entirely different from the one drawn up in his plans. Nietzsche had been writing again since mid-August, as we have said, committing to paper notes already present in a fair copy but now as individual, separate essays. A loose sheet of paper, on whose obverse side is printed only the title "Will to Power," contains on its reverse side a series of titles pointing toward an "excerption" of Nietzsche's philosophy:

Thoughts for the Day after Tomorrow
Excerpts of My Philosophy,

and

Wisdom for the Day after Tomorrow
My Philosophy
in Excerpts,

and finally,

Magnum in Parvo
A Philosophy
in Excerpts

are the experimental titles of the planned excerpt. More important is the list of chapters for it (on the same sheet, in fact):

1. We Hyperboreans
2. The Problem of Socrates
3. Reason in Philosophy
4. How the True World Finally Became a Fable
5. Morality as Anti-Nature
6. The Four Great Errors
7. For Us—Against Us
8. The Concept of a Decadent Religion
9. Buddhism and Christianity
10. From My Aesthetics
11. Among Artists and Writers
12. Maxims and Arrows

Numbers 2, 3, 4, 5, 6, and 12 are titles of identically named chapters, and number 11 is the original title of the chapter "Skirmishes of an Untimely Man," in *Twilight of the Idols;* numbers 1, 7, 8, and 9 are, however, the titles that—although stricken—we can still read in the printer's manuscript of *Antichrist:* "We Hyperboreans" for the current sections 1-7, "For Us—Against Us" for current sections 8-14, "The Concept of a Decadent Religion" for current sections 15-19, and "Buddhism and Christianity" for sections 20-23. Since Nietzsche dated a preliminary version of his foreword to "Idlesse of a Psychologist" (later *Twilight of the Idols*) as "the beginning of September," and since he also composed the foreword to "Revaluation of All Values" on September 3, in fact according to the plan of four books, the first of which was to be *Antichrist,* we may conclude from this that between August 26 and September 3 the following transpired:

1. Nietzsche abandoned any and all plans for "Will to Power."
2. For a brief period, he may have entertained the possibility of publishing the material already in fair copy as the "Revaluation of All Values."
3. He decided, however, on a selection of excerpts of his philosophy.
4. He named this selection of excerpts "Idlesse of a Psychologist."
5. Immediately thereafter he removed chapters 1, 7, 8, and 9 from the "excerpts," which yielded twenty-three paragraphs concerning Christianity, along with an introduction ("We Hyperboreans").
6. From then on, the magnum opus bore the title "Revaluation of All Values" and was planned in four books. The first book, *Antichrist,* was already a good one-third finished (the just-mentioned twenty-three paragraphs).
7. On September 3, 1888, Nietzsche wrote a foreword for the "Revaluation." The "Idlesse of a Psychologist" was, for Nietzsche, the "synopsis" of his "most characteristic philosophical heterodoxies," as he expressed it in his correspondence (September 12 to Köselitz and September 16 to Overbeck);

it was therefore a print-worthy production of the philosophizing in his last year of sanity. It consisted of notes intended purely for "Will to Power." The "Revaluation of All Values" in four books, however, was his new work project. A good one-half of the first book, *Antichrist,* comes from previous meditations—this origin understood in the sense allowed here, that of its literary origin, hence, its origin in earlier notes, "preliminary materials"—in fact, it had separated itself from the "excerpts" of his philosophy already committed in writing by Nietzsche; it was, though, in its literary intentions, a *new* beginning. In *The Antichrist* sections 1–7 present a sort of introduction (just as the chapter "We Hyperboreans" was the introduction for the "excerpts"), while sections 8–23 constitute a penetrating essay on Christianity, which Nietzsche now wished to employ for the same purposes—above all in terms of his stylistic intentions. With this he had discovered the "form" for the announcement of his "magnum opus." And we believe that his renewed reading of *Genealogy of Morals,* the work that so strongly resembles *Antichrist* in terms of style, helped him there.

Thus wrote Nietzsche to his friend, Meta von Salis, on September 7, 1888:

> Meanwhile I have been very productive—to such a degree that I have reason to withdraw the sighs in my last letter about the summer that "fell through." I have even achieved something *more,* something I did not believe myself capable of. [. . .] The repercussion was, I admit, that my life fell into disorder during the last couple weeks. Several times I stayed up until 2:00 A.M., driven by intellect, and wrote down what went through my head. Then I heard how my landlord, Herr Durisch, cautiously slipped outside to go on the hunt for gems. Who knows! Perhaps I, too, was on the hunt for gems. [. . .] The *third of September* was a quite remarkable day. Early on, I wrote the preface to my "Revaluation of All Values," perhaps the most exquisite preface written to this point in time. Afterward I went outside—and behold! The most beautiful day I have experienced in the Engadine—a luminosity of all colors, a blue in the lake and sky, a clarity of the air, perfectly incredible.

And further: "On September 15 I am continuing on to *Turin.* Concerning winter there, an experiment with Corsica would actually be still riskier, given my need for deep integration. [. . .] But who knows? I shall conclude my 'Revaluation of All Values,' the most independent book that exists, by bringing it to the printers in the next year. [. . .] *Not* without misgivings! For example, the first book is called *Antichrist.*"[18]

18

We are familiar with six versions of his new literary plan, meaning the "Revaluation of All Values" in four books. The books' headings clarify Nietzsche's intention; therefore, they are quoted here in chronological order:

1. First Book
The Antichrist. Attempt at a Critique of Christianity

   Second Book
The Free Spirit. Critique of Philosophy as a Current of Nihilism

   Third Book
The Immoralist. Critique of the Most Fateful Form of Ignorance, Morality

   Fourth Book
Dionysus. Philosophy of Eternal Recurrence

2. Book 1: The Antichrist

   Book 2: The Misosoph (Wisdom-Hater)

   Book 3: The Immoralist

   Book 4: Dionysus

3. The Antichrist. Attempt at a Critique of Christianity

   The Immoralist. Critique of the Most Fateful Form of Ignorance, Morality

   We Yes-Sayers. Critique of Philosophy as a Current of Nihilism

   Dionysus. Philosophy of Eternal Recurrence

4. Redemption from Christianity: The Antichrist

   Redemption from Morality: The Immoralist

   Redemption from Truth: The Free Spirit

   Redemption from Nihilism: Nihilism as the necessary consequence of Christianity, morality and the philosopher's concept of truth. Signs of nihilism. By "free spirit" I mean something quite specific: to be a hundred times superior to philosophers and other disciples of "truth," by means of a rigorousness toward them, by honorableness and courage, by the unconditional will to say No, where No is dangerous—I treat the past philosophers as contemptible libertines under the hood of woman, "Truth."

5. IV. Dionysus. Legislator-Type

6. Free Spirit. Critique of Philosophy as a Current of Nihilism.

   The Immoralist. Critique of Morality as the Most Fateful Form of Ignorance.

   Dionysos philosophos.

The final plan was apparently committed to paper after completion of *Antichrist*. We notice a shift in regard to the sequence of the second and third books: the critique of philosophy comes in the second position and that of morality in third position in the first, second, and sixth plans; in the third and fourth plans, the critique of morality comes first, and then that of philosophy. The general conception remained the same: after critiquing Christianity, morality, and philosophy, Nietzsche intended the announcement of his philosophy. This is the philosophy of Dionysus, the philosophy of eternal recurrence of the same. Viewed with respect to *contents,* the "Revaluation of All Values" was in a sense the same as the "Will to Power," but precisely for this reason was its *literary* negation. Alternatively, *Twilight of the Idols* and *Antichrist* were created from the notes for "Will to Power"; the rest is—*Nachlaß,* unpublished writings.[19]

19

With that, the history of "Will to Power" as one of Nietzsche's literary projects comes to an end. That Nietzsche considered *Antichrist* to be his "Revaluation of All Values," from at the latest November 20, 1888, onward, such that the main title, "Revaluation of All Values," became the subtitle, as he expressly wrote Paul Deussen (November 26, 1888: "My 'Revaluation of All Values,' with the main title, *Antichrist,* is finished"), that he altered the subtitle again at the end of December: all this, together with the history of his autobiography, *Ecce Homo, Dionysian Dithyrambs,* and the short composition *The Case of Wagner,* along with his political proclamations against the Germany of young Kaiser Wilhelm II, belongs to the ostensibly confused conclusion to Nietzsche's life-work, which spelled the end of his intellect. *The Turin catastrophe came when Nietzsche was literally entirely finished with everything.*

His unpublished writings remain behind for us, along with his other writings and works. This literary estate is, in the truest sense of the term, an *obligating inheritance,* because the questions posed by Nietzsche, whether in his works, his fragments, or both as a whole, drive us even today. Within the context of this obligation, however, the unpublished handwritten writings should be made known in their authentic form. Regarding the "Will to Power," after philological reconstruction of the unpublished writings from 1885 to 1888, the controversy about an alleged magnum opus has become pointless: Nietzsche scholarship may now move forward to its true daily business.

Notes

1. KGW VIII$_1$, pp. vif. (editor's prefatory remarks).
2. KGW VII$_1$, 5[1] <*Thus Spoke Zarathustra,* trans. Walter Kaufmann (New York: Penguin Books, 1954)>.
3. KGW V$_1$, 7[206] (end 1880).
4. For fragments in this section, see KGW VII$_2$, 26[259], 26[258], 26[243], 26[273], 26[274], 26[284], 26[293], 26[325], 26[465], 27[58], 27[80], 27[82].
5. KGB III$_1$, p. 567. Outline of letter to Julius Rodenberg, November/December 1884.

6. For fragments in this section, see KGW VII$_3$, 35[71], 36[75], 35[26], 35[47], 38[12], 39[1], 39[14], 39[15].

7. For fragments in this section, see KGW VII$_3$, 40[2], 40[53]; VIII$_1$, 1[36].

8. For fragments in this section, see KGW VIII$_1$, 2[73] and 2[122].

9. For fragments in this section, KGW VIII$_1$, 2[100] and 7[64].

10. KGW VIII$_1$, 5[71].

11. For the fragment in this section, see KGW VIII$_2$, 12[2].

12. KGW VIII$_3$, pp. 9–191.

13. For fragments in this section, see KGW VIII$_3$, 15[20], 16[51], and 14[169].

14. FNWdZ, p. 63.

15. GOA XVI, p. 432.

16. EBNN, pp. 149–60.

17. KGW VIII$_3$, 18[17].

18. For fragments in this section, see KGW VIII$_3$, 19[2], 19[3], and 19[4].

19. For fragments in this section, see KGW VIII$_3$, 19[8], 22[14], 22[24], 23[8], 23[13]; VIII$_2$, 11[416].

9   A New Section in Nietzsche's *Ecce Homo*

Until the summer of 1969 the final two unpublished fragments in the printer's manuscript of the new critical collected works of Nietzsche ran as follows:

> Here I will touch on the matter of race. I am a Polish nobleman *pur sang* <purebred>, without a drop of bad blood mixed in, least of all German. When I look for the most profound antithesis to me, for the incalculable commonality of the instincts, I always discover my mother and sister: to regard myself as related to such German *canaille* <rabble> was a blasphemy against my divinity. The treatment that I experience to the current day at the hands of my mother and sister instills me with a sense of incredible horror—I confess that the gravest objection against my idea of eternal recurrence, which I call an abysmal idea, was always, for me, the thought of my mother and sister. . . . However, as a Pole I am an uncanny atavism: one must go back centuries to discover in this noblest race of men pure instincts to the degree that I represent them. I have a sovereign feeling of distinction toward everything noble. I would not allow the young German kaiser to drive my coach. There are a few cases in whom I have found my equal—I admit it with gratitude. Frau Cosima Wagner is far and away the noblest type alive, and in relation to me, I have always considered her marriage to Wagner as mere adultery . . . the case of Tristan.[1]

On the same sheet of paper containing this fragment,[2] a second follows as well.

> All dominant ideas concerning degrees of relatedness are unsurpassed physiological nonsense. One is least of all related to one's own parents; sibling marriage as it was the rule with, for example, the Egyptian imperial family

is so little unnatural that in comparison to it, all marriage is well-nigh incest. . . . To resemble one's parents is the most typical sign of commonality: higher types have their origins infinitely further back, on which, at long last, an atavism—the greatest individual is the most ancient individual—must be unified, saved.

• • •

With the first reading it was already clear to the editors that the first fragment in particular had to belong to the climate of thought for *Ecce Homo*. The phrase "Here I will touch on the matter" indicates a probably discarded supplement to the printer's manuscript of *Ecce Homo*. Preliminary material for the dedication of *Dionysian Dithyrambs* to Catulle Mendès, dated January 1, 1889, and preliminary material for the conclusion of the dithyramb "Among the Daughters of the Desert"—both on the reverse side of the same sheet—suggest dating it around the day of January 1, 1889. The fragments' barely legible handwriting (in contrast to the thoroughly clear preliminary material for the dedication) may explain the fact that they escaped the belated, anxious, and relentless censure of the Nietzsche family and the archive.

A fortunate discovery in the Peter Gast literary estate—now appended to the Nietzsche collection of the Goethe-Schiller Archive in Weimar—entirely cleared up the matter in July 1969.

Gast's copies of Nietzsche's manuscript preserved between them a sheet of paper that, below the heading "Copy of a page that Nietzsche sent to Naumann during the printing of *Ecce Homo* (from Turin, end of December 1888)," offered the following text, which in fact is foremost an instruction: "For the first signature of *Ecce Homo*, in place of the current section three."

This instruction was meant for Constantin Georg Naumann in Leipzig, with whom Nietzsche—at his own cost—published his writing. On December 18, 1888, Nietzsche had returned the first and second signatures of *Ecce Homo* to Leipzig as "ready to print." Now Nietzsche wanted to replace "the current section three" (of *Ecce Homo*'s first chapter, "Why I Am So Wise") with the following new text:

> I consider it a great privilege to have had such a father: the farmers to whom he preached—since he was, after he had lived several years at Altenburg court, a preacher for his last ten years—said he appeared as must an angel. And with this I will touch on the question of race. I am a Polish nobleman *pur sang*, without a drop of bad blood mixed in, least of all German. When I look for the most profound antithesis to me, for the incalculable commonality of the instincts, I always discover my mother and sister: to believe myself related to such German *canaille* was a blasphemy against my divinity. The treatment that I experience to this moment at the

hands of my mother and sister instills me with a sense of incredible horror: perfectly hellish machinations are at work here with unfailing certainty, at the moment when I was vulnerable to bloody wounds—in my most elevated moments . . . because then I was completely powerless to deter the poisonous worm. . . . Physiological contiguity renders possible such a preestablished disharmony. . . . However, I confess that the gravest objection to the "eternal recurrence," my genuinely *abysmal* idea, is always my mother and sister. But as a Pole I am also an uncanny atavism. One must go back centuries to discover in this noblest race of men pure instincts to the degree that I represent them. I have a sovereign feeling of distinction toward everything considered noble today. I would not allow the young German kaiser the honor of driving my coach. There are a few cases in whom I acknowledge my equal—I admit it with gratitude. Frau Cosima Wagner is far and away the noblest type; and, although I say too little with this, I say that Richard Wagner was far and away the man most closely related to me. . . . The rest is silence. . . . All dominant ideas concerning degrees of relatedness are unsurpassed physiological nonsense. The pope traffics in this nonsense yet today. One is *least* related to his parents: to be related to one's parents is the most typical sign of commonality. Higher types have their origins infinitely further back, on which, at long last, an atavism must be unified, retained. Great individuals are the most ancient individuals: I do not understand this, but Julius Caesar could be my father—*or* Alexander, this incarnate Dionysus. . . . At the very moment I am writing this, the postman brings me a head of Dionysus.[3]

The extreme psychological stress and the uncanny euphoria in this text certainly cannot be overlooked as signs of the impending catastrophe; in this regard, though, it is scarcely distinguishable from many other passages in *Ecce Homo*. Since there could be no question as to its authenticity, and since it may be seamlessly inserted into *Ecce Homo,* this new text appears in the KGW in place of the previous section 3 in the chapter "Why I Am So Wise."[4]

· · ·

We may well guess at the background to Nietzsche's intentional, public, and irreversible separation from his mother and sister, but it can be verified by documentation only with enormous difficulty. Precisely those events of Nietzsche's final weeks in Turin were blurred and distorted through the fabrication and destruction of letters, in fact, by the downright crude fictions of his sister in her biography and her other writings "concerning Nietzsche's collapse":[5] this has long been well known. The entire extent of the sisterly mystification is seen clearly for the very first time through the *complete* publication of Nietzsche's correspondence (not only his own letters) in conjunction with all other available biographical documentation.[6]

Nietzsche's last known words concerning his sister and his brother-in-law, the anti-Semite Dr. Bernhard Förster, occupied at that time with the founding of a German colony in Paraguay, are in a letter to Overbeck at Christmas 1888:

> I venture to say that the situation in Paraguay is as bad as possible. The Germans trapped over there are in rebellion, they demand their money back—there is none. There has already been some brutality: I fear the worst. This does *not* hinder my sister from writing me with extreme derision on October 15 [Nietzsche's birthday] that I want to become "famous," as if that were something sweet! And that I have sought out only rabble, Jews who have licked every pot, like Georg Brandes. . . . Along with this, she calls me "the Fritz of my heart"! . . . This has gone on for seven years! My mother knows nothing of this—that is my masterpiece. She sent me a play for Christmas: *Fritz and Little 'Liza.*[7]

Passages from his sister's hitherto unknown letter that had provoked Nietzsche's wrath are witnesses who speak for themselves concerning the entirely "anti-Semitic, idealist" nature of Elisabeth Förster-Nietzsche (and her husband):

> I hear from mommy the many ways your fame increases, and it pleases me so very much, though, in the meantime, I have given up any hope of you coming over to see us because fame is a sweet drink! Of course, dearest mama must also remain there, even if it means I must accept that she would be more comfortable and care-free there than she could be here. . . . This week a dear Danish friend of ours is coming to visit, at which time, I hope, he will bring a Danish newspaper and translate for me what it says about you. I personally would have wished a different apostle for you than Mr. Brandes; he has licked too many pots and eaten off too many plates. Although, on the other side, he has countless admirers. And it is quite certain that he will make you fashionable because that is what he understands. But I cannot hold back one well-intentioned piece of advice: do not meet with him personally; "write thee thy feelings," but do not allow him in your immediate vicinity. Two friends of ours, Mr. Johannsen and Mr. Haug, know him personally and are not exactly impressed, although everyone agrees that he possesses an excellent sense for the most interesting phenomena of all time, and he makes himself interesting through them. It does my heart unlimited good that deadly silence is no longer the case and that through Brandes the genuine, good admirers who you deserve may now hear from you. Dear Fritz of my heart, now it's your dear birthday once again, and one thinks of how many years we have already spent together and have now, unfortunately, wandered so far from each other in life. How much joy and sorrow has already gone by for us; is life really worthwhile? For such highly sensitive human beings as we just are, life has more pain than joy, and it must be going wildly well for the pain to be entirely forgotten. One is able to over-

come much, but not everything, for example, a warm, indeed, occasionally indescribable desire to see you again.

This letter, in which <Bernd> Förster's opinion about the Jewish Brandes
resonates unmistakably, must have provoked Nietzsche's anger. As late as spring
1888, he had lauded in his correspondence both his friend's Copenhagen lectures "om den tyske Filosof Friedrich Nietzsche" <On the German philosopher
Friedrich Nietzsche> and the successful founding of the Paraguayan colony in
the same breath. In the summer he attempted to assuage his mother in the face
of the first unsettling news from South America. Foremost, the anti-Semitic
dispatch against Brandes renewed the feelings against his sister (and mother)
from 1882–83, which had never died. The no-longer-extant letter to his mother from October 9 must have already contained bitter words against the sister,
because she wrote in her answer on October 16:

> But it constantly hurts me when you rejoice over being freed from little
> 'Liza's presence, because I know that, next to your mother, no one could
> love you more dearly than she, and I will not go into how many tears of
> longing she has shed for you. We are few, but we three must remain inter-
> nally bound together, regardless of external separations, as is necessary for
> a sense of family. And blood relatives belong together, even if one mem-
> ber in such a family unit is not entirely agreeable to another.

Nietzsche finally gave air to his grievances, in a very harsh manner, in his final
letter to his mother, of which only the envelope with the postal mark, December 23, 1888, remains extant. The envelope arrived in Naumburg on December 25; Franziska Nietzsche answered him only on the thirtieth, since she had
been away on a Christmas visit:

> Your last letter has shocked me somewhat, because in it you seemed to real-
> ly be attacking me, I am not accustomed to hear such a tone from you any-
> more. And since I received your letter with great joy when I returned from
> my holiday journey of several days . . . my mood turned utterly sorrowful.
> But do you really mean the birthday letter that little 'Liza wrote to you? I,
> too, have read it, in fact, and have found nothing at all of what you read into
> her words. I even believe she intended to say something really quite sweet
> to you with it, granted that her letters are always somewhat disjointed, and
> she cannot weigh her words on golden scales, but otherwise she would not
> write at all. . . . Say anything else, my old Fritz, but not that she has treated
> you, or treats you, without love; I, who have been with her for thirty years,
> know better than that. She would give her *eyes,* her *life,* for you, and no hu-
> man being can offer more out of love; whether her behavior has always been
> proper is for God to decide, but it was from the purest motives, to serve you
> and keep you far from anything that might bring you harm. That will cer-

tainly become clear to you later as an "old philosopher." So think of her sympathetically, like your good heart does with others—for who is perfect? It pains my heart when things are otherwise, and my dear Fritz does not cause me heartaches! We would not choose it <the colonial undertaking in Paraguay> as a way of life, but when one gives one's hand to one's life partner at the altar to bear *everything* with him, there is no choice.

In a letter known only by its draft, Nietzsche broke contact with his sister; the cause was not her reaction to receiving *The Case of Wagner,* as she claimed,[8] but rather the events as they have been presented here.

Nevertheless, our description of the immediate biographical background is not able to clarify the entire significance of the new section of *Ecce Homo,* much less the place it occupies in the structure of this unique autobiography. To understand this, a brief description of its genesis is necessary.

• • •

"Well then, I am the opposite of a decadent, since I am describing myself"; these words close the brief self-description that Nietzsche sketched while still correcting *Twilight of the Idols* and that was said to constitute the core of *Ecce Homo.*[9] This "proto–*Ecce Homo*" is divided into eleven sections whose contents correspond to the following well-known texts in this order: *Ecce Homo,* "Why I Am So Clever," section 1; "Why I Am So Wise," sections 6, 4, and 5; *Twilight of the Idols,* the entire chapter "What I Owe the Ancients"; *Ecce Homo,* "Why I Am So Wise," sections 1 and 2.[10] When Nietzsche made the decision to "narrate his life story to himself," he took the section on his relation to the "ancients" from it and published that as the final chapter to *Twilight of the Idols.*[11] Corrections to *Twilight of the Idols* were concluded at the end of October, and on November 6 Nietzsche sent the self-description to his publisher, Naumann, in Leipzig with the following words:

> Wonder nothing more about me now! For example, that as soon as *Twilight of the Idols* is entirely finished, we must begin a new publication. I have completely persuaded myself that another writing is necessary, a writing *preparatory* to the highest degree, to be able to come before the public with the first book of the "Revaluation" within a year. It must create a real *tension*—otherwise, the results will resemble those from *Zarathustra.* In these last weeks, I have been inspired by the greatest happiness of all, thanks to an incomparable well-being, one unparalleled in my life, thanks equally to a marvelous autumn and to the most exquisite kindness that I have ever found in Turin. So I have an *extremely difficult task to solve*—specifically, to narrate myself, my books, my views, fragmentarily, so far as it allows me to narrate *my life* to myself—between October 15 and November 4. I believe

that will be heard, perhaps too much. . . . And then everything would be in order.

The printer's manuscript for *Ecce Homo* was in the Leipzig printing house shortly before mid-November, since on November 15 C. G. Naumann was in a position to inform Nietzsche about the projected completion of work.[12] From that point onward, the feeling of gratitude for the "gift of the last quarter-year" gradually turns to an extreme increase in egotism and finally to the outbreak of delusions of grandeur. Thus on November 26 Nietzsche wrote to Paul Deussen:

> My life is now reaching its culmination: a couple years more, and the earth will quake from a great lightning stroke. I swear to you that I have the power to alter the *calculation of time*. There is nothing in existence today that will not be toppled; I am more dynamite than human being. My "Revaluation of All Values," with the main title *The Antichrist,* is finished. In the next two years, I have to accomplish having the work translated into seven languages, the *first* edition in each language circa one million copies.

And directly thereafter to Georg Brandes, in a letter known only by its draft:

> We have entered into grand politics, even into the grandest of all. . . . I am preparing an event that will very probably split history into two halves, such that we would have a new calculation of time from 1888 as the year 1. [. . .] We shall have wars like there have never been, but *not* between nations, *not* between classes: everything will be tossed about into the air—I am the most dangerous dynamite that exists. I want to order the production of an edition of *The Antichrist: Revaluation of All Values* in three months;[13] it remains completely secret: it will serve me as an agitation edition. I require translation into all major European languages; when the work first appears, I estimate one million copies in each language as the first edition. I have thought of you for the Danish, of Mr. Strindberg for the Swedish edition. Since it is a *deathblow* to *Christianity,* it is in the cards that the single international power that possesses an instinctive interest in the nullification of Christianity is the *Jews.* [. . .] Consequently, we must secure for ourselves all the decisive power of this race in Europe and America—moreover, such a movement requires enormous capital. [. . .][14] All in all, the officer corps will share our instinct that it is in the highest degree *ignoble, cowardly, impure,* to be a Christian; one invariably carries away this judgment from my "Antichrist." [. . .] Concerning the kaiser, I know the art of handling such brown idiots: that makes an officer who has turned out well lose his moderation.

Nietzsche quotes several sentences from the "Decree against Christianity"—at the conclusion of *The Antichrist*[15]—and finishes with his vision of a future humanity: "We are victorious, so we have the government of earth in our hands—world peace added on to that. . . . We have overcome the absurd barriers of race, nationality, and class; there are still only orders of ranks between human being and human being, and indeed an incredibly long ladder of order of rank."

From now on *The Antichrist* is the entire "Revaluation of All Values" for Nietzsche, yet the revaluation itself is no longer a literary event but rather a geopolitical one; in *Ecce Homo* he wishes to enter as the man of destiny; *Thus Spoke Zarathustra* becomes the Bible of humanity; "*Ecce Homo,*" it is claimed in the previously mentioned letter to Deussen, "concerns only me; in the end I enter with a world-historical mission. [. . .] In it I will shed light for the first time on my *Zarathustra,* the premier book of all the centuries, the Bible of the future, the highest expression of human genius in which the destiny of mankind has been grasped."

We may rightfully claim that Nietzsche considered his lifework as completed now; we must not forget this fact "to be fair" not only to *Ecce Homo* but also to all the other outbreaks of the final Turin period. The second matter we must not forget is the "seventh solitude" in which Nietzsche completed his conscious life. A few days before the Turin catastrophe, he still wrote: "I am *solitude* as a human being."[16] A relation of alternating intensification existed between his feeling of loneliness, which forced itself on him despite everything (this period's "admiring" letters from Peter Gast, August Strindberg, Anna Tenischeff, Hippolyte Taine, Jean Bordeau, and others—to which he more or less attached too much importance), on the one side, and the feeling of having completed a work of world-historical significance, on the other side. It is as if Nietzsche sought to make himself heard from an ever-deepening abyss of solitude—hence the overly loud, sometimes shrill tone of his writings, letters, "laws," and proclamations. The third matter we rarely forget is the catastrophe itself, which unquestionably already now cast its shadow. This is, though, not the completion of Nietzsche's intellect but only its end, its destruction. And if we may speak in terms of an insane loneliness, it is only because he no longer had any contact with the human world, hence, also none with "the lonely." In spite of this, we should not draw hasty conclusions from the fact of the lurking delusion, in the light of everything that Nietzsche accomplished prior to his loss of world and very identity (somewhere around January 4, 1889, with the so-called delusional note).[17]

There is, for example (and in our case much hangs on this), the lucidity with which Nietzsche followed and directed the publication of *Ecce Homo* and *Nietzsche contra Wagner.* His numerous alterations and additions—without a single exception—may be seamlessly inserted into the two printer's manuscripts or the correction signatures; they stand in a logical literary relation to one another. Most definitely Nietzsche lost his "literary mind" only at the very end.

• • •

The revisions that in early December Nietzsche made to the printer's manuscript of *Ecce Homo,* returned to him by request, reflect the intensification of his self-image as a man of destiny.[18] On December 6 he sent the manuscript back to Leipzig. He no longer wished to alter anything, although on December 29, after he had already sent several additions, Nietzsche announced to his publisher "the remainder of the manuscript, nothing but extremely essential matters, among them the poem with which *Ecce Homo* should conclude." The very last alteration occurred on January 2, 1889, when Nietzsche requested that the concluding poems for *Ecce Homo* ("Fame and Eternity") and *Nietzsche contra Wagner* ("On the Poverty of the Wealthiest") be returned to him for his final work, *Dionysian Dithyrambs:* he did completely without publication of his "short composition," *Nietzsche contra Wagner.*[19]

In the printer's manuscript of *Ecce Homo* as we have it today, the later alterations and additions may be clearly distinguished from those Nietzsche had made up until December 6. Here the most important are as follows: in the chapter "Why I Am So Clever," sections 4, 6, and 7 were added as new text; in the chapter "Why I Write Such Good Books," section 2 was replaced by new text (the current one); in the chapter on *Human, All Too Human,* section 6 was added; and the conclusion to section 5 of the chapter on *Thus Spoke Zarathustra* was changed. All this occurred—as previously said—not in a single instant: still prior to December 20 Nietzsche had sent the current section of the chapter "Why I Am So Clever" to Leipzig,[20] whereas section 6 of the same chapter came later to the printer, although before section 4.

We cannot ascertain with certainty the nature of the parcel of December 29; in addition, we shall ultimately have to accept that much of this parcel no longer exists, whether as of early on or later. The new third section to the chapter "Why I Am So Wise," which we presented at the outset, was an additional alteration to the first, already typeset signature of *Ecce Homo,* the printing of which Nietzsche had authorized on December 18. Perhaps this text was already in the parcel of December 29; perhaps it was sent later. Both are possible, although it is not especially important; far more important, in contrast, is that the new section is intimately related to several of these very last alterations to the printer's manuscript.

• • •

The new conclusion to the fifth section of the chapter on *Thus Spoke Zarathustra* is well known. It reads:

> Thirdly, there is the absurd sensitivity of the skin to small stings, a kind of helplessness against everything small. This seems to me to be due to the tremendous squandering of all defensive energies which is the supposition of every creative deed, every deed that issues from one's most authentic, inmost, nethermost regions. Our small defensive capacities are thus, as it were, suspended; no energy is left for them. I still dare to hint that one digests less well, does not like to move, is all too susceptible to feeling chills as well as mistrust—mistrust that is in many instances merely an etiological blunder. In such a state I once sensed the proximity of a herd of cows even before I saw it, merely because milder and more philanthropic thoughts came back to me: *they* had warmth. <Kaufmann translation>

According to Nietzsche's instructions, this was to be replaced by the following passage, which he had composed with the revisions of early December:

> At that time what was most foreign to me launched itself recklessly against me in enmity. No great respect for my solitude. In the middle of Zarathustra's ecstasies, handfuls of rage and poison in the face—I even flatter it to call it poison; it was something else, it smelled horrific. . . . I am referring to the most horrible experience of my life, my single *bad* experience, which has worked an incalculably destructive effect on me. In every moment when I have suffered most monstrously from my own fate, some indecency from outside me was also turned loose. This experience has lasted for seven years now: when I was finished with the "Revaluation of All Values," I knew that I would not outlast it. The psychologist adds that in no set of conditions is the defenselessness, the exposure, greater. If there is a general method for killing those men *who are destinies,* the instinct of poisonous flies serves as this means. For those who have greatness, there is no fighting with the small; consequently, the small becomes master.[21]

Here Nietzsche spoke of a specific bad experience, the "single" one of his life, which further "lasted for seven years." He had also written, "This has gone on for seven years!" in his letter to Franz Overbeck (and to Meta von Salis) against his sister. That Nietzsche was thinking of the experience that began in autumn of 1882 with the so-called Lou affair and that created a division between him and those to whom he belonged—his mother and sister[22]—goes without question, especially when this replacement for the conclusion is compared with fragments and passages in his correspondence from the years 1882–85 (the emphases are mine and are intended to stress the similarity between what Nietzsche wrote at that time and the replacement passages for *Ecce Homo*):

> I have known for a long time that humans of my mother and sister's ilk

must be *my natural enemies. . . .* It fouls the air for me to be among such human beings.

(From unpublished writings, autumn 1882; KGW VIII, p. 113)

Consider that I *come from circles in which my entire development appears reprehensible and depraved;* it was a mere consequence of this that my mother previously called me a "curse to the family" and "a disgrace to my father's grave." My sister once wrote me to say that were she Catholic, she would enter a convent to make good my sins, which I create by my way of thinking; in fact, *she openly announced her enmity* until that point in time when I turn myself around and worry about becoming "a good and honest human being."[23] Both consider me as a "cold, hard-hearted egotist"; Lou also had that opinion before she came to know me better, I being "of an extremely common, low character, always out to exploit others for my own purposes."

(To Peter Gast, April 21, 1883)

My sister is a worm of misfortune: she has seen fit now six times in two years, right in the middle of *my highest and most blessed feelings*—feelings the likes of which have rarely been felt on earth—to have tossed into their midst a letter that has *the most despicable stench of the all-too-human. . . .* I constantly wondered in Rome [May 1883] and Naumburg about how rarely she says anything that does not go against my grain. . . . I was enraged after every letter over the *dirty,* slanderous manner in which my sister spoke of Fräulein Salomé. . . . That both of them [Lou and Rée] in concert had dazed me is true—but I had forgiven them, as I had forgiven my sister for worse behavior against me.

(Draft of a letter to Overbeck, January/February 1884)

As I read your letter, it came to mind once more why several of the finer minds in Germany consider me insane, or even say that I have died in a sanatorium. *It is one of those riddles about which I have reflected from time to time, as to how it is possible that we are blood relatives.*

(Draft of a letter to his sister, mid-March 1885)

I do not know which is worse, the boundless, audacious idiocy of my sister to wish to instruct a knower-of-men and renal expert like myself concerning two men whom I have had sufficient time to study at close quarters, or the unashamed tactlessness to *sling mud* at people in front of me with whom I share, in any case, an important part of my intellectual development and who are *a hundred times closer* to me than that idiotic, vengeful creature. *My nausea, to be related to such a miserable creature!* From whence did she get this nauseating brutality, from whence that mischievous art of the *poisonous sting?* . . . The stupid goose even went so far as to reproach me for envy of Rée!

(Draft of letter to his mother, January/February 1884)

We may extend our series of quotations of this sort as far as we wish; not one single credible piece of evidence from Nietzsche concerning his sister that could prove anything more than a "normal" relation between siblings stands in opposition. Even with the overcoming of a radical alienation to all those things decisive *for Nietzsche,* the so-called reconciliations occur (as in Rome, May 1883, under the auspices of the "idealist" Malwida von Meysenbug, or in Zürich, October 1884) only in the eyes of his sister at the expense of their friends (of the Overbeck couple in particular), who were "one hundred times closer."[24] The "normal" relation between brother and sister consisted of the simple human fact that, despite everything, Nietzsche maintained his interest in the destiny of his sister (and even in that of her anti-Semitic husband). That, on the other side, Elisabeth Förster-Nietzsche loved and worshiped her brother more than she did any other human being—albeit in the presumptuous conviction that she knew what was "best" for him—may shed generous light on this "*sœur abusive* <improper sister>," to use a phrase from Richard Roos.

On the threshold of his delusions, Nietzsche believed he had solved the riddle of his relation to the "miserable creature," having now considered it as a "question of race."[25] It is thus understandable why he included his mother in the opposition of "bad German blood" on his mother's side to an (allegedly) "Polish descent" on his father's side.

In this regard we may clarify precisely why Nietzsche now altered the opening of the revised section 2 to the chapter "Why I Write Such Good Books," which he had sent to Leipzig around the end of December. This opening runs as follows in its final, familiar form: "This was said for the benefit of Germans; for everywhere else I have readers—nothing but first-rate intellects and proven characters, trained in high positions and duties; I even have real geniuses among my readers. In Vienna, in St. Petersburg, in Stockholm, in Copenhagen, in Paris, in New York—everywhere I have been discovered: but not in the shallows of Europe, Germany" <Kaufmann translation>.

The replacement for the opening, in contrast, runs: "Finally, a matter of race has its say. Germans are not that closely related to me. I express myself cautiously: they are not whatsoever at liberty to understand me. . . . I am proud to be loved and distinguished everywhere *except* in Europe's shallows, Germany. . . . In Vienna, in St. Petersburg, in Stockholm and Copenhagen, in Paris, in New York—I have readers everywhere, *first-rate* intellects and proven characters, trained in high positions and duties; I even have real geniuses among my readers."[26]

Here, with its full consequences, enters the process of publication that led Nietzsche to draft a new section 3 for the chapter "Why I Am So Wise." The preliminary material—the first proffered by us at the outset—in fact treats "a matter of race"; it begins with the sentence "Here I will touch on the matter of race." Nietzsche did without reference to the question of race in section 2 of "Why I Write Such Good Books"; wrote a transition sentence ("I consider it a great privilege to have had such a father," etc.) to facilitate the insertion of the new text into the chapter "Why I Am So Wise," where he considered the "single bad experience" of his life in conjunction with the "question of race" (hence, the alteration to the conclusion of section 5 of the chapter on *Thus Spoke Zarathustra*); and finally executed still another correction in the subsequent section 4 that made the new section 3 necessary. Also, this correction comes down to us on the same sheet of paper on which Peter Gast had written down the new section 3. The correction concerns the following sentence: "One may twist and turn my life; in it one will only seldom, basically only once, discover a hint that someone had malicious intent against me." Instead of "in it one will only seldom, basically only once, discover a hint," it was then supposed to have read, "in it one will, *with the exception of that single case,* discover not a hint."

"You will discover in *Ecce Homo* an incredible page concerning *Tristan,* concerning my relation to Wagner in general. Wagner is, of course, the first name to appear in *E.H.* There, where I allow no doubts about anything, I have had courage in the extreme about this matter, too." These words of Nietzsche, in his letter of December 31, 1888, to Peter Gast, attain their full significance now that the history of the genesis of *Ecce Homo* and of the new section 3 to the chapter "Why I Am So Wise" is known to us. The "incredible page concerning *Tristan*" is section 6 of the chapter "Why I Am So Clever": as we know, one of the final additions to the printer's manuscript. We also discover a reference to it in his letter to Carl Fuchs on December 27: "*Tristan* . . . is a groundbreaking work and of a fascination not only in music, but is peerless in all the arts." We compare this to the following passage from the cited section: "But to this day, I am still looking for a work that equals the dangerous fascination and the gruesome and sweet infinity of *Tristan*—and look at all the arts in vain. All the strangenesses of Leonardo da Vinci emerge from their spell at the first note of *Tristan.*"[27] Typically enough, the sheet of paper that bears the preliminary material for this section also contains the draft of a brief announcement to Cosima Wagner that was never sent, since it had been considered as an accompanying note to *Ecce Homo:* "Honorable madam, the only woman, basically, whom I have ever respected . . . may it please you to receive the first copy of this *Ecce Homo.* In it the entire world is treated poorly, apart from Richard Wagner—and Turin. Also, Malwida comes forth as Kundry . . . [signed,] The Antichrist."[28]

Cosima Wagner had already been offered special respect in the second part of the second <*sic*> section of "Why I Am So Clever," a part that Nietzsche had composed as part of the revisions at the beginning of December: "The few cases of high culture that I have encountered in Germany have all been of French origin, especially Frau Cosima Wagner, by far the first voice in matters of taste that I have ever heard."[29]

Likewise at the beginning of December Nietzsche had reflected on his "intimate relationship with Richard Wagner" in the fifth section of the same chapter. "I'd let go cheap the whole rest of my human relationships; I should not want to give away out of my life at any price the days of Tribschen—days of trust, of cheerfulness, of sublime accidents, of *profound* moments. I do not know what experiences others have had with Wagner: *our* sky was never darkened by a single cloud."

We would also like to interpret a smaller correction to the first section of the chapter on *The Case of Wagner* in connection with longing memories of his days in Tribschen, which Nietzsche always carried about but which were expressed for the first time from the beginning of December onward, as well as in *Ecce Homo*. Nietzsche had written: "Everything decisive in this matter I held back—I can wait." Now he replaced the words "I can wait" with "I have loved Wagner." We may interpret another insertion into the fourth section of the same chapter—this section, by the way, came into existence only with the revisions from early December—in the same fashion: "Except for my association with a few artists, above all with Richard Wagner, I have not spent one good hour with a German."

In the end the chapter on *The Case of Wagner* was supposed to turn into a fierce attack—via this very fourth section—more on the entirety of German culture in general than on Wagner. At the end of December, Wagner—and with him, Cosima—was, "of course, the first name" to occur in *Ecce Homo*. There, where Nietzsche allowed "doubts about nothing whatsoever"—for us, it is out of the question that the allusion is *also* to the third section of "Why I Am So Wise"—did Cosima Wagner become the "most noble type," the single case where Nietzsche recognized "his equal," and Richard Wagner, "the man by far most closely related to me." The variations to the final version of this passage in the fragment, though, are striking. Whereas Nietzsche had written in the fragment, "Frau Cosima Wagner is far and away the noblest type alive, and in relation to me, I have always considered her marriage to Wagner as mere adultery . . . the case of Tristan," now he wrote, "Frau Cosima Wagner is far and away the noblest type alive; and to that I say not a word too little, I say that Richard Wagner is the man by far most closely related to me. . . . The rest is silence. . . ."

Precisely here is it impossible to determine—at least with the present state of biographical research—how much Nietzsche refers to an inner experience from the Tribschen period. It is this same problem—perhaps in still starker form—raised by the "delusional note" directed a few days later to Ariadne-Cosima.[30]

• • •

We have attempted to demonstrate the intimate relation of the new section to the textual history of *Ecce Homo*. The reconstruction of Nietzsche's life during the 105 days in Turin before his mental collapse is, however, a very complicated task; we will point out only a few aspects.[31] The place of *Ecce Homo* within the works and its value for biography may be determined in connection with the entirety of the unpublished fragments and the complete correspondence from this time. Also, Nietzsche's relationships to those in his immediate circle and to Cosima and Richard Wagner are treated here only in view of several of his final declarations. The discovery in the Peter Gast literary estate, however, offers us the opportunity to touch on one last important point. That sheet contains the copy of one last alteration on the first fair-copy sheet of corrections for *Ecce Homo*. This regards a passage in the brief prologue ("on this perfect day, when everything is ripening . . ."), which follows the preface, composed later, and which introduces the self-description. It is the passage where Nietzsche enumerates his last works. It reads: "The first book of the *Revaluation of All Values,* the *Songs of Zarathustra,* the *Twilight of the Idols,* my attempt to philosophize with a hammer." Now it should read: "*Revaluation of All Values, Dionysian Dithyrambs,* and, for convalescence, *Twilight of the Idols.*"

This correction, which Nietzsche had apparently forgotten in the fair copy of December 18, is in accordance with the equation "*Antichrist* = the entire 'Revaluation of All Values,'" as it stood in the letter to Paul Deussen on November 26 but also in other earlier and later letters and drafts of letters.[32] In addition we find the new title *Dionysian Dithyrambs* (in place of *Songs of Zarathustra*), which emerged around January 1, 1889, so the entire set of alterations must count as Nietzsche's final specifications.

After Nietzsche's mental collapse, Gast—in close association with Franz Overbeck—inspected the printer's manuscripts and correction sheets (to *Ecce Homo* and *Nietzsche contra Wagner*) that were located at the printing works of C. G. Naumann in Leipzig. In the case of *Ecce Homo,* the very first thing that struck him was Nietzsche's own announcement of the completion of the "Revaluation of All Values." Since Nietzsche had communicated absolutely nothing to him about the "advance in rank, or reevaluation" <*Aufwertung*>, of the *Antichrist* to become the "Revaluation" <*Umwertung*> in its entirety, Gast was, in his disciple mentality of that time, completely bowled over. He wrote to Overbeck concerning this on January 18, 1889:

If this work were finished—which I believe—then Nietzsche must have gone insane during the completion of the work, from jubilation over the triumph of human reason *in his own person*—we must remain content with this, as frivolous as it may sound. What now torments us is the dread that the collapse of the incarnation of these ideas has occurred *too soon.* I must confess, I am afraid that the manuscripts to the mentioned work are not among the items taken by you. Perhaps, though, with the packing up and sending away of his effects in Turin, the entrusted persons were not aware of the importance of the papers and notes, etc., such that everything hopefully arrives in its integrity.

One week later, after he had read *Ecce Homo,* Gast had become somewhat more skeptical about the "triumph of human reason" in Nietzsche, so that we read in his letter to Overbeck on January 25: "As soon as you have looked over the items from Turin, respected Herr Professor, please give me a brief note about them. In *Ecce Homo* the 'Revaluation' is described as complete; I am afraid that it refers only to the complex of ideas rather than to literary substance."[33]

As a matter of fact, Nietzsche had informed Gast very sparingly about the "Revaluation." Nietzsche had never communicated the title *Antichrist* to him but had spoken to him on September 27 only about the "process of finishing the first book of the Revaluation." In addition, from the period of his editorial work on *Twilight of the Idols,* Gast knew only of the evidence for the completion of the first book of the "Revaluation" that exists at the conclusion of the preface to the cited writing: "Turin, September 30, 1888, on the day that the first book to the 'Revaluation of All Values' came to an end."

Nonetheless, when we compare the alterations in *Ecce Homo*'s "prologue" to the cited letters and letter drafts (to Deussen, Brandes, H. Zimmern, C. G. Naumann, etc.), we can clearly see that with it Nietzsche wished to announce the completion of his "Revaluation of All Values." Gast must have missed a second, further, unmistakable expression that had led to his letters on January 18 and 15 to Overbeck. As a matter of fact, in a previously unpublished letter from November 17, 1893, Peter Gast wrote to Elisabeth Förster-Nietzsche: "The manuscript to *Ecce Homo* [which he had finalized and sent to Naumburg in 1889] has been proofread. I have allowed myself to make only one strike, on page 102, and to insert the three words 'the first book' on page 104."

As we may gather from the *Ecce Homo* manuscript (preserved at the Goethe-Schiller Archive in Weimar), both alterations involve the chapter concerning *Twilight of the Idols.* By way of the first, Gast wished to eliminate—apparently with his own hand—the phrase "which I demur to give their figures" (see KGW VI$_3$, pp. 352, 356). The second alteration related to a sentence from the third section that until today has always been known in this form: "On the thirtieth of September, great victory; seventh day; idlesse of a god along the Po." Gast's copy replaces "seventh day" with "completion of the first book of the Revaluation." Since Gast had spoken of an "insertion" in the cited passage from his correspondence, we have to accept that the words "completion of the Revaluation" originated with Nietzsche. Even today the printer's manuscript still shows traces of three words, written with a pencil but later erased, over the two words "seventh day," which once more show traces of an erased strike mark from a pencil. The initial letter of the first word placed over them is still recognizable as a *B* in Gast's handwriting. We may, then, reconstruct the entire course of events in this fashion: (1) The replacement of "seventh day" with "completion of the Revaluation" was Nietzsche's alteration, which he had sent—in the course of December—to Leipzig. (2) The sheet of paper or note on which Nietzsche gave his instructions for this alteration is, like so many others, missing and presumed destroyed. (3) Since the alteration was written on a separate sheet of paper or note, Gast immediately noticed it when he picked up the printer's manuscript for *Ecce Homo,* along with the numerous supplements to it from Naumann, and consequently wrote the animated letter of January 18, 1889, to Overbeck. (4) For the time being, Gast replaced the words "seventh day" with "Revaluation of All Values" (hence, in accordance with Nietzsche's instructions) in the original manuscript of *Ecce Homo.* (5) Later, however, when he finalized the copy, he wrote what seemed to him more correct: "completion of the first book of the Revaluation."

In the new critical edition of the collected works, Nietzsche's reconstructed alteration is given as follows: "completion of the Revaluation" in place of "seventh day."[34]

Concerning his own copy of *Ecce Homo,* Peter Gast wrote to Overbeck on February 27, 1889: "I only ask that you, respected Herr Professor, come to know the writing [*Ecce Homo*] initially by use of my own copy, hence, *without* those passages that give me the impression of too great a self-intoxication or become too contemptuous and commit injustices—in using it you would also receive that impression—which I can no longer recall, since I did not follow the train of thought in those eccentric matters."

This passage is of inestimable significance for the later textual history of *Ecce Homo.* Gast's copy, such as it comes to us *"without"* the offending segments, is, except for entirely minor differences, identical to the now familiar text of *Ecce Homo*! Those "eccentric matters," meaning the passages that gave Gast [!] "the impression of too great a self-intoxication" and that are "too contemptuous and commit injustices," would never again be included in later editions of *Ecce Homo*.

Here the concern is not about the few briefer passages that in part were mentioned in the earlier reports of the Nietzsche Archive editions and were made well known by Podach. The concern is far more about the texts that— as with the section that we were able to reconstruct here—were later *destroyed*.

When Elisabeth Förster-Nietzsche received possession of the *Ecce Homo* manuscripts in 1893, Gast's private censorship became censorship sponsored by the Nietzsche family (and by the Nietzsche Archive). A few scant fragments in barely legible handwriting, which do not belong in a final version of *Ecce Homo,* allow conjecture about the possible contents of several eliminated passages. However, they should no more be included in *Ecce Homo*'s text than should be the preliminary materials from which Nietzsche had worked and that belong in the critical apparatus. Apart from the section discussed here, *Ecce Homo* must remain as it is, as it is familiar. What is certain is that Nietzsche left behind a finished *Ecce Homo,* but we do not have it.[35]

Notes

1. See KSA 14, pp. 460–63 and 472–74. <This is not the third section of "Why I Am So Wise" with which readers of Walter Kaufmann's translation of *Ecce Homo* are familiar. In fact, Kaufmann's text is precisely what is referred to in this chapter as "the current section 3," which Nietzsche sought to replace. Stanford University Press will publish an English translation of *Ecce Homo* with the proper material in its *Complete Works of Friedrich Nietzsche.* This is my translation of preliminary material for *Ecce Homo.*>

2. See facsimile 22 in Erich F. Podach's *Friedrich Nietzsches Werke des Zusammenbruchs* (Heidelberg, 1961). Only the upper half of the page, however, is given in facsimile.

3. We have still not been able to determine what Nietzsche could have meant concerning this postal parcel. A hallucination cannot be ruled out. Among Nietzsche's acquaintances was numbered, from the Basel period, the "Dionysian" personality of Frau Rosalie Nielsen. Kurt Hezel reports: "Even today I myself recall, from among my student days, a photograph of a remarkable Dionysus head (a photographed sculpture) dedicated to me from Frau Nielsen. . . . If I recall correctly, Frau Nielsen had wanted Friedrich Nietzsche himself to own the photograph of the Dionysus head." See C. A. Bernoulli, *Franz Overbeck und Friedrich Nietzsche: Eine Freundshaft* (Jena, 1908), vol. 1, p. 117.

4. KGW VI₃, pp. 265–67.

5. See, for example, Paul Cohn, *Um Nietzsches Untergang* (Hannover, 1931), 121–59.

6. Since 1975 the Walter de Gruyter publishing house has been producing such an edition (namely, the *Kritische Gesamtausgabe Briefwechsel*).

7. This passage was left out of the *Briefwechsel Nietzsche-Overbeck* (Leipzig, 1916). It was made famous in Karl Schlechta's *Friedrich Nietzsche, Werke in drei Bänden* (Munich, 1956), vol. 3, p. 1345. See also Erich F. Podach, *Ein Blick in Nietzsches Notizbücher* (Heidelberg, 1963), 189f. Also, Nietzsche wrote Meta von Salis on December 29: "In addition, there is no absence of *contrasts!* My sister declared, with the greatest derision on my birthday,

that I had begun to wish to become 'famous.' . . . They would be a fine rabble who believed in *me* . . . This has lasted for *seven* years now." See Maria Bindschedler, "Nietzsches Briefe an Meta von Salis," *Neue Schweizer Rundschau* 12 (April 1955): 719. We find no comment concerning "the play *Fritz and Little 'Liza*" in the mother's Christmas letter. There is a one-act play by Jacques Offenbach entitled *Lischen und Fritzchen, conversation alsacienne* (1863).

8. See *Friedrich Nietzsches Briefe an Mutter und Schwester,* ed. Elisabeth Förster-Nietzsche, vol. 5 of the *Gesammelten Briefe* (Leipzig, 1909), 805: "Unfortunately, I had received *The Case of Wagner* earlier than his two letters of September 14 and 17 [this last letter is unquestionably a forgery] and positively shocked him and wrote him distressed about it, which greatly wounded him. Now he feared [!] the effects of the *Antichrist,* since Christianity and Wagner had become the most sensitive of matters for us [meaning, for Elisabeth and Bernhard Förster]." <The draft of Nietzsche's letter, in which he broke off relations with his sister, may be found in English in *Selected Letters of Friedrich Nietzsche,* ed. and trans. Christopher Middleton (Indianapolis: Hackett, 1996), letter 195.>

9. KGW VII$_3$, 24[1], pp. 427–44.

10. See KSA 14, p. 464.

11. On October 24, 1888, the printers sent Nietzsche the corrections to the new chapter "What I Owe to the Ancients," so we can accept his birthday—October 15—as the date on which he began his self-description, as he contended in his letter.

12. Between the original version and this printer's manuscript there were two other, incomplete versions of twenty-four paragraphs that are numbered continuously. Parts of them are published by Erich F. Podach in *Friedrich Nietzsches Werke des Zusammenbruchs,* 336–47; see, too, KSA 14, pp. 454–512.

13. Therefore, around the end of February 1889.

14. See Nietzsche to Peter Gast, December 9, 1888: "Do you know yet that for *my* international movement I shall require *the entire bulk of Jewish capital?*" In one folder we discover a note where Nietzsche wrote down several sentences to his "international movement," including this: "One final word. From this moment on, I shall require helping hands—undying hands!—without number—the Revaluation shall appear in two languages at a time. . . . One would do well to found associations everywhere, to secure for me, at the proper moment in time, several million followers. I foremost value having the officer corps and the Jewish bankers on my side" (KGW VIII$_3$, 25[1], p. 456).

15. The "Decree against Christianity" was published in Erich F. Podach's *Friedrich Nietzsches Werke des Zusammenbruchs,* 157–58. With regard to the reasons we have taken this text into our edition—and for the conclusion of the *Antichrist*—see volume VI$_3$, p. 161, as well as KSA 14, pp. 448–53.

16. See Erich F. Podach's *Friedrich Nietzsches Werke des Zusammenbruchs,* 318.

17. Fragments of his lost world also made themselves known in these announcements from delusion, as, for example, when Nietzsche, in a note he sent to Rohde (January 5, 1888) mentioned Rohde's "blindness toward Monsieur Taine"—which caused the breakdown of their friendship in spring 1887—and at the same time added, "Taine, who had previously composed the Vedas." See Hedwig Däuble, "Friedrich Nietzsche und Erwin Rohde," *Nietzsche-Studien* 5 (1976): 340.

18. The following sections came as new texts, or put more precisely, fundamentally revised parts (along with smaller alterations): in the chapter "Why I Am So Wise," section 8; in the chapter "Why I Am So Clever," the second, longer part of section 3 and

the entire section 5; in the chapter "Why I Write Such Good Books," section 3 and the conclusion to section 5; in the chapter on *Human, All Too Human,* section 2; in the chapter on *Thus Spoke Zarathustra,* sections 1 through 6; in the chapter on *The Case of Wagner,* chapter 4; at the conclusion, a "Declaration of War" and "The Hammer Speaks" (lengthy citations from *Thus Spoke Zarathustra,* part 3, "On Old and New Tablets," section 30). The last two mentioned texts were discarded at the end of December. Our commentary to *The Antichrist* (KSA 14, pp. 434–54) proves that the "Declaration of War" is not identical to the "Law against Christianity." Compare, in contrast, the astute remarks of Pierre Champromis, "Podach, *Friedrich Nietzsches Werke des Zusammenbruchs* oder Zusammenbruch der editorischen Werke Podachs?" *Philosophische Rundschau* 12, nos. 3–4 (January 1965): 250–54.

19. Compare this with KGW VI$_3$, p. 161. *The Case of Wagner* consequently would not be an "authorized unpublished work."

20. It concerns the section with the original title "Intermezzo," which Podach had left out of his edition of *Ecce Homo.* Compare this with P. Champromis, "Podach," 247f., whose remarks against omitting this section from *Ecce Homo* are correct. If *Nietzsche contra Wagner* should be edited, however—despite Nietzsche's abandonment of its publication—then the brief "intermezzo" would belong to it, as would the concluding poem, "On the Poverty of the Wealthiest" (contrary to the opinion of Champromis and with that of Podach).

21. See KSA 14, pp. 497f.

22. Compare this with *Friedrich Nietzsche–Paul Rée–Lou Salomé: Dokumente ihrer Begegnung,* ed. E. Pfeiffer (Frankfurt-am-Main, 1971).

23. The letters of his mother and sister to Nietzsche concerning the "Lou affair" have—with the exception of one fragment of a letter from his mother from autumn 1882—completely vanished. To the letter drafts cited here, compare KGB III$_1$, pp. 364, 471f., and 469f.

24. So Elisabeth Nietzsche wrote to her mother on April 4, 1883, before the "reconciliation" with her brother in Rome: "It is terrible for me; I cannot help that Fritz's opinions toward me become increasingly less sympathetic because I do not agree in the least whom they should help. You see, I only wish that Fritz had the views of Förster, who has ideals to promote, and which comply with humanity's betterment and pursuit of happiness. . . . You will see, Förster will one day be deemed one of the best men of Germany and the best benefactors of his people!"

25. Compare with this the following passages from Nietzsche's letter of December 29, 1888, to Meta von Salis: "My sister declared, with the greatest derision on my birthday, that I had begun to wish to become 'famous.' . . . They would be a fine rabble who believed in *me.* . . . This has lasted for *seven* years now. . . . Still *another* case. I seriously consider Germans as a *dog-common* <hundsgemeine> sort of human being and thank the stars that in all my instincts I am Polish and am nothing else." Here the motives are tellingly touched on one after the other, which Nietzsche should have then developed in his new section 3 of "Why I Am So Wise."

26. See Erich F. Podach's *Friedrich Nietzsches Werke des Zusammenbruchs,* 253.

27. In this context, Leonardo da Vinci's name achieves a special significance when we reflect that Nietzsche had imagined Zarathustra's appearance as that of Leonardo in his self-portrait: "Nietzsche saw it in 1885 in my room," reports Gast, "in the Röthel reproduction by Ongania in Venice, and said: 'Ah! That is Zarathustra, indeed! I have imag-

ined him roughly like that!'" Compare also Gustav Naumann, *Zarathustra-Commentar* (Leipzig, 1899), pt. 1, p. 25 <Kaufmann translation of the Gast report>.

28. See Erich F. Podach's *Friedrich Nietzsches Werke des Zusammenbruchs,* 166, where, however, this letter draft is given with errors and lacunae.

29. The entire passage was inserted into the new text as a supplement by Nietzsche <Kaufmann translation>.

30. The delusional notes to Cosima Wagner are given in facsimile by Curt von Westerhagen in *Richard Wagner* (Zurich, 1956), 471.

31. The difficult task would entail, for example, the break in relations with Malwida von Meysenbug in connection with *The Case of Wagner* (the decisive letters on both sides remain unknown today); the disagreement with F. Avenarius, which led to the creation of *Nietzsche contra Wagner;* the break in relations with the Leipzig publisher Ernst Wilhelm Fritzsch and Nietzsche's subsequent attempt to regain control over his "literature"; the brief correspondence with August Strindberg; the "negotiations" for translations of *Ecce Homo, The Antichrist, Twilight of the Idols,* and *The Case of Wagner,* with which Nietzsche occupied himself especially in December; the "promemoria" against the German Reich, which he in fact composed in the closing days of December and sent to a "translator," the French publicist Jean Bordeau (who wrote on January 4, 1889: "J'ai reçu également votre manuscrit de Turin, qui témoigne de vos sentiments anti-prussiens. . . . Il ne me semble pas de nature à pouvoir être publié" <I also received your manuscript from Turin, which testifies to your anti-Prussian feelings. . . . It doesn't strike me as publishable>); the entire Turin scene: funerals, weddings, operas, concerts, particular buildings such as the "Galleria Subalpina," but especially "Mole Antonelli," that work of the "age-old" Piedmont architect Alessandro Antonelli (1798–1888, died October 18), whose funeral Nietzsche attended (cf. letter to Burckhardt, January 6, 1888); Nietzsche had christened his edifice "Ecce Homo." And others besides. Compare with this KSA 15, pp. 176–210 (the chronicle).

32. See Nietzsche's letter and letter draft to Helen Zimmern, mid-December, as well as the letters of November 20 to Georg Brandes and of December 27, 1888, to C. G. Naumann.

33. The correspondence between Franz Overbeck and Peter Gast is of inestimable significance for Nietzsche research. Gast's letters are preserved in the Basel University Library; we thank Herr Dr. Max Burckhardt, who placed these letters at our service. Overbeck's letters exist—but only in part—as copies, also at the Basel University Library. All original letters from Overbeck to Gast are part of the Gast literary estate, hence in Weimar. This correspondence is already known through its partial publication. A complete edition is planned by de Gruyter Publishers. What strikes us is how the main argument used later by the Nietzsche Archive in its slander against Overbeck is already present here in embryonic form in the cited passages from Peter Gast's letters: if Nietzsche had completed work on the entire "Revaluation" (at least on the complex of ideas), manuscripts must necessarily have been lost.

34. The equation *The Antichrist* = the "Revaluation" was proposed for the first time by Ernst Horneffer, *Nietzsches letztes Schaffen* (Jena, 1907), 17–19, on the basis of the final title page for *The Antichrist,* which had as its subtitle—later stricken—"Revaluation of All Values" (in the end Nietzsche replaced these words with "Attack on Christianity"). The title page in its first version accords perfectly with the passage from the November 26 let-

ter to Paul Deussen printed by us: "My 'Revaluation of All Values,' with the main title, *The Antichrist,* is finished." This letter was never published by the Nietzsche Archive, for otherwise Elisabeth Förster-Nietzsche would have had to abandon one of her main arguments in her hateful campaign against Franz Overbeck, her brother's best friend. In the cited letters to Brandes and Naumann, Nietzsche had spoken of a completed "Revaluation," without, however, mentioning the "main title," so that his sister contended that Nietzsche could only have meant by this his work on a project in four volumes (in accordance with the final plan for the "Revaluation"), of which only the first book—*The Antichrist*—remained at hand, other important manuscripts having been lost due to Overbeck's carelessness when he picked up his mentally ill friend from Turin. Förster-Nietzsche herself—mark well!—had received Nietzsche's letters to Deussen as a gift from the latter *between 1896 and 1901.* Concerning the "conflict over the lost manuscripts," see Elisabeth Förster-Nietzsche, *Das Nietzsche-Archiv, seine Freunde and Feinde* (Berlin, 1907); C. A. Bernoulli, *Franz Overbeck und Friedrich Nietzsche: Eine Freundshaft* (Jena, 1908); Ernst Holzer, "Antichrist und Umwertung," *Süddeutsche Monatshefte* 5, no. 8 (August 1908): 162–69. Peter Gast participated in the entire campaign as an official of the Nietzsche Archive. Thus, for example, in his work Ernst Horneffer states, precisely in accord with the facts presented here: "Peter Gast himself told me, though, that Nietzsche had characterized the Revaluation as finished in *Ecce Homo* and that he, namely Peter Gast, had inserted 'the first book of the revaluation' in his copy *out of his own free will,* Nietzsche's statement being false" (26). Gast answered this in the brief essay, "Die neueste Nietzsche-Fabel," *Die Zukunft* 16, no. 1 (October 5, 1907): 29: "In *Ecce Homo* Nietzsche devoted a chapter to each of his finished works. Since the 'Revaluation' was not finished by the composition of *Ecce Homo,* it does not receive its own chapter. Only at the conclusion of the *Ecce Homo* chapter on *Twilight of the Idols* is the 'Revaluation' conceived. . . . In the original manuscript of *Ecce Homo* one finds the following sentence at the passage I am thinking of: 'On the thirtieth of September, great victory; seventh day; idlesse of a god along the Po.' The two words 'seventh day' were struck by Nietzsche but not replaced with anything new. As I copied the work in 1889, it appeared impossible to me that Nietzsche would have allowed the abbreviated sentence to go to the printers in that condition. The divine rest was appropriate to only the seventh day, but not to victory. Obviously, Nietzsche had arrived at the expression 'seventh day' because it could give the impression of the 'Revaluation' being completed; perhaps the replacement words did not come to him immediately, or the ones that occurred to him did not yet suffice. I am convinced even today, too, that Nietzsche would have filled in the lacuna at the printing. And then there in the preface to *Ecce Homo,* and in fact in the still extant corrections proof as well . . . among the enumerated works of 1888, one could clearly read: 'The first book of the Revaluation of All Values,' so because it was my opinion that the struck phrase was to be replaced by something or another, I took it on myself to write the entire phrase there thusly: 'On the thirtieth of September, great victory; completion of the first book of the Revaluation; idlesse of a god along the Po.' I told the Horneffers of this insertion. They were alerted to it for the first time by me. But what do I experience now? It becomes clear from the mentioned work that Horneffer has gotten it fixed in his head that, of the six words 'Beendigung des ersten Buches der Umwerthung,' only the second, third, and fourth words were inserted by me and that 'completion of the Revaluation' was the way it stood with Nietzsche. However, with Nietzsche there was nothing there except what had been struck by him, the 'seventh day' awaiting some replacement." Peter Gast himself later gave the proper commentary to this prose:

"Why should not one, as a former archivist, jointly support everything that one could *never* support as a decent human being?" (to Ernst Holzer, January 1910; see this volume, pp. 166–68).

35. See Erich F. Podach's *Friedrich Nietzsches Werke des Zusammenbruchs,* 184: "What is certain is that Nietzsche did not leave behind a finished *Ecce Homo,* but we have one." As we have seen, Podach proceeded from the proper perspective, Peter Gast being the key figure to the later history of *Ecce Homo.* His edition of *Ecce Homo,* which also brought the last preliminary materials to the texts—and in fact mixed them together with the final versions—did not, however, provide the decisive proof of Peter Gast's manipulations.

Documentary Supplement

Nietzsche's harshest reckoning with his mother and sister arrived by mail in Leipzig "on one of the last two days of December, 1888"; C. G. Naumann, made aware of this text's "highly injurious nature" by a supervisor, did not initially allow it to be taken into the fair copy made by Nietzsche; he intended, rather, to elicit information about the matter from Nietzsche himself. Directly afterward came news of Nietzsche's mental collapse. This page was not missing from Peter Gast's copy of *Ecce Homo;* as a matter of fact, it belonged to those passages that gave him the impression of being "too contemptuous" and of committing "injustices." So the page remained in Naumann's writing desk until Peter Gast, on orders from Nietzsche's sister, picked it up at the beginning of February 1892. He sent it to Naumburg on February 9, 1892, with the accompanying note: "I went to Naumann the first thing early on Monday. His nephew <Gustav Naumann, later author of a four-volume commentary on *Zarathustra*> was also called by telephone. Next, I acquired, with Naumann's consent, the accompanying page to *Ecce Homo*. I do not believe that Naumann has a copy of it: it still lay in the box and in the same position where it had been when he had showed it to me previously. Let us rejoice that we have it! But now it must also *really be destroyed*! Even if it is clear that it was written in complete madness, there will always be people, nonetheless, who say that it is still of value *precisely for this reason* because the instincts speak in their full truthfulness here, without inhibition."

At this opportunity, Gast probably finalized his copy of the page, which we have recovered from his effects. The heading already quoted by us, which Gast set at the top of his copy, reads: "Copy of a page that Nietzsche sent to Naumann during the printing of *Ecce Homo* (from Turin, end of December 1888)."

Later Gast struck the words "in complete madness," which he had used in the accompanying note from 1892 against better knowledge of *Ecce Homo*'s textual history, out of deference to Nietzsche's family.

After his final break with Förster-Nietzsche in the summer of 1909, Gast no longer needed to withhold his true opinion about all this. The fifth volume of the *Gesammelten Briefe* appeared at that time; it contained Nietzsche's letters to his mother and sister and was—as we know today from Karl Schlechta's reports—a masterpiece of falsification. On this occasion Peter Gast wrote to Ernst Holzer (June 23, 1909): "In your last card you said that letter 5 showed Nietzsche's close relationship to his sister beyond any doubt. Ha, ha, ha, ha, ha! The close relationship, though, cost him great efforts. How convulsive the efforts were for Nietzsche was made plain shortly before the outbreak of his delusions: namely, Nietzsche's large folio page of additions to *Ecce Homo,* which Nietzsche sent to Naumann, concerning his mother and sister. Finally nauseated at his own good sportsmanship, Nietzsche spoke frankly and freely there, and nothing more devastating has ever been said about anyone than on this page."

Our remarks on the authentic text to the third section of the chapter "Why I Am So Wise" in *Ecce Homo* should be supplemented with several additional letters from the year 1908. They come from the period in which the Nietzsche Archive was preparing the publication of *Ecce Homo* and are taken from the correspondence of Peter Gast with Raoul Richter (professor of philosophy in Leipzig and the first editor of *Ecce Homo*) and from that of Elisabeth Förster-Nietzsche with Raoul Richter and Constantin Georg Naumann. In this way several important details from the history of the mentioned text become known and sufficiently testify to what Peter Gast ironically called "Frau Förster's sense of truth." These documents are preserved at the Goethe-Schiller Archive in Weimar.

1. Peter Gast to Raoul Richter (letter fragment)

Weimar, May 5, 1908

[++] the still-extant correction sheet number one, I can no longer recall, nor is it even conceivable to me.

Since the day you were here, I have searched and searched to find a clue about the alterations written down by me on the first page of signature number one. I finally found them in one of my pocketbooks from that period—for the first time on the day before yesterday. I am certain that this one alteration, namely, the phrase "and for convalescence," was not one of my own. But to explain them by documentation, or for me to remember from whence I got those alterations, was completely impossible.

Now I know that this alteration (with several others) was on a sheet of paper that Nietzsche had sent to Naumann at the end of December 1888 and that contained such horrible things about his mother and sister. Because of these things, I was instructed by Frau Förster-Nietzsche at the beginning of the nineties to take the page away from Herr Naumann and bring it back to Weimar. Whether the page still exists or not, I do not know: Elisabeth Förster-Nietzsche wanted to burn it. To be brief, in my notebook there was written, probably during the train ride, the following:

On the page for *E<cce Homo>*
with the altered opening from section three in signature one,
one still reads,
Other corrections on signature one.
Page 1, line 8: The Revaluation of All Values,—

2. Raoul Richter to Peter Gast

Leipzig, May 16, 1908

Dear Herr Gast,

With my best thanks for your detailed and friendly explanation, I beg your pardon that I must reply here so briefly. But I hope to speak with you personally on Thursday.

It is indeed very pleasant that no slanderous voices have emerged in the press concerning the mutilation of *E<cce Homo>*, and in the evaluative report, a consideration of such accusations may well fail to materialize. I believe that we can find formulations for the destruction of the page in mind that will render insightful readers unable to disapprove of the action and that nevertheless do not silence the fact. This does not seem to me advisable to do, in the interests of your affairs, of the archive, and of its director. We would only have to do something with the explanation *later,* which we could have given in a more delicate manner previously in a tone that is no longer entirely available to us, because of the initial really impolite, adversarial tone—it really concerns only a couple of words about the matter—as an answer to certain attacks.

By your remark that Nietzsche never again saw the manuscript to *Ecce Homo* after December 7, 1888, I was all the more strengthened in my belief that the December 16, 1888,* dispatch to Naumann—"manuscript back, everything revised"—refers to *Nietzsche contra Wagner.* That can be ruled out with certainty by Naumann's correspondence alone.

With friendly greetings to your wife and children, too,

Yours sincerely,
Raoul Richter

[*Peter Gast's marginal remark: "The telegram on this date only announces to Naumann that Nietzsche had just sent off *Ecce Homo* from Turin to Leipzig. It must read instead, December 6, 1888."]

3. Raoul Richter to Peter Gast

May 27, 1908

Dear Herr Gast,

Many thanks for your friendly lines. The belated correction to page 1, line 17, will not, of course, be incorporated, in accordance with our principles: neither, of course, that concerning the "Songs of Zarathustra." If one were to further question this, the alteration, without any details about the "one case" on page <read "line"> 17, would result, in fact, in nonsense.[1] But if one abandons this correction, one need not bring up the others, either. I believe this will clarify things for you,

With thanks and regards,

Yours,
Raoul Richter

4. Elisabeth Förster-Nietzsche to Constantin Georg Naumann

Weimar, June 18, 1908

To the Firm of C. G. Naumann, Leipzig
Dear Sir,

Today I must ask you for a very precise piece of information about a very important matter; in the year 1891 or early 1892, Herr Constantin Georg Naumann gave one page of a manuscript to Herr Peter Gast, which he has claimed was accidentally left to lie in a drawer and would have arrived there for you in Leipzig in early 1889, when Professor Nietzsche was already ill. I have seen the page only fleetingly, but our mother had it in hand for a longer period, and what was on the page I know only through her account. I remember only one sentence, with the approximate content that he had been elevated to become God and that we were no longer worthy of being his mother and sister. It had those capital letters with which he wrote everything once he had taken ill. Our mother burned the page. When I returned from Paraguay in 1893, it was no longer present, and she could no longer recall exactly why she had destroyed it. Herr Gustav Naumann, whom I questioned, told me to my great astonishment how the firm of C. G.

Naumann had come to hold back a page of manuscript, obviously with a content that was highly objectionable to our mother, for a period of three years—he declared that he could give me no information about this matter. But he did claim to know one thing for certain: that the page had belonged to neither *Ecce Homo* nor *Nietzsche contra Wagner*. Both of these manuscripts have been completely withdrawn from the Naumann firm; yet it is ridiculous that the firm suppressed one of those pages and has returned it only once queried by Peter Gast, because he had heard of this page through others who had been shown it.

Well, now I hear to my great befuddlement that Herr Constantin Georg, as well as the former supervisor of your publishing house, has spoken of this page as if it were part of *Ecce Homo*. I am outraged by this, because then it could not be destroyed in any case after all—let it contain whatever it will. Only I cannot recall it, unless the page is one of those like my husband received in Paraguay after the illness of my brother. I found them for the first time after the death of my husband, which followed five months after the onset of my brother's illness; and since the contents, in fact, were full of confusion, and in addition, full of insults against my husband, I burned them uncopied, except for two. One bore a precise designation for the chapter of *Ecce Homo* concerning *The Case of Wagner*—but in spite of that could not be inserted and published, since it was extraordinarily insulting to my husband, to Peter Gast, but above all to Overbeck.[2] The other page, which I still possess from this packet, is, as it appears, an addition intended for *Nietzsche contra Wagner*. I admit that I took it for an addition to *Ecce Homo* at the time.

Now I would like to ask for information as to why the Naumann firm's previous statement about the aforesaid page contradicts its current one and how the firm allowed the pages to be withheld and shown to complete strangers, further, with what must have been its disagreeable contents. It was suggested to me at the time that Herr C. G. Naumann was exemplifying in himself Nietzsche's intellectual confusion—all the same, more excusable than when he now designates it as a part of *Ecce Homo* that he illegally withheld at that time and would not have returned on demand of the legal guardian.

Therefore, I must ask you most politely to give me the exact information about these individual points, since the matter must be properly settled before publication of *Ecce Homo*.

It has just occurred to me whether the sheet in question bore the instruction that it belonged to *Ecce Homo* and whether the place where it should be inserted was indicated. I do not remember seeing anything of the sort, but as I said, I had it in my hand only momentarily, because I, in colonial circumstances, wanted to travel immediately to Berlin.

5. Elisabeth Förster-Nietzsche to Raoul Richter (draft of a letter)

June 18, 1908

My Dear Professor,

The affair with that page of which C. G. Naumann has spoken is, quite the contrary, a very serious matter. I am enclosing your copy of a letter that I have sent to Naumann in this regard. He is returning tomorrow from a long journey;

consequently an answer to it will not come right away. In any case, we—I mean you and I—must speak once more about this entire *Ecce Homo* affair. I request most fervently that you specify a date to me when you would like to come here, and then I will show you what is still present of the preliminary materials to *Ecce Homo,* along with what I have purchased of it. But you should again bring the goods, the printer's manuscript, with you.

6. Constantin Georg Naumann to Elisabeth Förster-Nietzsche

Leipzig, July 2, 1908

Frau Dr. Elisabeth Förster-Nietzsche
Weimar
Respected Frau Dr.,

After having returned home from my summer vacation only a few days ago, I now hurry to begin an answer to your letter of June 18.

I would gladly have avoided—so as not to relive old things—a pronouncement on your brother's manuscript page in question, but because you place so much importance on the matter yourself, nothing remains for me to do other than speak openly and honestly about everything that enters into the matter here.

Herr Professor Dr. Raoul Richter, who visited me at your instructions several times with regard to *Ecce Homo,* requested from me the most exact data in this regard, and I have, at the cost of at least one week of time, occupied myself with it, painstakingly gone through selected correspondence between your brother, Professor Overbeck, Peter Gast, your mother, and so on, and sought after explanations. After all the basic points of interest were established in association with Herr Professor Dr. Richter, everything was read over again from the beginning, and the result of the entire experience was that, *twenty years after the fact,* I could not say more than I had before. Also, I must decline to consider it any evidence of a loss of professional abilities when I investigate and discuss the same case again and again from the beginning to the end.

Given the importance of the matter, your brother's manuscript page could not have been withheld, because knowing something and not saying it is the same as giving a false statement; I can't be expected to do that!

In my considered opinion, the page belongs to *Ecce Homo.* On one of the last two days of December 1888, my supervisor, Herr Haupt, came to my city office to inform me under forfeiture of the page that he could not allow the questionable sentence to be accepted in its given, highly injurious form. I took the page and told him that I would correspond directly with Herr Professor Nietzsche concerning the matter.

By the way, the two other books were, in fact, on the one side finished (*Twilight of the Idols*) and on the other side set in fair copy up to the final page (*Nietzsche contra Wagner*). Also, the contents of the page would have made no sense at all in these books.

At this point I must interject that the manuscript page (of strong handmade paper with deckle edges, around 17–23 cm large—a rough edge at the right, containing around 35–38 *very tight* lines of text) was written calligraphically in impeccable purity and bore the traits of your brother's clear handwriting; large capitals and other conspicuous characteristics untrue of earlier manuscripts were completely absent; *the evil phrase* merely had to be looked at somewhat more carefully, because it came at the end of the deckle edge of the paper; all considered, though, another reading of the word had to be completely excluded, as Peter Gast can attest to, in any case.

An orderly, smooth-running business would have required me to have sent a query about the additional sentence to your brother and to have asked for another, exact proposal. This would not be the first time I had entered into this practice in such cases! In fact, the same likewise happened with you, when I made you cognizant, during the Lou affair, that one does not speak of lies, and so on, in published books, and so forth, without damaging oneself in the eyes of others.

The course of events that the entire matter with your brother took after the outbreak of his catastrophic illness came about entirely otherwise than could have been anticipated.

Herr Professor Nietzsche wrote me *no earlier than December 31,* 1888, the business letter you have in your hand, in which there was a remark about *the marketability of Zarathustra and its value for the publisher,* and this letter was the first one that I did not take entirely in earnest but as really quite humorous, such that I made note of it to myself. Given the long journey for this letter, it could have reached my hands on January 2, 1889, at the earliest.

From that point in time onward, the news came fast and furious; the fateful manuscript page lay in my desk and was not given another consideration, particularly when, no later than a few months afterward, the entire manuscript for *Ecce Homo* was sent to Basel.[3]

A conscious suppression on my part can be completely ruled out, for otherwise I would not have given notice to Herr Gast later on discovering the document.

Only those who have survived the tumultuous times after the catastrophe can have any idea of the continually changing picture, and those who understand such a business as mine at that time can appreciate that in the course of one day, with around eighty letters and the delivery of around 100 commissions, one is not in the position to concentrate all his thoughts merely on one extraordinary case of this sort.

Enough—the page went into my writing desk when my own letter to Herr Professor Nietzsche became superfluous in the first days of January 1889, many business papers were piled on it, and when I found it again years later, the *Ecce Homo* affair had long passed by, but the ominous passage prevented me from letting the page out of my hands, or rather to say, handing it over to your mother; despite all that, I gave notice of it to Peter Gast during one of his visits. This must have been after your return to Germany, because Peter Gast wished that I myself turn over the page to you; this, too, I declined, because of the nature of the affair, and I urged Herr Gast to take over this dire mission himself.

In any case, I had the occasion during one of the named gentleman's visits to be told by him that, having had a consultation with you about the case, he hesitated not one moment to return it to its destination.

Thus and in no other way does the affair remain fixed in *my memory*. Whether Peter Gast has given the document to you or your mother, I cannot, of course, know, nor does it matter to me.

However, because the written piece was, according to your letter, *burned* and is no longer extant in the archive, its publication perforce remains impossible—just as you wish, by your statements, to take over another passage unconnected to *Ecce Homo,* although you describe such an omission, "regardless of what it concerns," as thoroughly improper in the same letter several lines above.

The fact is that you recited its contents quite accurately, in one sense, though of course the wording read somewhat differently, and there was a pause to the concluding sentence somewhat like the following version: "*to feel related . . . would be an attack on my divinity.*"[4]

I can offer nothing further, especially whether the page at issue bore specific instructions for *Ecce Homo* or clues thereabout, as I have also told Herr Professor Dr. Raoul Richter.

On the contrary, the tone of your letter is highly injurious, although, on the other side, I do not believe that you consciously wished to slander me but rather that the honor-offending passages have grated on your impulsive temperament.

If you wish to confirm that you have reputed all the slanders against my person by your letter, the affair shall be considered at an end; if you do not, you will force me, regardless of whether such a measure leads to further actions, to consult with my attorney, with whom I will ascertain whether I must tolerate your sort of insinuations without defending myself.

I hope to resolve this matter peacefully. Looking forward to your reply, and greetings,

Respectfully,
C. G. Naumann
For the firm of
Constantin Georg Naumann Publishers

7. Elisabeth Förster-Nietzsche to Constantin Georg Naumann, Dictated
Weimar, July 3, 1908

To the Firm of C. G. Naumann, Leipzig
Dear Sir,

You would have cause to play the injured one if the matter were as harmless as you have presented it to be. Unfortunately, it is something else entirely. But first of all I wish to correct a misunderstanding; I consider it an extraordinary stroke of luck that Professor Richter has researched this matter so precisely, and thus were you led to express yourself precisely about the matter—it would have been desirable to me if your current statements had agreed with your earlier ones. It was simply your duty, and I agree completely that you said everything you believed to remember. <Frau Förster means here that Naumann did not lead the research but only aided Richter, and was obligated to do so at that. Also, her carefully chosen wording, "believed to remember," insinuates that Naumann's memory is selective.> Therefore, we will leave the inquiry and your answer to

Professor Richter out of the discussion, and you need not have outdone yourself. Something completely different is the concern.

1. You now claim that you first withheld the page out of sensitivity, and then it was forgotten in your writing desk. That is accurate on neither count. You showed the page to complete strangers at a time when you were entrenched in battle with me and my mother because of your irresponsible business practices toward our dear patient, and I remember quite well that, when I paid you a visit in spring 1891, you had made a veiled reference to it <the manuscript page>—in order to create a sort of impression on me—but I thought it applied to letters, unknown to me, to you from my brother. You handed over the page only when the battle had been decided to your disadvantage, and you wanted to gain a certain sort of gratitude whereby your firm, and not E. W. Fritzsch, became the publishers of my brother's works. Herr Gustav Naumann had said at the time that it must have been a page outside any printed work, which, in fact, made surrender of the page more explicable and led to the gratitude; *I* have certainly not seen the least printed line of this, nor any indication where it should be inserted. Also, Professor Richter has given the entire printer's manuscript of *Ecce Homo* the most exact examination without having found the slightest hint that this page should or could have been somehow inserted. He has taken the greatest trouble over it.

2. This, then, is how the matter stands: if the page belongs to *Ecce Homo,* your business practices at that time were illegal and inexcusable; in addition to that, you showed this page to strangers. Unfortunately, your letter confirms, and I would only like to express the hope, that you are not certain about what you say. If the page is, as Herr Gustav Naumann said at that time, a page *outside of* any printer's manuscript, then your business practices—of which, by the way, Herr Gustav Naumann very nobly and powerfully disapproved at the time—are all the same pardonable. Therefore, I shall direct you once again to the specific questions:

a. Can you definitely remember that there had been a note on the page that it ought to be added to *Ecce Homo*?

b. How could you bring yourself to show this page to complete strangers?

c. Have you or any other member of the C. G. Naumann firm withheld a copy of your own, and why do you not turn it over to us?

What you recited from your memory does not agree with mine; consequently, it would be desirable if you could produce a copy that would appear differently under the circumstances of the time.

Therefore, I request that you give me a very exact answer on these three points. I do not see why I should not press for your account of this affair in the strongest tone—I even *must* do so to redeem our dear mother, who would have reconsidered her incineration, if one had told her, or such an interpretation had been at hand, that the page belonged to *Ecce Homo.* At that time you could have set aside all other conjectures, but we knew nothing of it. I certainly do not want to be unfair to you, and I give you my best thanks, for example, that you aided Professor Richter in his research, but I cannot regard your business practices at that time as anything other than how I expressed it, and in the recent letter still in very mild words. You forget entirely what a chain of unpleasant events you caused us at that time and still now continue to do so.

8. Elisabeth Förster-Nietzsche to Raoul Richter (draft)

My Dear Herr Professor,

My best thanks for your return of my brother's letter to C. G. Naumann and of both of my handwritten notes, the first a supplement to my brother's letter to C. G. Naumann and the other page that additional passage concerning my husband, Gast, and Overbeck, originally intended for *Ecce Homo*. I must tell you once again how thrilled I am by your report. You struck upon such a fine tone, effective in both scholarly and philosophical manner and certainly so warm and persuasive in its cordiality. I thank you mostly warmly for it.

As of late, I have smiled a bit about our negotiations. We never choose to discuss something ahead of time, until the wording of what it roughly is we wish to say has been determined. We are so fundamentally similar in sentiment on all main points that in truth no differences can express themselves. That also gives me a wonderful confidence in the future, because when the scholarly edition comes out, I would hope so very much that you will be its editor. How we will work with the preliminary materials and additions at some point is, of course, not entirely clear to me at the moment, but there is time for that, too. I recently read something in the preliminary materials and again have found confirmed how much milder and happier the first notes are formulated. I almost believe we could assemble a second *Ecce Homo* from the preliminary materials and additions in such a way that the tones of the first and the last would be entirely, extraordinarily different from each other.

As I had already imagined, Herr Naumann—because you apologized in such a friendly fashion—wrote me a letter as if he were some wounded nobleman. So I have written him that everything he has said to you was completely correct; I also had to thank him for his helpful aid. But I also had to tell him the complete truth, because, as I have told you, the reason that I turned my energetic rebuke against Naumann was not you but rather news from an entirely unrelated quarter ~~which I have already mentioned to you~~.[5] Well, I hope that he answers the three questions that I have posed to him very precisely this time. Finally, I request that you send back both copies of the letters to Naumann once you have read them.

Now I must change the topic, however; you were recently so dear as to offer to search for the original letter whereby I had first learned of *Ecce Homo*. Now the situation is as follows: through one Herr Johann Reinelt in Neisse, whose *nom de plume* was "Philo of the Forest," I became quite absorbed in the outstanding psychiatrist Professor Wernicke in Breslau. This Herr Reinelt—whom I had already met earlier—at one time ~~spring 1898~~ came directly to Weimar, where it had been going remarkably well for my brother. Consequently, I believed a cure to be possible, and Philo of the Forest, who was a natural healer, bolstered my belief in it. He considered my brother's last letter noteworthy precisely in its happiness and its clarity, such that I decided to give the letter to Professor Wernicke. ~~Well, at that time came the so-~~ Wernicke agreed to come for a fee of 800 marks, which was quite affordable in comparison with other psychiatrists because Kreplin <sic> wanted 3,000 marks. But after this so-called "remission" there came relapses, such that the house physician became very skeptical of my hopes and advised me to move him to Leipzig, that he might be treated sooner. This caused me to forget the entire matter with Professor Wernicke. I must even admit that it had been completely lost on me that I had given the letter to Herr Philo of the Forest. My first attempts to assemble all the letters in the spring co-incided with a visit from Dr. Sandberg, from Schlesien, who had obtained for me one of my brother's last letters—in fact, the one I had sent from Paraguay to Biswanger—and it occurred to me that both of the other letters from the final period had likewise fallen into the hands of psychiatrists.

Well then, I would be very grateful to you if you would place the inquiry to ask for the letters to be returned—but it *must* be emphasized that I have no right to them. At that time I was foolish, and it could even be that I had promised me-diation of the original letter, if not to Professor Wernicke, then to Herr Reinelt. So at the most I can only ask for a photographic copy. Dr. Sandberg, for example, has agreed to this.[6]

9. Elisabeth Förster-Nietzsche to Constantin Georg Naumann (draft)

CGN July 6, 1908

In the meantime I have thought that if I advance against you "fully ar-mored, weapons glistening," then I will never hear ~~the truth about the entire~~ the real course of events to this affair, and to me, everything rests above all on finally getting a little clarity in the story and whether those statements I have heard from others are true or not. Therefore, I shall give you my assurance that if you send the copy and divulge precisely to whom you showed it, and whether instructions were given on it as to whether or not it was for *Ecce Homo,* you shall certainly not suffer legal difficulties from it. From the exact portrayal of the page that you gave in your last letter, it seems that despite all this, you are quite famil-iar with it ~~although the wording that you recall does not seem quite accurate to my ear~~. What do you really mean, then, by the "ominous phrase"? In short, I would like to offer you this—we certainly want to resolve the affair in a friendly manner, or at least insofar as it is possible for me with these highly unpleasant discoveries—that it is possible the page may have belonged to *Ecce Homo* and that it is said to be distinctively marked as such. And in this regard, I expressly note that destruction and nonpublication are two very different things and that, by the way, compositions such as those from the final period, which I have already mentioned in the biography, page 921, wherein, for example, poor Over-beck and other friends are called *canaille*—as are, by the way, various Germans, for example, Wagner, Bismarck, and, astoundingly, Stöcker[7]—certainly do not belong in publication ~~and it certainly does not condemn our mother~~; our moth-er would ~~certainly~~ not have destroyed these pages, despite everything, if she had known that they were parts of a manuscript.[8]

So, in conclusion, the most important thing is whether you can remember specifically whether there was an instruction at the top of the page. I will then back off from the other questions and forgive you entirely if you bring me a copy. Perhaps it would really be better if you came in person, and then I will show you the pages that come into question, and you can tell me whether your page is similar in appearance.

From your description I cannot gather anything specific.

10. *Constantin Georg Naumann to Elisabeth Förster-Nietzsche*

Leipzig, July 7, 1908

Frau Dr. Elisabeth Förster-Nietzsche
Weimar
Respected Frau Dr.,

No answer is also an answer: I have done nothing improper and consequently decline to enter into your new inquiries, particularly since my last letter *precisely presented the affair according to my memory.*

Herr Peter Gast, who had the manuscript at issue in his hands at my counter and read the text, will, as a Nietzsche scholar, know exactly to which book the contents of the page at issue belongs, and I must accordingly request that you make all related inquiries to the aforementioned gentleman, while I refuse an answer to any question personally involving me because such a final and *really conclusive* one can only be given in a legal venue.

<interruption in document>

I was about to answer your letter of July 3 in the manner above—to be short and concise—honorable madam, when your letter of July 6 arrived! I must admit now, of course, that a quiet, dispassionate tone speaks to me more, and since the tone of your letter today convinces me that you did not wish to consciously libel me, I am entirely ready to take up again the previous manner of factual discussion, only I cannot really satisfy your wish because I am *not* able to give anything definite as to whether there had been a direct instruction for *Ecce Homo* on the manuscript page.[9]

In my opinion, it was exactly one continuous manuscript page, and I cannot give you *a copy,* because *I never finished one!* Had I purloined a copy for any intention whatsoever, then the guile <*dolus*> would represent dishonesty, and in my own opinion I would be a pathetic figure were I ever to misuse the intellectual property of another; yet the page and its contents meant nothing to me. However, by accident I was put into a forced position; I could not give away the page without deeply wounding a third party.

Indeed, you claimed that I should have notified your mother of the incident but overlooked the fact that my correspondence with her and that with Herr Professor Overbeck concerned two entirely different matters. When I recall in what an intimate manner Frau Pastor Nietzsche complained to me of her pain over the—in her view—probably inevitable fates of her children, then, you, too, honorable madam, would not have further burdened a mother's wounded heart and would not, at that time, have demanded such a thing.

How careful I have been on this sort of occasion should be sufficiently familiar to you, also, from correspondence relevant to the Nietzsche Archive, "Dr. Langbehn, Naumann, and Frau Pastor Nietzsche" and the reverse series, in which as mediator I had to copy selected letters, and in the evening hours, so to speak, carried out the functions of a copyist.

Your concern about the making known of the manuscript is certainly un-justified because only very few people come into question. I simply do not go to the marketplace and show such a written work in an offhand manner. Do you believe, then, that I have the time at my business for a little *"gossip"*?! It has never been so in my entire life; I have continually worked honestly and utilized each day to its fullest.

In my estimation, aside from the firm's departmental personnel, approximately 4–8 persons have seen the manuscript, among them Peter Gast, Professor Hausdorff, Paul Lauterbach, and Moritz Wirth—who at that time had a great interest in the accident that met your brother—coming into question. I showed the page only when the conversation turned to many inquiries about Nietzsche's medical situation—I may even have previously made remarks about the unevenness of business activity; from the given number, you can appreciate that only a few exceptional cases were involved because my tight schedule forbids me to enter into long conversations with every inquirer.

So much for today on the affair of the manuscript; I will write you tomorrow about concerns for the edition of volume 1,[10] about which we are not entirely in agreement, until then, I remain respectfully yours,

C. G. Naumann Publishers

11. Elisabeth Förster-Nietzsche to Raoul Richter (draft of a letter)

July 8, 1908

My Dear Herr Professor,

It has occurred to me in the meantime that Naumann is telling me nothing definite because he fears that I shall take him to court over this matter. So I have written him again and given my solemn assurance that I would not do this and suggested to him that we certainly ought to discuss the matter with each other in a friendly fashion. He answered me very quickly after that. The affair is as I have already said: there was no instruction or page number on the sheet, and it was one of those pages without instructions, just as I had received in Paraguay.[11]

Well, I do not know, of course, what Naumann means by "the ominous phrase" <Frau Förster blurs Naumann's *"evil phrase"* and "ominous passage">, but it probably will be the same that occurs again constantly in this section four.

By the way, there is something I must tell you; on one page of the preliminary material to *Ecce Homo* from the final period, one finds the expression "royal idiot," and on the same page there is a remark from me: "an expression that occurred on the page that our mother burned because of royal defamation."[12] Thus, it appears correct that the main contents of that page—as you had already opined—was directed against the kaiser, and I am certain that we finally have found the original composition.

I am happy that Havenstein's article pleased you as well as it did us. But I must still add that this article was written five weeks ago, and in the meantime everything has been gone through in accordance with those passages that have been discovered, and nothing has been found, so that I have replied to a genuinely vile attack in the Jena newspaper with the following attachment.[13]

12. Elisabeth Förster-Nietzsche to Constantin Georg Naumann (draft of a letter)
July 9, 1908

Very respected sir,

First of all, I will answer your letter of yesterday; I read it groaning, so to speak, at what people occasionally have for their own strange notions of "sensitivity." You indicate that there was something slanderous to our mother on the page and wished to withhold the page, only out of sensitivity, from my mother. On the contrary, your sensitivity did not hinder you from showing it to at least a half-dozen of your close pals or from displaying it to the eyes of strangers behind her back. You would not make it through court with this conception of sensitivity. All the same, I shall keep my promise not to draw further consequences from the prior course of events. I also want, right away, to correct a confusion relating to that course of events; you returned the page not in 1897 but instead at the beginning of 1892, when the first contract for ~~several of~~ my brother's writings was to be finalized and Herr E. W. Fritzsch passionately sought that for himself. At that time, Herr Gustav Naumann was the mediator.[14]

• • •

Apart from Peter Gast, there was someone to whom the history of *Ecce Homo* was very well known; that was the author of the first *Zarathustra* commentary, Gustav Naumann, nephew and business aide to Nietzsche's publisher, Constantin Georg Naumann. Around 1940 he put his testimony in the form of short essays at the disposal of the University of Basel Library, where they are accessible today. In one of the essays, "Naumburg Virtue," he wrote: "If nothing in the Nietzsche Archive has been destroyed, then one should still find the manuscript line from the *Ecce Homo* manuscript, which Peter Gast took with him to Naumburg as an olive branch when he reconciled with the director of the archive, who had previously dismissed him very sharply." In another essay, "Peter Gast and Nietzsche's Sister," he comes to speak of the mysterious "manuscript lines" in greater detail:

> In June 1897, I left the firm at the very point in time I was to have become its part owner.[15] This in the face of the unreasonable demand from my uncle to abstain from all independent activity in future matters related to Nietzsche. Yet Frau Förster would continually contend. . . . What happened after then, I did not experience firsthand. I spent most of my time abroad. However, I did hear that Gast had concluded a peace with Nietzsche's sister. I learned as well that he took those lines from the *Ecce Homo* manuscript, which already had a special history of their own, with him on the first trip to visit her. It concerns the sentence that said it had been his mother and sister who had poisoned his existence. I myself had the lines in front of my own eyes and know with certainty that it spoke in terms of poisoning. The wording itself has escaped me. It was so harsh, in any case, that the typesetter took exception to it as being unfit to print. He alerted the business manager and as a result the lines were deleted from the manuscript page. My uncle guarded them in a safe like something to be kept secret for a time. Yet he was very uneasy about this; he could not, and he

dared not, destroy them; nor could he withhold it over the long run. He was certainly happy to get rid of this text by having Gast take it away, who in turn was done a favor by this. Gast was already familiar with it. I do not know whether the lines were taken away at my uncle's own urging or by the suggestion of the other. But afterward it is not hard to imagine for what reason the appeasement of Peter Gast and Frau Förster came about.

The "lines" referred to here are doubtless the third section of the chapter "Why I Am So Wise" in *Ecce Homo,* which we have reconstructed here. What Gustav Naumann has been able to tell concerning the contents of the lines, after nearly fifty years, agrees well with our text; so, for example, the "poisoning" agrees with the phrase "because then I was completely powerless to deter the poisonous worm." Naumann's memory is, despite unavoidable inexactitudes—the reconciliation between Peter Gast and Elisabeth Förster-Nietzsche, for example, occurred in 1899 in Weimar and not in Naumburg—a further confirmation of the authenticity of the reconstructed section. Concerning the value of those Nietzsche omissions, Naumann wrote with right: "What one thinks of the manuscript itself plays no role in it. Its sharpness of tone may be considered pathological in view of the place where it was supposed to appear. The omission may be defended, therefore, should the need arise. All the same it remains awkward. Why should we be ready to note his mental illness here of all places but everything else is written without being affected by it? In fact, it is now well known that Nietzsche had already expressed very similar things about his nearest relatives much earlier."

That the reconciliation of Frau Förster and Peter Gast presented a sort of "non-aggression pact" in which the silence of both sides would be ensured concerning certain unpleasant statements by Nietzsche can be confirmed by the circumstantial fact that his sister possessed letters in some of whose passages Nietzsche spoke very disparagingly of Peter Gast. These passages were actually made public in 1893 as part of a "mailing" to Nietzsche's friends (including, among others, Overbeck) in order to discredit Gast as an editor, although they were not published by the Nietzsche Archive in later editions of the letters.

In conclusion, it should be noted with the highest probability that Overbeck, too, was made well aware of Nietzsche's statements against his mother and sister in *Ecce Homo,* as a matter of fact by Peter Gast's letters, which today are missing from the collection of the University of Basel Library and which, by all appearances, were entered into the files of Peter Gast's legal action against Carl Albrecht Bernoulli and Eugen Dietrich in 1908 as pieces of evidence against the Nietzsche Archive.

Notes

1. See *Ecce Homo,* "Why I Am So Wise," section 4, KGW VI$_3$, p. 267, l. 14. <Montinari refers here to Nietzsche's correction that included the phrase *"that single case."* Richter argues that the phrase would have no reference if the other corrections were not also accepted. See page 112 of this volume for the full context.>

2. This concerns the so-called Paraguay note, which Podach has already published (*Friedrich Nietzsches Werke des Zusammenbruchs,* 314). Since this passage, in contrast to the reconstructed section in *Ecce Homo,* is produced only as a copy by the sister, it was not included in the *Ecce Homo* text of the KGW; see KSA 14, pp. 506–9.

3. Naumann did not send the printer's manuscript of *Ecce Homo* to Basel (to Overbeck) but rather handed it over to Peter Gast.

4. Naumann quotes the "ominous" passage from memory: "to believe myself related to such <German> *canaille* was a blasphemy against my divinity" (KGW VI$_3$, p. 266), yet out of deference to Elisabeth Förster-Nietzsche, he deletes the "evil" phrase "to such <German> *canaille.*" <Here Montinari uncharacteristically leaves out the word *German*, which occurs in both versions of the third section to "Why I Am So Wise" in *Ecce Homo*. See this volume, pages 103–5>

5. The crossed-out passages in this letter draft were struck by Elisabeth Förster-Nietzsche.

6. See the details in our remarks to Nietzsche's alleged letter to his sister "whereby I had first learned of *Ecce Homo*" (KGW VIII$_2$, p. 475). Johann Reinelt had died in the meantime, so Förster-Nietzsche could let her fantasies rule over Raoul Richter. Quite the contrary; on the so-called original copy of the alleged Nietzsche letter we discover the remark, "Original burned by our dear mother"!

7. Every scholar of Nietzsche's notebooks knows to the contrary that Nietzsche always energetically attacked court minister Adolf Stöcker and, with him, anti-Semitism.

8. See the previously cited letter from February 9, 1892, which Peter Gast sent to Naumburg with the page to *Ecce Homo* (Gast unmistakably wrote "the accompanying page to *Ecce Homo*" in it).

9. A sort of "*reservatio mentalis*" evident in the phrases "*not . . .* definite" and "direct instruction" is noteworthy in this formulation from C. G. Naumann; nevertheless, from this Förster-Nietzsche achieved what she had desired—see her next letter of July 8, 1908, to Raoul Richter.

10. The pocketbook edition.

11. See note 9.

12. See KGW VIII$_3$, p. 450, l. 29.

13. This concerns publications about the so-called Koegel Excerpts, which was the object of polemics and a legal action between Carl Bernoulli and the Nietzsche Archive.

14. Förster-Nietzsche's memory here is exemplary; compare to it the cited letter of February 9, 1892, by Gast.

15. Gustav Naumann was estranged from the publishing house as a friend of Koegel; at that time he collected a selection of pieces of evidence concerning the "editorial" activities of Nietzsche's sister under the title "The Case of Elisabeth." Copies of it are present in the Goethe-Schiller Archive and in the central library of the German classics in Weimar.

Nietzsche and National Socialist Ideology:
Alfred Bäumler's Interpretation

1. A national socialist "ideology" in the current sense of the word could, perhaps, be reconstructed. But it would be impossible, on the contrary, to speak
of a genuine national socialist assimilation of Nietzsche's ideas. As recent research has determined, Nietzsche was as good as alien to the founders of national socialism. Alfred Rosenberg, who laid claim to him as a forerunner to
"the movement" in *Mythos des 20. Jahrhunderts,* placed Nietzsche in the dubious company of Paul de Lagarde (whom Nietzsche despised) and Houston
Stewart Chamberlain (who, from his Wagnerian and racist standpoint, rejected Nietzsche). Hitler himself had no relation to Nietzsche; it is questionable
whether he had read him at all. The entire ideology of race was profoundly
alien to Nietzsche. It would be carrying coals to Newcastle if I were to cite the
countless passages in which Nietzsche spoke out against the racial theories of
the true forerunners of national socialism in general and anti-Semitism in
particular. He even had occasion to correspond with someone who later was
a national socialist representative, Theodor Fritsch; his two letters to the latter are a complete mockery of the muddled racial theories of the eighties in
the previous century, with their—as Nietzsche said—dubious concepts of
"Aryanism" and "Germanism." Shortly after his correspondence with Nietzsche, Theodor Fritsch reviewed *Beyond Good and Evil* in 1887 and found in it
(with good reason!) a "glorification of the Jews" and a "harsh condemnation
of anti-Semitism." He disposed of Nietzsche as a "philosopher-fisherman of

the shallows" who had abandoned "any and all understanding for national essence" and who cultivated "old wives' philosophical twaddle in *Beyond Good and Evil*." According to Fritsch, Nietzsche's pronouncements concerning the Jews were the "flat twaddle, too forced, pretending to be intellectual, of a Judaized type, self-taught in some apartment"; luckily, he believed, "Nietzsche's books will be read by scarcely more than two dozen men."[1] This was Nietzsche's actual relationship to anti-Semitism and Germanism as long as he lived. And yet still today, among the wider public, Nietzsche is considered an "intellectual pathfinder of national socialism."

2. We owe Hans Langreder credit for having carefully examined "the confrontation with Nietzsche in the Third Reich" using the methods of historical-empirical research in his dissertation at Kiel from 1970. In this way he was able to determine that there was no consensus in the Third Reich in the evaluation of Nietzsche. He spoke of a "positive" (in the sense of national socialist ideology) and a "negative" image of Nietzsche in the Third Reich. Among national socialist ideologues, there were several who endeavored to win him for Hitlerism; others who on the contrary opposed the unsettling, cosmopolitan, decadent, individualistic Nietzsche; and as a result, still others who sought to mediate between the two positions. The so-called positive image of Nietzsche officially won the upper hand and unfortunately still holds it today. Langreder rightfully named the "conservative revolutionary" Alfred Bäumler as the key figure in Nietzsche's appropriation into the Third Reich. "At the inception and at the mid-point of the development of a positive Nietzsche image in the national socialist period stands [. . .] Alfred Bäumler": thus Langreder in his dissertation. After the "seizure of power," Bäumler was called to the newly founded academic chair for political pedagogy at the University of Berlin; soon afterward he became head of the science department in the governmental office of the "führer's deputy for oversight of the general spiritual and philosophical schooling and education of the NSDAP," hence in the so-called Rosenberg bureau <*Amt Rosenberg*>.[2]

3. At the beginning of the thirties, Bäumler presented himself as the editor and interpreter of Nietzsche's works. The latter occurred first by publishing, with Reclam Publishers, two arrangements of texts, chiefly from Nietzsche's so-called magnum opus, "The Will to Power," in fact with the title, *Nietzsches Philosopie in Selbstzeugnissen. Erster Teil. Das System; Zweiter Teil, Die Krisis Europas.* Immediately thereafter, still in the year 1931, appeared Bäumler's own interpretation, which corresponded exactly to the twofold division

of the Reclam edition: *Nietzsche der Philosoph und Politiker.* That was a period of frequent Nietzsche discussions. One reason for this was the release into the public domain <*Freiwerdung*> of his works (thirty years after the death of the author, as per the law at that time, and Nietzsche died August 25, 1900). "When the works of a genius become the free property of his people and of the entire world of ideas, thirty years after his death," remarked Hans Prinzhorn in the *Deutsche Rundschau* (1932), "then the brains and hands of those who live in this world of ideas understandably stir. How many opportunities offer themselves there: knowledge, abilities, opportunities to mediate—but also opportunities to maintain the craving for admiration and private spitefulness, at the same time to make a profit from this opportunity and to strengthen hidden cultural-political trends." As a matter of fact, the argument over Nietzsche experienced a very powerful reanimation. Erich Podach published the Jena medical reports from the first years of Nietzsche's illness: the sensation with the public was great; countless discussions began; and Nietzsche's elderly sister, with her accomplice, sought once again to take active measures toward the imaginary rescue of her brother's moral honor. After a twenty-year silence, one of the best Nietzsche experts and critics, Josef Hofmiller, took pen in hand once more to express his uneasiness with Nietzsche; he condemned the philosopher and wished only, in polemic with Bäumler, to validate the moral thinker and writer. Nietzsche's private life became the object of a demythologization of the alleged "saint," as the Nietzsche Archive in Weimar had presented him; I need only recall H<ellmut Walther> Brann's book *Nietzsche und die Frauen.* Nonetheless, anyone who could have interpreted the genuine signs of those times would have come to the conclusion that a new corner had been turned in the diverse history of Nietzsche's reception in Germany. Even if the significant and in many respects still valid philosophical research of Karl Jaspers and Karl Löwith (who wrote his important review and dispatch of Klages's book in 1927) was conceived in those very years—on account of which Alfred Bäumler did not need to take Nietzsche "seriously" as a philosopher—it was not the sensationalist discussion of Nietzsche's illness and private life that bore the signature of those fateful years but rather Nietzsche's suitability for the "demands of the day," for those not really well hidden "cultural-political trends" that grew from the seething soil of the dying Weimar Republic. And nothing signified this so much at that time as the newly created Nietzsche interpretation of Alfred Bäumler.

4. He was completely conscious of his deed. As an answer to the attack of the generally conservative-minded Josef Hofmiller, Bäumler wrote:

It belongs to the destiny of Nietzsche's effect on the German spirit that the gigantic work of his unpublished writings has not, to the present day, exerted its effect. (His sole and best readers to this point have still been Klages and Spengler.) For the vast majority, Nietzsche has remained the poet of *Zarathustra;* but he has worked his effect on subtler minds through, above all, two of his masks: through "Dionysus" (*Birth of Tragedy*) and the "free spirit" (the aphoristic books). This free spirit became master of a stylistic genre still scarcely known in Germany: the genre of moralistic, psychological essays. As the virtuoso of an intellectually rich and tight style of thought, Nietzsche won his generation, who, after his death, entered into the German literary public life. He worked his effect as a poet and writer at that time; he is honored still today as a poet and writer. A special appreciation for the middle, most personal works follows directly from this. [. . .] We ascertain today that this appreciation was tied to an underestimation of the works of the later Nietzsche and of his unpublished works.

We for our part would ascertain that Nietzsche's extreme revision as a Germanic thinker, his "recasting as Nordic"—as one could have called it a few years later—was something quite new for the intellectual public at the beginning of the thirties; writers and literati (as Bäumler scornfully remarked) found themselves confronted with an image of Nietzsche previously unknown to them. Of course, the development of this image, too, lay with Bäumler several years earlier; it began just as it had earlier for Warner, when he wrote his work on Bachofen and Nietzsche. I recall the pages by Thomas Mann in his *Pariser Rechenschaft* of 1927, with the ponderable words directed at Bäumler: "Nietzsche's elevated and cultured Germanism knew, as did that of Goethe, other ways of expression than that of the great retreat into the mythic-historical-romantic womb." I further recall still more explicit advice about the politics of the day:

> The scholar's fiction that the intellectual-historical moment belongs to a purely romantic reaction against idealism and rationalism, against the receding decades of the Enlightenment, as if "nationality" stood against "humanity" once more again today with perfect revolutionary right as the new, the youthful, the timely: this scholar's fiction must be recognized for what it is, namely, a fiction filled with the trend of the day, which is neither the spirit of Heidelberg nor that of Munich. Whatever wishes to become genuinely new connects itself not to Bachofen and his grave symbolism but instead to the heroic, most awe-inspiring event and theater of German intellectual history, to the self-overcoming of romanticism in and through Nietzsche; and nothing is more certain than that in the humanity of tomorrow, which must be not only beyond democracy but also beyond fascism, elements of a new idealism will grow strong enough to hold the ingredients of romantic nationalism in the scales.

Unfortunately the "humanity of tomorrow" prophesied by Thomas Mann had to wait for the time being: in the meantime, what was "timely" in Germany turned into the philistines' standoff against spirit and humanism.

5. Bäumler's Nietzsche interpretation is based on two premises. The first is that Nietzsche's genuine philosophy is concealed in his unpublished writings (as Bäumler knew them at the time). The second is that if one wishes to evaluate Nietzsche's works, "one must take over for oneself the logical arrangements for which he had no time." Bäumler's real desire was, of course, to prepare Nietzsche's published and unpublished writings as the foundation for a particular "Germanic" political philosophy written for him. Two questions that must be answered arise from this. First, did Bäumler correctly grasp the significance of Nietzsche's unpublished writings? Second, what becomes of Nietzsche on the basis of the "logical arrangements" of his ideas that Bäumler has taken over for himself? Above and beyond all else to be investigated, however, is whether Bäumler's *politicizing* of Nietzsche's thinking, as it was carried out, was justified.

6. Bäumler and Nietzsche's unpublished writings: Bäumler took over the compilation, which has made history under the name of "Will to Power," completely uncritically (in comparison to Jaspers, for example, but also Heidegger). He did this as well after World War II as editor of the widely known Kröner edition of Nietzsche's works. It is interesting, though depressing, to compare Bäumler's afterwords written before and after World War II. For example, after the German collapse he deleted the following sentences: "The young Nietzsche distinguished between a romantic, 'decorative' concept of culture and a Greek-German concept of culture as one of a higher nature. His final systematic philosophical work turns the Greek-German concept of education into intellectual reality." Yet precisely these sentences capture the "complete" Bäumler. In them the main features of his Nietzsche interpretation are recollected; the antihistorical equation of Greek and German (rejected by Nietzsche after the break with Wagner) is laid down as the foundation of Nietzsche's alleged "system" in the "Will to Power." Of course, after 1945 this was not up to date. Another passage from the afterword of 1930 may not go unmentioned: "In the current form of the 'Will to Power,' we can easily recognize one grand train of thought, and we can also distinguish between completely worked out smaller sections, but we must never forget that we do not have before us a finished book by Nietzsche. Even if many further improvements on this work are produced by a later, critical edition of the collected works, it still would not achieve what Nietzsche had

planned and what he himself would have been in a position to provide." Here Bäumler rightfully indicates the objective limits that doom every such reconstruction to failure, but he himself, by speaking of a "work," remains imprisoned in the fantasy that there was, hidden in the papers left behind, a mere torso of a work by Nietzsche under the title "Will to Power."

Ernst Horneffer has already shown that this work does not exist; Karl Schlechta did it once again fifty years later. We notice, nonetheless, the one time as with the other, a remarkable resistance to the matter that it really concerned. In the polemics of both times, two fundamentally different questions were being confused: on the one side, that concerning the significance of Nietzsche's unpublished writings for his philosophy; on the other side, that concerning the editions of those unpublished writings. Alternatively: on the one side, the will to power as philosophical doctrine; on the other side, the "Will to Power" as a work, as a "book." It is of course possible to hold fast to the central significance of the will to power in Nietzsche's thinking and simultaneously maintain that Nietzsche—as in fact the manuscripts prove—never wrote a work under this name (nor did he want to). Unfortunately, in 1907 Ernst Horneffer and his brother August, like Schlechta in 1956, were also not without guilt in this confusion. The Horneffer brothers (Nietzsche Archive editors of the first "Will to Power" in 1901, incidentally) inferred from their philological determination of the systematic work's non-existence Nietzsche's inability to write such a one and the fragmentary character and indeed short-winded nature of his thinking itself. For them, Nietzsche was not a systematic thinker and therefore not a philosopher in the genuine sense, since he was unable to write a systematic work. For Elisabeth Förster-Nietzsche and her literary followers, in contrast, Nietzsche was a philosopher precisely because he had left behind a systematic work, even if unfinished. Yet in the philistine equation "philosopher = system = a work," their two standpoints met each other most happily; a typical *querelle alle-mande* <German argument> arose by reason of an even more common *niaiserie allemande* <German foolishness>. Fifty years later, another former Nietzsche Archive editor, Karl Schlechta, adduced all the proof one would ever want that *the work* did not exist.[3] Schlechta, however, wanted to prove something further, namely, that Nietzsche's unpublished writings are uninteresting (of course, with the qualification, *so far as he knew them*). His opponents— Löwith, Wolfram von den Steinen, Pannwitz, and others—protested against this devaluation of the unpublished writings but once again confused the two questions: on the one side, the edition of the unpublished works (and here Schlechta was undoubtedly correct; there was no "Will to Power"); on the other side, the philosophical *significance* of the same unpublished writings (and here not a little could be directed against Schlechta).[4] Schlechta's service—having made the publication of the *Nachlaß* in chronological order his principal editorial goal, and having supported himself with irrefutable arguments—remains intact, even if he did not fulfill this goal with his edition. We must not overlook this in the polemical fervor concerning the philosophical significance of the unpublished writings.

Bäumler's publisher did not wish to abandon the "beautiful" title "Will to Power." And in 1964 Bäumler once again edited Nietzsche's "magnum opus." Of course, he did replace the previously quoted passage from the afterword as follows: "The 'Will to Power' that Gast left behind to us is a historical document that will keep its significance once all the handwriting has been deciphered and published. Someone who has lived as long in Nietzsche's proximity and participated as much as has Peter Gast has handed down to us something that will remain indispensable for the understanding and reconstruction of the 'Will to Power.'" The Bäumler of 1930 held fast to the compilation just as did the one of 1964, even with his qualification that Nietzsche did not carry out this "philosophical magnum opus"; Gast, however—Elisabeth Förster-Nietzsche's philosophically insignificant, will-less tool—became the indispensable mediator for the "reconstruction" of this magnum opus in 1964. We find a copy of Bäumler's book, with a dedication to Nietzsche's sister, in Weimar even today, but what she thought of the indispensable mediator of the "Will to Power" can be discovered, for instance, from a letter in which she expresses herself on the question of a future critical edition of Nietzsche's collected works. On September 16, 1915, Elisabeth Förster-Nietzsche wrote to her counsel, Karl Theodor Koetschau:

> Now it would be necessary, though, too, that the editorial activity begin anew from the beginning. [. . .] You can get some idea of how much there is to do in view of the manuscript only if you come here yourself and I can lay out for you the materials and future plans. Peter Gast was simply not a scholar, and even if he had the personal legacy, he still lacked philological scholarship, which he replaced with a sort of contrived willpower. But the most diverse, labor-intensive proofreading is unconditionally required, as long as I live, since I have the entire legacy of the collected edition and, unfortunately, also of the mistakes which have been made. <Frau Förster used the German word *Tradition* twice, which generally means simply "tradition," but I believe she meant that, although Gast had a Nietzsche legacy by virtue of having known the philosopher personally, she had the legal guardianship of the literary estate as her undeniable Nietzsche legacy; note that she did not assert her family bond as the legacy.>

We should take note of this letter's date; it was written scarcely five years after the appearance of the so-called critical edition of the "Will to Power" by Otto Weiss!

But Peter Gast himself conceded the scholarly untenability of his compilation, too. In his copy of Ernst Horneffer's short written work *Nietzsches letztes Schaffen,* which he used and is still preserved in Weimar, he commented on the remark therein, made with reference to "Will to Power," that "Nietzsche's manuscript must be edited abandoning any organization and arrangement, word-for-word, precisely as it is," by writing in the margin, "If it had been made public *in this fashion,* then Horneffer would have declared the exact opposite as proper. The public did not request such an edition. The experts, for whom such an edition would be genuine ecstasy, are in too small a minority." The unpublished fragments, above all those of the "Will to Power," had in reality a sort of esoteric value for Bäumler; for him, Nietzsche expressed his real opinions in the unpublished writings for the first time. He felt bolstered in this perspective by the artificially produced system of the "Will to Power"; for him it was a mere torso of a work that contained the authentic Nietzsche.

This very optic is nevertheless a distinctly falsifying one. As Horneffer had postulated in 1907, publication of the literary estate would have demonstrated the complete brittleness of the construction "Will to Power"; it would not, for instance, have brought about "many improvements" (thus Bäumler in 1930) but instead would have proved the *negative* significance of the "historical document" that Peter Gast allegedly left behind (thus Bäumler in 1964).

And this would have made the experts ecstatic—but probably not the crude falsifier à la Bäumler—when seen in the following way.

Nietzsche's manuscripts, read in their chronological order, result in an exact, nearly seamless presentation of his creation and his intentions. The unpublished works in their chronological form stand in an illuminating and complementary relation to the published (or ready-to-print) works. This is true for the *Nachlaß* of the eighties, too, from which the "Will to Power" was compiled. Two approaches to Nietzsche's unpublished writings are possible. One understands the totality of the handwritten notes—apart from their employment in the works—as the more or less unified expression of Nietzsche's thought in process. The other emphasizes Nietzsche's literary intentions, meaning his plans for publication, insofar as we may detail them; consequently, it searches for the preliminary material to his works and concerns itself with the reconstruction of their compositional process.

What Nietzsche incorporated in his works, what was simply rejected or postponed for later use, what was ultimately unused and why—all this is the subject the second approach seeks to investigate. Each approach must complement the other in a complete interpretation of Nietzsche's thinking. Nevertheless, the second one is the distinctive modus operandi of the critical edition, whose purpose it is to mirror, in a "objective" manner, the subtle differentiation among the notes in their relations to the published works or extant finished works. This occurs through publication of the rejected or unused notes left as "unpublished fragments" and through evaluation, in the critical apparatus, of the preliminary material to the works.[5]

This constitutes the sole possible manner, presented as succinctly as possible, of occupying oneself in a critical way with the manuscripts of a multifarious and multivalent author such as Nietzsche. This would not have enticed Bäumler the systematic thinker, of course; he far more diligently prepared Nietzsche's "main prose work"[6] and made it into a best-seller, which his publisher did not want to strike from their program even after World War II.

And with that we arrive at what became of Nietzsche when the "logical arrangement" of his ideas was taken over by someone else: that is, at what Bäumler called "Nietzsche's system."

7. "Nietzsche's System": One of the best current Nietzsche interpreters, Wolfgang Müller-Lauter, placed the following sharp-witted fragment by the romantic Friedrich Schlegel as the motto of his introductory observations to *Nietzsches Philosophie der Gegensätze* <*Nietzsche: His Philosophy of Contradictions*>: "It is equally disastrous for the mind to have a system and to have none. Surely, then, it will have to decide to combine the two."[7] That is spoken as if from the spirit of Nietzsche, who in fact fought the romantics but who had more than a merely negative relation to them.

In the summer of 1888 Nietzsche sketched a sort of preface to the book that he was directly thereafter to drop from his plans, namely, to the "Will to Power." This preface is particularly important because it informs us about Nietzsche's "intentions," much discussed by Bäumler, with all the clarity for which one might hope. According to the text of the current critical edition, it reads:

> A book for thinking, nothing else; it belongs to those for whom thinking is a delight, nothing else—
> That it is written in German is untimely, to say the least; I wish I had written it in French so that it might not appear to be a confirmation of the aspirations of the German *Reich*.
> The Germans of today are no thinkers any longer: something else delights and impresses them.
> The will to power as a principle might be intelligible to them.
> It is precisely among the Germans today that people think less than anywhere else. But who knows? In two generations one will no longer require

the sacrifice involved in any nationalistic squandering of power and in becoming stupid.

(Formerly I wished I had not written my *Zarathustra* in German.)*

I mistrust all systems and systematizers and move out of their path: perhaps one will still discover the system to this book, which I have *eluded*. . . .

The will to a system: expressed morally, a more refined corruption with
philosophers, an illness of character; expressed unmorally, his will to appear stupider than he is. Stupider, that means stronger, simpler, more dominating, less cultured, more commanding, more tyrannical.[8] <*End of Kaufmann's translation; the remainder is my translation.>

Müller-Lauter, too, observes the meaninglessness of Nietzsche's just-quoted
sketch in his subsequent discussion by commenting on the sentence "The will
to power as a principle might be intelligible to them" as follows: "For the un-
thinking Germans, talk of the will to power, insofar as power is discussed, could
seem to be 'a confirmation of the aspirations of the German *Reich*.' Besides, they
are accustomed to using the term 'will' in the sense of Schopenhauer and his
successors. Therefore, what Nietzsche says of the will to power must be *hard* for
them to understand. Is the will to power, then, precisely not a 'principle' in the
sense of traditional metaphysics?"[9] Not a trace of the intellectual tension that
Schlegel's phrase ("equally disastrous [. . .] to have a system and to have none")
betrays, and that we detect very easily in Nietzsche's ("perhaps one will still discover the system to this book, which I have *eluded*"), can be found in Bäumler's
account of "Nietzsche's system." What Bäumler required was a Nietzsche who
"appears stupider than he is," meaning, "stronger, simpler, more dominating,
less cultured, more commanding, more tyrannical." This Nietzsche cannot be
found, especially in the unpublished notes—always assuming that we have
decided to reconstruct not a *definite* Nietzsche but rather the entire Nietzsche
as he was, as he opened himself up in his intimate notes but also in his books,
his letters. In contrast, Bäumler wanted a fundamentally unproblematic Nietzsche, a Nietzsche in halves, not the Nietzsche who wrote of "a profound aversion to resting once and for all time in any one general observation on the
world. Magic of the opposing mode of thought: to never allow the appeal of
an enigmatic character to be lost."[10]

Bäumler designs his image of Nietzsche with the formulation of a "heroic realism." The matter was not such that Bäumler could have gained no insight whatsoever into Nietzsche's world of ideas, but there are only a few aspects that he brings up with relish. Nietzsche becomes the radical, pathetic
atheist; he has, in contrast to philosophers such as Plato, "courage in the face
of reality"; he, like Heraclitus, is a philosopher of Becoming and war, of the
will to power. Bäumler is a well-read Nietzschean; thus, for instance, he is able

to present the essential viewpoints of Nietzsche's epistemology with precision. The contemporary problematics of natural science, from which Nietzsche drew his insights concerning knowledge of the world, are of course completely lost to him in this regard. Here the historical sense that he lauds in Nietzsche appears to have gone astray. To mention only one name, it is as if Ernst Mach had never been Friedrich Nietzsche's contemporary at all, as if he had never written *Analysis of Sensation,* and as if Nietzsche had never read this book. And yet the natural scientist and philosopher Mach—well-known to Nietzsche— was the representative of a radical critique of causalism, of the mechanistic conception of physics in general at this time. Examples such as this could be presented at will. For Bäumler, Nietzsche the "good European" does not live in the Europe of the nineteenth century. He has precious little to do with great minds such as Stendhal, Baudelaire, Dostoyevsky, or Tolstoy or with other authors, poets, and philosophers such as Mérimé and Taine, the Goncourts and Renan, Sainte-Beuve and Flaubert, Guyau and Paul Rée, Bourget and Turgenev. The thoughtful and thought-provoking pronouncement that Nietzsche voiced in *Ecce Homo*—"Apart from my being a decadent, I am also the opposite"[11]—appears to him, once Bäumler has systematized Nietzsche, to have never been said.

Bäumler speaks of furthering one of Nietzsche's confrontations against consciousness <*Bewußtsein*>, against spirit <*Geist*>—a confrontation that Nietzsche led both in theoretical and practical spheres—in favor of "life" "on the guiding path of the body." What Bäumler wants to overlook is the painful tension that rules between the poles "spirit" and "life" in Nietzsche's entire philosophy, as when Nietzsche's *Daybreak* speaks of a passion for knowledge being the unconscious happiness of barbarism, or when his *Zarathustra* pronounces "spirit" and "life" as one inseparable unity—namely, in the statement "Spirit is life which cuts into itself."[12] Nietzsche the spiritualized philosopher appears to have never existed for Bäumler. Also, the two-thousand-year-long moral vivisection that Nietzsche received as his own personal premise does not exist for Bäumler. And yet Nietzsche himself defined his philosophy in the late preface to *Gay Science* with these words: "A philosopher who has traversed many kinds of health, and keeps traversing them, has passed through an equal number of philosophies; he simply *cannot* keep from transposing his states every time into the most spiritual form and distance: this art of transfiguration *is* philosophy. We philosophers are not free to divide body from soul as people do; we are even less free to divide soul from spirit."[13]

In the end Bäumler even had to allow the fundamental idea of *Zarathustra* to disappear from his systemization of Nietzsche: the doctrine of eternal recurrence of the same, the entire philosophy of Dionysus—and this even though Nietzsche occupied himself in his later notes with that fundamental idea, indeed, wanted to dedicate the fourth and last book of the "Will to Power" to it. In his final plan dated "Sils-Maria, on the last Sunday in the month of August, 1888," meaning directly before the abandonment of the publication of a work under the title "Will to Power,"[14] that fourth book bore the title "The Great Noon"; its third and final chapter was called "The Eternal Return." Bäumler resisted the inclusion of this idea; he identified the system that he had constructed, with help from Nietzsche's alleged magnum opus, the compiled "Will to Power," with Nietzsche's system and opined: "There is nothing in his philosophical system with which this eternalization of Becoming can be brought into connection—the idea of eternal recurrence exists in 'Will to Power' as a solitary erratic block."[15] This might be correct, if we possessed what Bäumler called "Nietzsche's system," or if we even had a book written by Nietzsche from which the idea could be removed as an erratic block. However, we have neither the system nor the book. But since the entire Nietzsche interests us and not Nietzsche's "system," we are forced to question Bäumler's interpretive skills. In this regard we will do well for ourselves to become acquainted with the weighty arguments of a far deeper interpreter—I mean Karl Löwith. Concerning Bäumler, Löwith wrote:

> The will as power takes over the function of the eternal recurrence, and in place of the self-willing Dionysian world. [. . .] This will made innocent is the dubious foundation of Bäumler's entire interpretation of Nietzsche's beheaded philosophy. [. . .] Only in the ring of this eternal recurrence of the same can the existence of the agonal, "wrestling" man, too, "will itself" beyond the first liberation from the "Thou shalt." Nietzsche's formula for this willing of the eternal recurrence is no mere will to "destiny" but *amor fati,*" whereas Bäumler can picture under the term "love" not love of eternity but only a bourgeois sentimentality.[16]

But once again we hear Bäumler's involuntary confession about the breakdown of his own interpretation on "Zarathustra's fundamental idea" (for so Nietzsche called the doctrine of eternal recurrence of the same in *Ecce Homo*): "Such a world [of eternal recurrence] can never be presented *philosophically,* and it is impossible, in this Dionysian world of 'eternal self-creating, eternal self-destroying, this world secret of doubled lust,' to recognize the *world as battle* [. . .] that world of conflict and tension which is ruled by the rigorous law of unity, of justice, which results in the meanwhile out of this tension."[17] All the worse for that world which Bäumler has prepared, we may well say!

Yet Nietzsche is readied to the condition where he can be used by Bäumler only under the presuppositions treated to this point. His "beheaded phi-losophy" can now easily be turned into a pseudorevolutionary gesture, into—as Bäumler expressed it—"a Siegfried-like attack on the urbanity of the West." Nietzsche has been transformed into "horned Siegfried"; every irony, every ambiguity, every sort of *Geist* or *esprit* has been driven from him. Nietzsche has become a warrior; he has even become a Teuton.

8. Nietzsche, Teuton and Political Thinker: With this we come to the most unpleasant part of our observations, for once Bäumler gave a one-sided view of Nietzsche's philosophy, he then presented him "as a political thinker," as an utter Teuton, intelligible only against the background of the mistaken hodge-podge of Rosenberg's *Mythos der 20. Jahrhunderts.* If there had been presentation of evidence here, however meager, where Bäumler troubled himself with Nietz-sche, now "every trace of intellectual integrity"—to use Nietzsche's words—has disappeared from his presentation. What remains is his evil <*übel*>, all too trans-parent political disposition.

Nietzsche's Teutonism is presented by Bäumler as an apodictic certainty. Here are a few samples.[18] "Nietzsche's philosophical this-world-liness must be seen in conjunction with its positing of a heroic goal. Nietzsche's Teutonism consists in this." "Nothing was more despicable to Nietzsche's Nordic, tense being than the Oriental notion of blissful peace. [. . .] His doctrine of the will is the most perfect expression of his Teutonism." "From the core thought of Nietzsche's Greek-German metaphysics comes forth his great doctrine that there is not *one* morality but only one morality for the *masters* and a morality of the *slaves*." "What a genuinely Germanic sentiment speaks from Zarathus-tra's defense of the people against the state. [. . .] Nietzsche is not aware that he declares the secret of German history" (hence Nietzsche as an "unself-con-scious Teuton"!). "The same aversion to the universality of the state that we notice in the Germans we find in the *Greeks,* who share a blood relation with the Germans." Bäumler sets the Greeks against the Romans and would very much like Nietzsche to join him in it, since they <the Romans> appear in his eyes as the founders of that non-German creation, the "state." Unfortunately none of it works without "a trustworthy reconstruction"—as Bäumler's pre-sentation in *Nietzsche als Politiker* calls it—of Nietzsche's political thought. The reconstruction appears, then, with Nietzsche's pensive pronouncements, as follows: "And even in my *Zarathustra* one will recognize a very serious ambi-tion for a *Roman* style, for the *aere perennius* in style. [. . .] To the Greeks I do not by any means owe similarly strong impressions; and—to come out right with it—they *cannot* mean as much to us as the Romans. One does not *learn* from the Greeks—their manner is too foreign, and too fluid, to have an imperative, a 'classical' effect. Who could ever have learned to write from a Greek?"[19]

Bäumler commented on this passage from Nietzsche's *Twilight of the Idols* with the following sentences: "The passage is completely misunderstood if one relates it simply to the Romans; it is solely the Romans as *literary ideal* that is meant, as masters of the noble form, of the perfect literary demeanor. Nietzsche [. . .] learned something essential [. . .] from them." "The substance of his doctrine is non-Roman, in fact anti-Roman—this is expressed most strongly in his animosity to the state as an institution" (96). Bäumler completely forgets that Nietzsche experienced "form" and "substance" as the same thing, that for him the "form" was the "thing itself <*Sache selbst*>." Bäumler is not even embarrassed by the following, still more unambiguous passage from *Antichrist,* in which Nietzsche declares what the Romans were to him:

> That which stood there *aere perennius,* the *imperium Romanum,* the most magnificent form of organization under difficult circumstances that has yet been achieved, in comparison with which all before and all afterward are mere botch, patchwork, and dilettantism—these holy anarchists made it a matter of "piety" for themselves to destroy "the world," that is, the *imperium Romanum,* until not one stone remained on the other, until even Teutons and other louts could become masters over it. [. . .] Christianity was the vampire of the *imperium Romanum:* overnight it undid the tremendous deed of the Romans—who had won the ground for a great culture that would have time. Is it not understood yet? The *imperium Romanum* [. . . ,] this most admirable work of art in the grand style, was a beginning; its construction was designed to prove itself through thousands of years: until today nobody has built like this again, nobody has even dreamed of building in such proportions *sub specie aeterni.*[20]

Bäumler's commentary to this runs thus: "Compared to the Jews and Christians, the Greeks and Romans move onto the same level. Against a stronger opponent, old rivals must also tolerate each other" (113). Thus a sort of people's front, or better put, the people's front against Christianity! And when Nietzsche the "unself-conscious Teuton" speaks of "Teutons and other louts," or of "Teutons and other lead boots," his attack on Christianity remains yet a Siegfried-like attack: "Nordic paganism is the vast, dark underground from which the bold warrior against Christian Europe emerges forth" (103). That is, of course, spoken mythically and darkly. The "thing itself" is quite another matter for him.

"Psychology is, for Nietzsche, always merely a weapon," says Bäumler at one point (111), because he cannot possibly fathom the full depths of his author's psychological vision; Nietzsche could not possibly be a psychologist because otherwise his educators would have to be sought somewhere entirely different from the forests of Germania, in France, for instance. But "he who knows Nietzsche"—after the fashion of Bäumler—must accept that he is an "admirer of French culture" (112). Psychology and French culture—we prefer once again to fall back on Nietzsche (who speaks of himself in this passage from *Ecce Homo*):

> The Germans [. . .] shall never enjoy the honor that the first *honest* spirit in the history of the spirit [. . .] should be counted one with the German spirit. The "German *Geist*" is for me bad air: I breathe with difficulty near the now instinctive uncleanliness *in psychologicis* which every word, every facial expression, of a German betrays. They have never gone through a seventeenth century of hard self-examination, like the French—a La Rochefoucauld and a Descartes are a hundred times superior in honesty to the foremost Germans—to this day they have not had a psychologist. But psychology is almost the measure of the *cleanliness* or *uncleanliness* of a race. [. . .] And when I occasionally praise Stendhal as a deep psychologist, I have encountered professors at German universities who asked me to spell his name.[21] <Kaufmann translation>

One must not speak of Nietzsche's "partiality to the Renaissance," in Bäumler's estimation, because otherwise one would also have to accept that Nietzsche was partial toward the "Mediterranean priesthood" and against the "advances of the Reformation." What is more, the aristocracy "in the upper and central Italian city-states [. . .] with *extreme likelihood* originated from Germanic blood" (97). I think that any commentary would only spoil this!

And when Nietzsche's patience came to an end with such sentences as "The Renaissance *and* Reformation constitute a whole only when taken together" (so much so in fact that he referred to this sentence by the "aesthetically Schwabian Vischer" as an "idiotic judgment *in historicis*"), Bäumler found that Nietzsche wanted not merely to "return to the Reformation" but instead to "go further than it" (112). In the fifth book of *Gay Science,* Nietzsche developed his position toward Luther and the Reformation with all the clarity for which we could hope, namely in the aphorism "The peasant rebellion of the spirit."[22] There we discover a characterization of the "*southern* freedom and enlightenment of the spirit" on which the edifice of the Church rests as well as on a "southern suspicion of nature, man, and spirit." "It seems the Germans do not understand the nature of a church." In regard to this sentence, intentionally negative to Germans, Bäumler finds hidden praise (109). It's too bad that Nietzsche moderated the tone of the final version of his aphorism! Otherwise Bäumler could have hardly been able to speak of any praise of the north and Teutonism. We read in the preliminary material to this aphorism: "But in the north one believes with Rousseau, 'man is good.'" Moreover, "Luther's Reformation was from its inception onward Nordic numbskullery."[23]

Enough! Enough! A little fresh air!—we would like to call out thus, as with Nietzsche at another occasion. Here I will break off my confrontation with Nietzsche's putative Teutonism; I almost want to apologize for having taken up time with such uninspiring polemics concerning rightfully expired concepts such as Romanism and Teutonism. For these concepts come from a more than dubious grasp of history and have nothing to do with integrity in research—which begins where ideology, meaning false consciousness, ends. Today they sound merely ridiculous and philistine. We must never forget in the meantime that Nietzsche's "forced conformity" <Gleichschaltung> to national socialist ideology was made possible in the first instance by preparatory work, most notably by Bäumler's propaganda book.

Marxism and Nietzsche: Georg Lukács's Interpretation

1. Whoever seeks to explain the significance of renewed interest in Nietzsche's philosophy will quickly discover two sorts of explanation for it. One sort: the received image of Nietzsche no longer suffices for us today, either as the crude simplification of his theory of will to power into *Realpolitik,* as a memorial to Brownshirts, or—in the better case—as an aesthetically sensitizing enthusiasm for his "style" or his philosophy of art. With regard to the other sort, we want moreover to move beyond even those grand philosophical interpretations originating in the thirties of our century, although far removed from Nazi pseudophilosophy (I refer to the interpretations by Karl Jaspers and Karl Löwith, in many respects still relevant today). And we also want to move beyond them to a new, critical mode of contemplating Nietzsche and of being fair to him.

Within the framework of this critical confrontation with the received image of Nietzsche, the interpretation by Georg Lukács occupies an especially important position for the following reasons. First, Lukács was one of the most significant Marxist theoreticians of our time, and as a philosophy and worldview, Marxism plays a decisive role in our times across the entire world. Second, Georg Lukács's interpretation of Nietzsche has exercised a very powerful influence on Marxist and non-Marxist scholars. This is so not least of all because his sharp-witted applications of the Marxist method to the most diverse areas of cultural history, philosophy, and aesthetics have long been the orthodox ones and continue to have such an influence today—even where his Marxism, as a consequence of his views about the events of 1956, is no longer undisputed, hence, in the socialist lands (wherein Hungary itself has constituted an exception for several years).

The difficulties confronting the application of the Marxist method to phenomena of the so-called superstructure are well known. A principled confrontation with the type of historical-materialist approach that Lukács applies to art, literature, and philosophy, as well as the manner in which he does so, does not fall within the framework of my discussions. But perhaps they will be able to afford a tangible concrete contribution to this general issue.

2. We find occasional references to Nietzsche in all the writings of Lukács, including the "pre-Marxist" essays of the collection *The Soul and the Forms*. These references bear testimony to a deep-running knowledge of and unceasing confrontation with Nietzsche that would warrant the efforts of a complete reconstruction. The works in which Lukács expressly gave his Nietzsche interpretation, however, are the following:

1. the essay from 1934 titled "Nietzsche as Predecessor of the Fascist Aesthetic," later reprinted in the collection *Essays on the History of Aesthetics;*
2. an essay from the war years, written in 1943, with the title "German Fascism and Nietzsche," which five years later—1948—was to start a series of "essays toward a new German ideology," as the subtitle to the collected volume *Schicksalswende* declared; and finally,
3. the comprehensive work *Die Zerstörung der Vernünft*. Here Lukács delivers the "new German ideology" announced in the subtitle to *Twist of Fate* in the form of a monograph on—as per its subtitle—the "path of irrationalism from Schelling to Hitler." (Incidentally, this subtitle recalls the work of the American historian Peter Viereck that appeared in 1941 under the title *Metapolitics: From the Romantics to Hitler* and that likewise provided an intellectual genealogy of Hitlerism wherein Nietzsche—in polemics against the Nazi pseudophilosophers and historians—is nonetheless distanced quite decisively from the intellectual predecessors of national socialism.) The key chapter to *Die Zerstörung der Vernünft* is doubtless the one about Nietzsche: "Nietzsche as the Founder of Imperialistic Irrationalism."

The three cited depictions of Nietzsche are as many stages in one increasingly more powerful and consequential speech for the prosecution of Nietzsche.

If Lukács attempted, especially in the first of his Nietzsche essays, to ascertain some measure of "difference" between Nietzsche and national socialist ideology, and even conceded misuse at the hands of Alfred Rosenberg and Alfred Bäumler, he later no longer saw any essential difference. Nietzsche's thought became ceaselessly identified with fascist and imperialistic ideology because it had been on the path of a so-called indirect apologetics for capitalism, on the path to an ideological anticipation of fascism and imperialism. In fact, there are cases in which Lukács's Nietzsche is more of a strict national socialist than is Alfred Bäumler's Nietzsche. For instance, when, as has been shown, Bäumler sought to simply discard from Nietzsche's philosophy what was to him the personally disagreeable idea of "eternal recurrence of the same" in favor of the far more personally appealing principle of will to power (more on this principle later!), Lukács hurried to point out the allegedly fascist characteristics of this idea.

Lukács delivered his final and most radical pronouncement against Nietzsche in *Die Zerstörung der Vernünft*. Let us consider this pronouncement seriously. I devote the following reflections to him, although from the onset, they do not go beyond a discussion supported by the most concrete, critical, and philological data possible.

3. Our subject matter has truly far-reaching implications, because it concerns not only the general problem of the relationship between what Marxists call the "economic-social base" and what they call the "superstructure" but also, in connection with the same problem, the still more general question of the relationship between materialist conceptions and philosophy in general. This question, genuinely at the frontiers of Marxist philosophy, concerns itself, in fact, with the extent to which the historicity of all human thought postulated by historical materialism logically implies its own historical conditionality as well, hence the historicity of Marxism itself. Thus, Antonio Gramsci, the great Italian theoretician of Marxism, wrote that historical materialism "developed as an expression of the inner contradictions that tear our society apart [. . .], unable to abandon the ground of those contradictions"; it is itself provisional, because of the "historicity of every conception of the world and of life." One could even maintain—I quote again from Gramsci—that "while the entire system of historical materialism can be invalidated in a united world, many idealistic worldviews, or at least several aspects of them, which in the realm of necessity are utopian, could become a reality."[24] We consider true of some things from Marx and Engels, but not—so far as we know—from Lukács, what Engels once said of Hegel: "In human history, unending progress is the single true form of existence recognized by the *Geist,* only assuming an end, fantastically, to this development—in the presentation of the Hegelian philosophy."[25]

A fundamental pillar of Lukács's Nietzsche interpretation is what he calls the "indirect apologetic." I quote from the conclusion to the chapter on Kierkegaard in *Die Zerstörung der Vernunft:*

The indirect apologetic refers, in general, to entirely rejecting, negating reality (society in general) in such a way that the final result of this negation leads to an affirmation of capitalism, or at least to its benevolent toleration. In the realm of morality, the indirect apologetic defames, above all, social behavior, especially every tendency to want to change society. It achieves this goal through isolation of the individual and through erection of such a higher ethical ideal that, before its sublimity, the petty nullity of social norms would appear to fade away and distinctions between them blur. But should such an ethic work a real, wide, and deep effect, then it would have not only to erect such an ideal but also simultaneously (even with the help of ethically sublime arguments) to exclude compliance with it. Because realization of such an ideal could place the decadent bourgeois individual before just as personally challenging a task as was social behavior. The reality of the disconnective function of the indirect apologetic would become problematic in this way.[26]

In this way Lukács gained two sorts of results in relation to Nietzsche. On the one side, he refuted in advance any attempt to portray Nietzsche as a sharp-witted critic of bourgeois society and morality, as Thomas Mann, for instance, undertook in his 1947 essay "Nietzsche's Philosophy in Light of Contemporary Events." On the other side, Nietzsche, as soon as he abandons society and morality or considers society and morality in the light of several of his philosophy's unique frontier notions—for instance, "eternal return of the same," the "overman," the "will to power," "nihilism," and so forth—must push forward the "indirect apologetic" of capitalism. That which informs the issues of Lukács's interpretation is not what Nietzsche actually said or meant but rather what he *must* have said and meant within the framework of an ideological, ostensibly Marxist publication, which in itself allows no concrete verification, since everything has already been prescribed and predetermined in it. The argumentation with which Lukács introduced his observations about Nietzsche, is, from this perspective, typical unto paradox, Nietzsche's lifework being, so we are told, a continual polemic against Marxism—and that despite the fact that he never read a line of Marx or Engels, in fact never knew of the terms "Marxism" and "historical materialism" at all! This circumstance may, nonetheless, be explained away. "Against the class enemy," Lukács thought, "all things appear permissible; here all objective morality ceases."[27] And literally: "What Engels said of lawyers is true in a higher degree for philosophy, 'The mirroring of economic relations as legal principles [. . .] proceeds without their becoming conscious for the ones who perform actions, which lawyers imagine to operate with *a priori* principles, though they are but economic reflexes.'"[28]

Lukács quotes from a letter of October 27, 1890, from Engels to Conrad Schmidt, in which, contrary to Lukács's claim ("What Engels said of lawyers is true in a higher degree for philosophy"), Engels nevertheless does not tire of warning about pedantry "concerning all this primordial nonsense"—Engels means "seeking economic causes for ideological areas that hover still higher in the clouds [higher than jurisprudence]," such as "religion, philosophy, etc."

In view of this statement, to speak of "economic reflexes" as Lukács does seems to me highly questionable. The elder Engels directed his polemics (as we may infer from letters to Joseph Bloch on December 21, 1890; to Franz Mehring on July 14, 1893; and to Heinz Starkenburg on January 25, 1894) against the simplifying enthusiasm of many "Marxists" who set off blustering right away, who degrade historical materialism by mechanical and dogmatic applications to—as he says—"empty phrases." This is especially explicit in his letter to Joseph Bloch: "According to the materialist conception of history, production and reproduction of real life is the determining moment in history *in the last instance.* Neither Marx nor I have ever maintained more than this."

4. According to Lukács, Nietzsche availed himself of two means to refine his unself-conscious, "indirect apologetic" for developing imperialism and fascism: the aphoristic, unsystematic form of writing and *myth*. Or put more properly: Nietzsche expressed his mythmaking in his preference for the aphorism, since in this way he makes everything into myth: history, society, natural science, and indeed even his "agnosticism"; there is, in addition, his myths of "will to power," "overman," "death of God," and so on.

Karl Löwith once remarked quite rightly about Ernst Bertram: "The historical insight of Hegel and Burckhardt that nothing distinguishes us so much from antiquity as precisely the lack of a truly mythical way of thinking, is ignored in Bertram's presentation."[29] This insight of Hegel and Burckhardt was also shared by Nietzsche, so much so that it had to destroy his youthful belief in the possibility of a resurrection of Teutonic myth in the Wagnerian form and in the tenability of myths in general. This is the meaning of the second of the *Unfashionable Observations,* that there is no longer any possibility for modern man to win back the limiting—and therefore life-promoting—horizon. The "historical illness" was portrayed there, though, by one who—as he says of himself—did not whatsoever renounce the "historical sense." And whoever knows the preliminary material to *Thus Spoke Zarathustra* knows that the "ugliest man" in part 4 personifies this "historical sense";[30] this "ugliest man" is now the "murderer of God," meaning that the historical sense has killed God, the myth of myths. After that, there is no longer a return to any sort of myth whatsoever! The happiness that myth afforded the men of antiquity is closely related to the "happiness without knowledge" of barbarism, but Nietzsche said in a previously cited aphorism from *Daybreak* (number 429): "Knowledge has in us been transformed into a passion which shrinks at no sacrifice and at bottom fears nothing but its own extinction; we believe in all honesty that all mankind must believe itself more exalted and comforted under the compulsion and suffering of *this* passion than it did formerly, when envy of the coarser contentment that follows in the train of barbarism had not yet been overcome. [. . .] Yes, we hate barbarism—we would all prefer the destruction of mankind to a regression of knowledge" <see this volume, p. 58>. In his unpublished writings from 1875 until his mental collapse at the beginning of January 1889, Nietzsche himself wrote down accounts regarding what his Wagnerian and mythical period meant to him. We will take only three such pieces of evidence. 1883: "After my first phase smirks the face of Jesuitism: I mean, the conscious holding fast to an illusion and the compulsory application of the same as the basis of culture. [. . .] Wagner was bagged by this very hazard. [. . .] To the position of philosopher, I would raise the free spirit, who, *without turning Jesuit,* nonetheless penetrates the irrational constitution of existence."[31] 1885: "One day—it was during the summer of 1876—a disgust and insight suddenly came to me: I have mercilessly surpassed the beautiful objects of desire and dreams as I had loved them in my youth; mercilessly I continued on my way, a path of 'knowledge at any cost.'"[32] 1888: "Around 1876 I was terrified to see all I had desired hitherto *compromised,* as I grasped which way Wagner was going now [. . .]: what I valued most in Wagner was the bit of Antichrist that he represents with his art and style."[33]

The emphasis certainly shifted in the course of these years from the attempt—*without turning Jesuit*—not only to penetrate the illogical character of existence but to affirm it as well. The experiment itself, though, remained supported by what Nietzsche called the "passion for knowledge" and contains nothing mythical or of mythmaking in itself. We find myth, of course—the Nietzsche myth—in many Nietzsche interpretations, from Klages, to Bertram, and up to Bäumler and even Lukács. What we scarcely ever find, by contrast, is an attempt to historically and critically approach the real Nietzsche living at a definite time.

5. We discover two ideas at the frontiers of Nietzsche's philosophy that can awaken impressions of mythmaking: that of the "eternal return of the same" and that of the "overman." And yet, if one were to refer less to the crude simplifications that these ideas have undergone in the heads of literati, fashion philosophers, and other "Nietzscheans" of the late prior century and rather give them the significance that Nietzsche gave them in the framework of his observations, then one would prefer myth less and knowledge more.

How did Nietzsche regard his idea of the eternal return of the same? He said it himself: as the ultimate conclusion of the mechanistic worldview, hence in close association with the natural scientific notions of his time. (I am setting aside the question as to what actual philosophical meaning befits this idea: I want only to emphasize its origin—the historical origin, mind you, not the personal—of the experience at Sils-Maria in August of 1881.) That this is so is verified from a corner that we certainly cannot suspect as being sympathetic to myth, namely, from Engels. He wrote in a note to his *Die Dialektik der Natur* (which may be dated to the period between 1878 and 1883!): "Impossibility of conceiving the infinite. As soon as we say matter and motion are not created and are indestructible, we are saying that the world exists as infinite progress, i.e., in the form of bad infinity, and thereby we have conceived all of this process that is to be conceived. At the most, the question still arises whether this process is an eternal repetition—in a great cycle—or whether the cycles have upward and downward portions"<Dutt translation>. One page later, Engels quoted from the Italian of Abbé Galiani: "Questa infinità che le cose non hanno in progresso, la hanno in giro" ("This infinite, which things do not have in progress, they have in circling").[34] This frontier notion of an "eternal repetition of the same" <ewige Wiederholung desselben> does not inspire Engels further, yet it is—and it comes to—a thoroughly scientific notion that has nothing to do with myth. For Nietzsche it has ramifications, one of those ramifications being the overman. The world of immanence, the world after the death of God, the world, therefore, of natural and human history (the historical sense—the murderer of myths): to man it poses the challenge of a qualitative change, of a radical overcoming of himself. Nothing signifies the overman other than that he must be able to bear life—Nietzsche denied it of himself once—to the finale of just this mythical period, the time of God, but also of art, morality, and all remaining illusions. Lukács's explanations quite properly demonstrate, contra Bäumler, that there is no contradiction between the idea of eternal recurrence and that of the will to power. In this way, however, Nietzsche became a still better fascist for Lukács than for Bäumler:

> Nietzsche's pseudorevolution originates in the "innocence of becoming," the crossing-over of the bourgeoisie from the liberal period of "security" to the "grand politics" of the struggle for world domination. With the overload of revaluation pathos, however, this upheaval is still merely a pseudorevolution, a mere intensification of reactionary contents of capitalism, embellished with revolutionary gestures. And eternal recurrence has the function of explicating this myth's ultimate meaning; the existing social order, created as it is by barbarian tyrants, is said to be the decisive one, a conscious realization of which failing in most cases and being only now and then partially successful. When one considers the methodological structure of this intellectual system, one observes that it corresponds perfectly with Hitler's, only [let us pay close attention to this "only"!] that, for Hitler, Chamberlain's racial theory is built in as the new explanatory element

to replace eternal recurrence. Nietzsche's intellectual proximity to Hitlerism cannot, therefore, become lost on the world due to refutation by the false claims, fabrications, and so on, of Bäumler or Rosenberg: it is objectively still greater than they have imagined this to be.[35]

6. I resist Georg Lukács's total political revision of Nietzsche because I give priority to a method that seeks foremost to understand this thinker in and through his own times and, from their problems, to explain the framework of his issues. Discussions about Darwinism in Nietzsche's day, for instance, may afford us a more valid perspective than the purely intellectual historical genealogy by which Lukács perceived in Nietzsche's views about Darwin "the methodological 'model' for fascist racial theory and especially for its practical application." To this end Lukács cites the following passage from *Twilight of the Idols* (one of Nietzsche's last works, written in 1888): "Assuming, however, that there is such a struggle for existence—and, indeed, it occurs—its result is unfortunately the opposite of what Darwin's school desires, and of what one *might* perhaps desire with them—namely, in favor of the strong, the privileged, the fortunate exceptions. The species do *not* grow in perfection: the weak prevail over the strong again and again, for they are the great majority—and they are also more *intelligent.*"[36] We may compare this passage with the following, which comes from the pen of an illustrious Nietzsche contemporary:

> Darwin's mistake lies precisely in lumping together in "natural selection" or "survival of the fittest" two absolutely separate things:
>
> 1. Selection by the pressure of over-population, where perhaps the strongest survive in the first place, but where the weakest in many respects can also do so.
> 2. Selection by greater capacity of adaptation to altered circumstances, where the survivors are better suited to these *circumstances,* but where this adaptation as a whole can mean regress just as well as progress (for instance adaptation to parasitic life is *always* regress).
>
> The main thing: that each advance in organic evolution is at the same time a regression, fixing *one-sided* evolution and excluding evolution along many other directions. This, however, *a basic law.*"

The contemporary's name is Friedrich Engels, once again. The note comes from *The Dialectics of Nature.*[37]

We must not overlook the differences, neither here, nor with all the previous cited parallel passages, nor with those parallel passages that could be quoted in addition. But it seems important to me that we recapture the atmosphere in which Nietzsche's philosophy breathed, not to carry out any sort of ideological mission against it—whether for condemnation or absolution.

7. For Lukács, the "fight against the proletariat worldview" represents the entire content of Nietzsche's philosophy. But where was this "worldview" hiding, that Nietzsche should have known and fought against it? Lukács has already told us: Nietzsche fought against it without knowing about it!

I recommend that we introduce some history here, too. Nietzsche had a very limited knowledge of the socialist movement in Germany. Still further, he grew up in an environment—the parsonage in Röcken and later the administrative city of Naumburg—that we might very well describe with Thomas Mann's later famous phrase "inwardness supported by power": a nonpolitical environment par excellence, indeed, a petty bourgeois one. Then in Leipzig and Basel, Nietzsche shared all the political prejudices of his academic colleagues. When he spoke of "the masses" and "public opinion" or "the herd types," he understood by this—according to one of his last published notes—the philistine, the "middle class" (hence, his own class).

As a young man Nietzsche admired the "irrational grandeur" of Lassalle (who died in a duel in 1864 when Nietzsche was twenty years old). We may very well imagine that socialism was a topic of discussion with the Wagners in Tribschen every now and then between 1869 and 1872: Cosima Wagner had known Lassalle, Lothar Bucher, and Georg Herwegh—through her <former> husband Hans von Bülow—during her Berlin days. In addition, the old revolutionary of 1848, Richard Wagner, may have talked occasionally of his acquaintance with Bakunin and his experiences during the Dresden uprising of May 1849. The idealist Malwida von Meysenbug mediated Nietzsche's knowledge of Alexander Herzen's works and certainly of other revolutionary, more or less socialist literature of Europe at that time. We also know that Nietzsche had a conversation with a Proudhonist in Basel during 1875, at the home of his motherly friend Marie Baumgartner. It remains for us to mention that a series of later leaders of Austrian worker movements in the seventies were Nietzsche admirers: Heinrich Braun, Victor Adler, and Engelbert Pernerstorfer.[38] (Thus was fulfilled what had been said by Marxist Franz Mehring, to the great horror of Georg Lukács in *The Destruction of Reason,* that Nietzsche has been a good preparation for becoming socialist, specifically for the discontented bourgeois youth.)

Of Marx, Nietzsche could have known at most only the name, if he had in fact read the entire thick tome by Karl Eugen Dühring, *Kritische Geschichte der Nationalökononomie und des Socialismus*—which is doubtful despite this work's presence in his library. Through Dühring's other writings and the personal proximity of his own brother-in-law, Bernhard Förster, Nietzsche knew what was for him—understandably—an especially unappetizing variation of socialism: the anti-Semitic one.

It will not surprise us, then, when, from the period of *Human, All Too Hu-*

man onward, meaning from 1878 until the end of his sane life in January 1889, Nietzsche raised his famous dictum "As little state as possible!" against the socialism known to him. And at that time in the German social democracy, the question of the state did not command very much clarity, and the decisive document on the subject—Marx's *Critique of the Gotha Programme* (1875)—was published for the first time in 1891, sixteen years after its composition (and additionally not in its full text!). This "whole programme," wrote Marx in his critique, "for all its democratic clang, is tainted through and through by the servile belief in the state of Lassalle's sect, or, what is no better, by democratic miracle-faith, or rather it is a compromise between these two kinds of miracle-faith, both equally remote from socialism."[39] The socialism of which Marx spoke existed at that time—as a theory—only in London, in fact, only for him and for Engels.

At the most Nietzsche himself knew—recall the political narrowness of an academician at that time—either state socialism à la Lassalle or democratic phrases of equality, but mediated by the political agitation of the *Eisenachers,* for instance. And in fact it is not difficult to find quotations against the equality of man in Nietzsche's writings, as Lukács does. But the formulations of equality popular in the German social democracy had, in Marx's estimation, "become obsolete rubbishy phrases." And in March 1875 Engels wrote to August Bebel: "'The removal of all social and political inequality' is also a very questionable phrase in place of 'the abolition of all class differences.'"[40] As if more evidence were needed, we read in his notes to *Anti-Dühring* several years later: "To willingly set up 'Equality = Justice' as the highest principle and ultimate truth is absurd. Equality merely exists as a contrast to inequality, justice to injustice; they are, therefore, still linked to ancient history and to ancient society itself." And further:

> Mankind must bring about several generations of social development under a communist regime and under increased aid, until this insistence on equality and justice appears just as laughable as does the insistence on noble, royal privilege, etc., today; until the opposition of the old inequality versus old positive justice has disappeared, even if only to a new, transitional justice out of practicality; until whoever insists on his equal and fair share of the product, on entirely pedantic grounds, shall be doubly mocked. [. . .] And where, then, will equality and justice persevere, other than in the rag drawer of historical memory? Since the same are crucial today for agitation, they are not eternal truths. [. . .] Further, the abstract theory of equality is, and shall remain for the long term, an absurdity. It would not occur to any socialist proletariat or theoretician to wish for an abstract equality between himself and a bushman or Tierra del Fuegan, or even between himself and a peasant or semi-feudal day laborer; and from

that moment on, when it has been overcome on European soil alone, the abstract standpoint of equality itself will be overcome.

Engels expressly declares once more: "The equality of the bourgeoisie (disso-lution of class privilege) is very different from that of the proletariat (dissolu-tion of the classes themselves). Further examined, meaning, abstractly con-sidered, this latter type of equality becomes nonsense."[41]

8. In this way the problematic of equality was nuanced and complex for Engels and Marx; for the practical socialists in Germany and Europe at that time—for understandable reasons—the agitation was simplified and direct-ed toward propagandistic effect. But Nietzsche was familiar with only the lat-ter, and with them never precisely! It is no use, then: Nietzsche's battle against the proletarian worldview, of which Lukács speaks, takes place in the intellec-tual, historical, almost metaphysical constructions from Lukács himself, in-sofar as every philosophy of history that avoids a real confrontation with his-tory and its facts is, in the final analysis, a disguised metaphysic. On historical grounds, in any case, that battle never took place.

This becomes all the more evident when we more closely examine the ar-gumentation with whose assistance Lukács seeks to interpret, in his own sense, Nietzsche's relationship to the concrete German history of his day, hence Bis-marck's era. For him, Nietzsche's critique of Bismarck's *Reich* is a critique from the right. (Incidentally, exactly the same thing was said—with different circum-stances—by Bäumler's national socialist Nietzsche interpretation.) To unmask Nietzsche as the preacher of Wilhelmian imperialism, Lukács quotes from the philosopher's letter to his sister of October 1888. The quoted passage runs: "Our new kaiser [meaning Wilhelm II] pleases me very much more. [. . .] He would easily understand the will to power as a principle *<Der Wille zur Macht als Prin-zip wäre ihm schon verständlich>*." In Lukács's estimation, understanding the will to power means understanding the "ever increasingly powerful imperialistic strivings of the German bourgeoisie; and this understanding"—according to Lukács—is what "Nietzsche misses in Bismarck."[42]

We must immediately notice that Lukács quoted this passage from corre-spondence in a tendentious manner, because he intentionally left out the reason Nietzsche found something attractive about the young kaiser: specifi-cally, the position Wilhelm II initially took up against court minister Adolf Stöcker and the anti-Semites. But concerning the sentence "He would easily understand the will to power as a principle," we must make note of the follow-ing: *the alleged letter of October 1888 to the sister is a fabrication.* Of course, we do not mean that this letter was a complete falsification; Nietzsche's sister constructed it with a technique of quotation montage, that is, from drafts of letters to other persons, out of unpublished passages that were still unknown, and so on. However, we do have the testimony of one of Elisabeth Förster-Nietzsche's close collaborators, Nietzsche's pupil and later editor, Peter Gast, to this of all sentences, "He would easily understand the will to power as a principle." On January 26, 1910, he wrote to Ernst Holzer, a fellow Nietzsche Archive colleague at that time:

> With regard to the chapter, "Frau Förster's Sense of Truth," I simply must tell you of an instance that I recalled just now and that brings a smile to my face. Why should not one, as a former archivist, jointly support everything that one could *never* support as a decent human being? When we were print-ing the second volume of the biography in 1904, Nietzsche's letter entered into consideration, the one in which our kaiser, twenty-nine years old at that time, was praised for disparaging remarks about anti-Semites and the *Kreuz* newspaper. Well, you know how frequently she burned with desire to interest the kaiser in Nietzsche and to possibly get him to make an ac-knowledging remark in Nietzsche's direction. So what did she do toward this goal? . . . She inserted a sentence that *did not exist at all* in the relevant letter: she wrote, "He would easily understand the will to power as a princi-ple." You will recall where this sentence comes from: out of the preface sketch to the "Will to Power," which is printed in volume 14, page 420. The composition of this sketch [. . .] belongs among the most difficult tasks in deciphering Nietzsche. The Horneffers had attempted it before me, but their deciphered text had more lacunae than words. They fully wrote out *this very sentence alone!* Such preliminary work more often than not proves a hin-drance rather than a furtherance to the one who comes afterward. Enough then: as the final arbitrator in deciphering this piece, it did not escape my attention that the Horneffers' decipherment, "They [Germans] would eas-ily understand the will to power as a principle," could in no way be correct within the context of the preface sketch. And when I had the notebook back in my hands in April of last year, my suspicion was *confirmed* that it did in-deed unquestionably have to read "hardly understood <*schwer verständ-lich*>" instead of "easily understood <*schon verständlich>*"! Isn't the joke *very* good indeed that, if Frau Förster wanted to be exact, she would now have had to print, "He [the kaiser] would hardly understand the will to power as a principle"?![43]

The objective basis for Georg Lukács's one-sided Nietzsche interpretation comes into view here. Lukács has—this is what associates him with Bäumler—undervalued the entire philological problematic connected to Nietzsche's "philosophical main prose work," "Will to Power," and to the editing of his unpublished works in general. Karl Schlechta rightfully emphasized that the overestimation of the unpublished writings within Nietzsche's works is a distinctive trait of those who wanted Nietzsche to fit the momentary needs of the day. We should qualify this determination by saying that it is not valid for serious Nietzsche interpretations, such as those of Karl Löwith, Karl Jaspers, Edgar Salin, and others, but all the more for fascist Nietzsche interpretations. They and their kind in no way consider the complete *Nachlaß* as a problem but instead rest perfectly content with the dilettantish compilation by Elisabeth Förster-Nietzsche and her tool until 1909, Peter Gast, both of whom compiled "Will to Power" out of remaining fragments from the eighties. For this reason, it seems to me that the new Nietzsche edition should be understood within the progress of that new valuation of Nietzsche's thought about which I spoke at the beginning of this second section.

Notes

1. See R. F. Krummel, *Nietzsche und der deutsche Geist* (Berlin, 1974), 65f.

2. See R. Bollmus, *Das Amt Rosenberg und seine Gegner: Zum Machtkampf im nationalsozialistischen Herrschaftssystem* (Stuttgart, 1970).

3. See Karl Schlechta's "Philologischen Nachbericht," *Friedrich Nietzsche, Werke in drei Bänden* (München, 1956), vol. 3, pp. 1393ff.

4. Compare this to Eckhard Heftrich, *Nietzsches Philosophie, Identität von Welt und Nichts* (Frankfurt, 1962), esp. pp. 273–75, 277, and 290–95.

5. See KGW VIII$_1$, page vif., as well as this volume, page 80.

6. The noteworthy phrase is from Elisabeth Förster-Nietzsche, introduction to volume 9 (1906) of *Nietzsches Werken* (Leipzig, 1905 ff.), the so-called Taschen-Ausgabe <pocketbook edition>, p. vii: "Already in the spring of 1883, when I was with my brother in Rome, he said that, once *Zarathustra* was finished, he wanted to write his theoretical-philosophical main prose work."

7. See Wolfgang Müller-Lauter, *Nietzsche: Seine Philosophie der Gegensätze und die Gegensätze seiner Philosophie* (Berlin, 1971), 1. <See Müller-Lauter, *Nietzsche: His Philosophy of Contradictions and the Contradictions of His Philosophy*, trans. David J. Parent (Urbana: University of Illinois Press, 1999), 1.>

8. KGW VIII$_2$, 9[188], pp. 114f. Compare also in this volume pages 166–68. <Walter Kaufmann does not indicate that he truncated this passage in his translation, pp. xxii–xxiii.>

9. See Wolfgang Müller-Lauter, <*Nietzsche,*> 28 <Parent trans., 18>.

10. KGW VIII$_1$, 2[155], p. 140 (autumn 1886).

11. KGW VI$_3$, p. 264.

12. KGW VI$_1$, p. 130.

13. KGW V$_2$, p. 17.

14. Compare to this page 53.

15. See A. Bäumler, *Nietzsche der Philosoph und Politiker*, 82.

16. See Karl Löwith, *Nietzsches Philosophie der ewigen Wiederkehr des Gleichen* (Stuttgart, 1965), 212 <*Nietzsche's Philosophy of the Eternal Recurrence*, trans. J. Harvey Lomax (Berkeley: University of California Press, 1987), 212>.

17. Bäumler, 84.

18. The numbers in parentheses refer to pagination in Bäumler's book.

19. KGW VI₃, pp. 148f. <*Twilight of the Idols,* "What I Owe the Ancients," secs. 1, 2>.

20. KGW VI₃, pp. 243f. <*The Antichrist,* sec. 58>.

21. KGW VI₃, pp. 359f. <*Ecce Homo,* trans. Walter Kaufmann (New York: Vintage Books, 1967), "Case of Wagner," sec. 3>.

22. See *Gay Science,* aphorism 358.

23. See KSA 14, p. 274.

24. See Antonio Gramsci, *Quaderni del carcere,* critical edition of the Gramsci Institute, ed. Valentino Gerratano (Turin, 1975), vol. 2, pp. 1487ff. <Montinari translated the Italian into German in his book.>

25. See Friedrich Engels, *Dialektik der Natur, Marx-Engels Werke* (MEW) (Berlin, 1958ff.), vol. 20, p. 504 <*Works of Marxism-Leninism,* trans. C. P. Dutt (New York: International, 1938), 248>.

26. Georg Lukács, *Die Zerstörung der Vernunft* (Berlin, 1955), pp. 242f.

27. Ibid., p. 247.

28. Ibid.

29. Löwith, <*Nietzsches Philosophie,*> p. 206 <Lomax translation, 204>.

30. KGW VII₃, p. 76.

31. KGW VII₁, p. 533.

32. Variation to fragment 2[9], KGW VIII₁, p. 68. See vol. XIV, p. 386, of the *Großoktavausgabe.*

33. KGW VIII₂, p. 18.

34. MEW, vol. 20, pp. 503f. and 505 <Dutt translation, p. 248>.

35. Lukács, <*Zerstörung,*> p. 304.

36. KGW VI₃, p. 114 <Kaufmann translation>.

37. MEW, vol. 20, p. 564 <Dutt translation, p. 236>.

38. KGW IV₄ (M. Montinari, "Nachbericht zur vierten Abteilung"), pp. 12 and 36f.

39. MEW, vol. 19, p. 31 <Dutt translation, p. 21>.

40. MEW, vol. 19, p. 7 <Dutt translation, p. 31; and Karl Marx, *Critique of the Gotha Programme,* in *Works of Marxism-Leninism,* vol. 11, trans. C. P. Dutt, rev. trans., p. 10>.

41. MEW, vol. 20, p. 580f. <*Anti-Dühring* and *Dialectics of Nature,* in *Works of Marxism-Leninism,* trans. C. P. Dutt, p. 314.>

42. Lukács, <*Zerstörung,*> p. 270.

43. Compare KGW VIII₂, p. 475 (Konkordanz, Anm. 2).

SOURCES

1. "Reading Nietzsche": lecture held in Munich (September 1981), at the Wissenschaftskolleg in Berlin (January 1982), and at the Philosophy Faculty of the University of Tübingen (February 1982).

2. "The New Critical Edition of Nietzsche's Collected Works" appeared as "Nietzsche" in *Literatur-Magazin* 12 (1980): 317–28; see also KSA 14, pp. 7–17.

3. "Nietzsche's Recollections from the Years 1875–79 Concerning His Childhood": lecture held at the University of Basel (June 1980) and at the University of Münster (July 1981).

4. "Nietzsche and Wagner One Hundred Years Ago" appeared in *Aneignung und Umwandlung: Friedrich Nietzsche und das 19. Jahrhundert,* Proceedings of the International Nietzsche Conference, Berlin, 1977; and *Nietzsche-Studien* 7 (1978): 288–302.

5. "Enlightenment and Revolution: Nietzsche and the Later Goethe" appeared in *Deutsche Klassik und Revolution: Texte eines Literaturwissenschaftlichen Kolloquims* (Rome: Edizioni dell'Ateneo, 1981). The colloquium took place in May 1978 at the Istituto Italiano di Studi Germanici (Rome).

6. "Nietzsche's Philosophy as the 'Passion for Knowledge'" appeared in *Studi germanici* 7 (1969): 337–52.

7. "Zarathustra before *Thus Spoke Zarathustra*": lecture held in Sils-Maria (September 1981).

8. "Nietzsche's Unpublished Writings from 1885 to 1888; or, Textual Criticism and the Will to Power" appeared in *Jahrbuch der Internationalen Germanistik,* ser. A (Congress Report), vol. 2, issue 1, Proceedings of the Fifth International Congress of Germanists, Cambridge, 1975, pp. 36–58; and "Nietzsche," ed. Jörg Salaquarda, *Wege der Forschung* 521 (1980): 323–49 (Darmstadt: Wissenshaftliche Buchgesellschaft; see also KSA 14, pp. 383–400.

9. "A New Section in Nietzsche's *Ecce Homo*" appeared in *Nietzsche-Studien* I (1972): 380–418.

10. "Nietzsche between Alfred Bäumler and Georg Lukács" appeared in *Basis: Jahrbuch für deutsche Gegenwartsliteratur,* ed. Reinhold Grimm and Jost Hermand, vol. 9 (Frankfurt-am-Main: Suhrkamp, 1979).

NAME INDEX

Adler, Victor, 164
Albert, Paul, 10
Alexander the Great, 105
Anders, Anni, x, xiii, xiv
Andler, Charles, 1
Andreas-Salomé, Lou. *See* Salomé, Lou von
Antonelli, Alessandro, 123
Augstein, Rudolf, 7
Avenarius, Ferdinand, 123

Bachofen, Johann Jacob, 144
Bäumler, Alfred, xi, xv, xvi, xviii, 93, 142–57, 161–63, 166–67
Bakunin, Michail, 42, 164
Balzac, Honoré de, 10
Baudelaire, Charles, 10, 93, 151
Baumgartner, Marie, 164
Bebel, August, 165
Beethoven, Ludwig van, 72
Benn, Gottfried, 76
Bernoulli, Carl Albrecht, 11, 120n.3, 123–25n.34, 139, 140n.13
Bertram, Ernst, 160–61
Bindschedler, Maria, 121
Binswanger, Otto, 135
Biser, Eugen, 79
Bismarck, Otto von, 135, 166
Bloch, Joseph, 160
Bohley, Reiner, 26–27, 30
Boscovich, Roger J., xv, xix
Bourdeau, Jean, 110, 123n.31
Bourget, Paul, 10, 151
Brandes, Georg, 106–7, 109, 118, 123–25n.34
Brann, Henry W., 143
Braun, Heinrich, 164
Brenner, Albert, 36
Broch, Hermann, 55

Brunetière, Ferdinand, 10
Brutus, Marcus Junius, 75
Bucher, Lothar, 164
Bülow, Hans von, 164
Burckhardt, Jacob, 53, 55–56n.5, 56n.6, 123n.31, 160
Burckhardt, Max, 123n.33
Byron, Lord (George Gordon), 54, 60

Caesar, Gaius Julius, 105
Carlyle, Thomas, 44, 51
Chamberlain, Houston Stewart, 141, 162
Champromis, Pierre, 121–22n.18, 122n.20
Claudius, Matthias, 27
Cohn, Paul, 120
Colli, Giorgio, ix–x, 6, 13, 20–21
Constant, Benjamin, 93

Däuble, Hedwig, 121n.17
Daechsel, Friederike (née Nietzsche), 27–28
Dante, 23
Darius the Great, 69
Darwin, Charles, 51, 163
de Custine, Astolphe, 10
Democritus, xii, 38–39, 48n.3
Deussen, Adam, 32
Deussen, Paul, 32, 101, 109, 110, 117–18, 123–25n.34
Descartes, René, 155
Diederichs, Eugen, 139
Dietze, Walter, 22n.16
Dostoyevsky, Fyodor, 10, 93, 151
Dühring, Karl Eugen, xvi, 201
Durisch, Gian Rudolf, 99
Dutt, C. P., 162

Einaudi, Giulio, 14, 20
Emerson, Ralph Waldo, 10, 71–72, 77

MAZZINO MONTINARI was the editor of the critical edition of Nietzsche's collected works and correspondence, for which, after Giorgio Colli's death, he was entirely responsible. The international journal *Nietzsche-Studien* and its companion, *Monographien und Texte zur Nietzsche-Forschung,* were founded on Montinari's suggestion in 1972.

GREG WHITLOCK teaches philosophy at Parkland College in Champaign, Illinois. He is the translator and editor of Friedrich Nietzsche's *Pre-Platonic Philosophers* (University of Illinois Press, 2000).

INTERNATIONAL NIETZSCHE STUDIES

Schopenhauer and Nietzsche   *Georg Simmel; translated by Helmut Loiskandl,*
   Deena Weinstein, and Michael Weinstein
Nietzsche's Revaluation of Values: A Study in Strategies   *E. E. Sleinis*
Making Sense of Nietzsche: Reflections Timely and Untimely   *Richard Schacht*
Nietzsche and the Problem of Sovereignty   *Richard J. White*
Nietzsche: His Philosophy of Contradictions and the Contradictions of His
   Philosophy   *Wolfgang Müller-Lauter; translated from the German by David J. Parent*
Nietzsche's Perspectivism   *Steven D. Hales and Rex Welshon*
The Pre-Platonic Philosophers   *Friedrich Nietzsche; translated from the German*
   and edited by Greg Whitlock
Nietzsche and the Transcendental Tradition   *Michael Steven Green*
Reading Nietzsche   *Mazzino Montinari; translated from the German and*
   with an introduction by Greg Whitlock

The University of Illinois Press
is a founding member of the
Association of American University Presses.

————————————————————

Composed in 9/13 ITC Stone Serif
with ITC Stone Sans display
by Celia Shapland
for the University of Illinois Press
Designed by Paula Newcomb
Manufactured by Thomson-Shore, Inc.

University of Illinois Press
1325 South Oak Street
Champaign, IL 61820-6903
www.press.uillinois.edu